Forgotten Victims

Forgotten Victims

Victims

The Abandonment
of Americans
in Hitler's Camps

Mitchell G. Bard

Westview Press
Boulder • San Francisco • Oxford

Copyright © 1994 by Westview Press, Inc.

Published in 1994 in the United States of America by Westview Press, Inc., 5500 Central Avenue, Boulder, Colorado 80301-2877, and in the United Kingdom by Westview Press, 36 Lonsdale Road, Summertown, Oxford OX2 7EW

Library of Congress Cataloging-in-Publication Data
Bard, Mitchell Geoffrey, 1959–
Forgotten victims : the abandonment of Americans in Hitler's camps
  / Mitchell G. Bard.
    p.   cm.
  Includes bibliographical references and index.
  ISBN 0-8133-2193-X
      1. Jews, American—Crimes against—Germany—History—20th century.
2. Holocaust, Jewish (1939–1945)   3. World War, 1939–1945—Prisoners
and prisons, German.   I. Title.
D805.G3B284   1994
940.53' 18—dc20   94-745
                                                                                  CIP

Printed and bound in the United States of America

The paper used in this publication meets the requirements
of the American National Standard for Permanence of Paper
for Printed Library Materials z39.48-1984.

10   9   8   7   6   5   4   3   2

This book is dedicated to Marcela,
whose good heart reassures me about the future
and whose support keeps me going.
And to Ariel, who is my hope for the future.

The book is also dedicated to the American victims
whose names will never be known.

When our country called for men
We came from forge and stone and mill
From workshop, farm, and factory,
The broken ranks to fill.
We left our quiet, happy homes
And the ones we loved so well
To vanquish all the Union's foes
Or fall where others fell.
Now as in prisons drear we languish
It is our constant cry,
O, ye who yet can save us
Will ye leave us here to die?

The voice of slander tells you
That our hearts were weak with fear,
That all, or nearly all of us
Were captured in the rear.
The scars upon our bodies,
From the musket ball and shell
The missing legs and shattered arms,
A truer tale will tell.
We have tried to do our duty
In the sight of God on high
O, ye who yet can save us,
Will ye leave us here to die?

From out our prison gate
There's a graveyard near at hand
Where lie ten thousand Union men
Beneath the Georgia sand.
Scores on scores are laid beside them
As day succeeds today,
And thus it will ever be
Till they all shall pass away
And the last can say when dying,
With upturned gazing eye,
Both love and faith are dead at home,
They have left us here to die.

—**Anonymous Union soldier in
the Confederate POW camp
at Andersonville, Georgia**

Contents

Illustrations

Preface

Americans in Hitler's death camps? Who ever heard of such a thing? The Holocaust was a European phenomenon that affected only the Jews who lived in areas occupied by the Nazis. Could it be true that American Jews were also subject to the "Final Solution"? Scholars have documented how the U.S. government abandoned the Jews of Europe: Could it be that this same government forsook its own citizens? If it is true, how could it happen?

These were the questions I sought to answer in this book. The disclosures will shock most people who never had any idea that Americans died at the hands of the Nazis other than in combat. Even Holocaust scholars will be surprised to learn how many American Jews suffered. Most Americans are likely to find it disturbing that U.S. citizenship was not a reliable shield; scholars already know that Jews could not depend on anyone or anything to save them.

My interest in this subject was provoked by the 1987 television documentary *P.O.W.—Americans in Enemy Hands*. In it, one World War II veteran gave a startling account of how he and his fellow Jewish prisoners had been segregated from their comrades in a prisoner of war camp and sent to a slave labor camp where they were beaten, starved and many literally worked to death.

This was the first I had ever heard of American victims of the Holocaust, and it stimulated me to investigate whether there indeed had been American Jews among the six million exterminated by the Nazis. I contacted Holocaust research institutes, survivors' organizations, military archives and veterans' groups and discovered only a few oblique references to American Jews who might have been killed as part of the "Final Solution." Rather than indicating that no American Jews died at the hands of the Nazis, the lack of information reflects the sad fact that these victims' stories have gone untold.

In spite of these difficulties, I wrote a short article, "American Victims of the Holocaust," for the now defunct *Present Tense* magazine. It took nearly three years for that article to actually appear in print. That day, I received a call from a radio talk-show host who wanted me to speak about it. At that point, I had not even seen the article. At midnight on a Sunday, I went on the air to talk about the article. One caller asked if I planned to write a book. I had not given the idea much thought because it had been so long since I worked on the project, but after reading the article over I became convinced it was a story that demanded a fuller investigation. And so it began.

If it were easy to find documentation on this subject, others would no doubt have already written books. In fact, material is scattered throughout various archives, and I spent hours sifting through thousands of documents to find even one relevant piece of evidence. Often, key documents were missing. This was particularly frustrating when a document mentioned an American who was believed to be in a concentration camp but no other leads were to be found. Undoubtedly, a great deal more can be learned about this tragic story, and I hope this book will encourage others to probe for additional information about American victims.

Ideally, historical studies rely to some degree on eyewitness accounts. In this case, however, such accounts were hard to find. Given the passage of more than four decades, it was next to impossible to locate American survivors. Those I did find were often hesitant to speak. During a training session for interviewers I attended, Linda Kuzmack, formerly director of the oral history project for the U.S. Holocaust Memorial Museum, gave three reasons for the reluctance of survivors to talk about their experiences: a) they could not cope with the trauma; b) no one believed them; and c) they wanted to get on with their lives. I found this to be true of many of the civilians and ex-POWs I spoke to as well.

The memories of people who went through a traumatic experience forty-odd years ago are not always reliable. Fortunately, contemporary documents written during the war and after liberation could often be found to resolve discrepancies.

Initially, I had wanted this book to be titled *American Victims of the Holocaust.* A debate has long raged about the definition of the Holocaust. Some universalists believe that it should apply to the 12 million people who died at the hands of the Nazis, whereas the majority opinion is that the term "Holocaust" should only be used in reference to the six million Jews murdered as part of the "Final Solution." I have always taken the latter view, being convinced by Emil Fackenheim's explanation of the unique character of what happened to the Jews:

> The "Final Solution" was designed to exterminate every Jewish man, woman and child. The only Jews who would have conceivably survived had Hitler been victorious were those who somehow escaped discovery by the Nazis.
>
> Jewish birth (actually, mere evidence of "Jewish blood") was sufficient to warrant the punishment of death. With the possible exception of Gypsies, Jews were the only people killed for the "crime" of existing.
>
> The extermination of the Jews had no political or economic justification. It was not a means to any end; it was an end in itself.[1]

In this book, then, I only describe Americans who were Jewish as Holocaust victims. But many non-Jews discussed here, particularly those who were POWs, were targeted for death or mistreatment and became subject to the methods used in the "Final Solution."

Mitchell G. Bard

Notes

1. Emil Fackenheim, *To Mend The World* (NY: Schocken Books, 1982), p. 12.

Acknowledgments

A LARGE NUMBER OF PEOPLE contributed in various ways to the completion of this book. The original stimulus for expanding on my early work on the subject came from someone who called in to a radio show I was doing and asked if I was going to do a book. I am grateful that *Present Tense* was able to get my article in its last issue before closing shop.

Rabbi Abraham Cooper of the Simon Wiesenthal Center was particularly helpful at the outset of the project by disseminating a note to the press asking for people with knowledge of the subject to contact me. I am grateful to those papers that published the notice. Aaron Breitbart of the Center answered many of my research inquiries.

The U.S. Holocaust Memorial Museum staff also contributed to various aspects of the project. Bob Kesting was a wealth of information about archival material and gave me some clues to sift through Suitland's vast files. Linda Kuzmack and Sybil Milton offered suggestions and guidance. John Ferrell produced lists of files to search, and Elizabeth Koenig gave me access to the Museum's library. Peter Martz and Andrew Campana assisted in making photographs available. Most importantly, Brewster Chamberlain read the manuscript and provided valuable suggestions. David Altshuler of the Museum of Jewish Heritage also was generous enough to read the manuscript and recommend changes that enhanced the work.

The archivists at Suitland were patient and helpful, and Robert Wolfe, in particular, was a valuable resource in Washington. Hadassah Modlinger at Yad Vashem forwarded several useful documents, as did archivists in several museums in Europe.

Veterans organizations provided me with valuable information and helped spread the word of my research. The Jewish War Veterans of the USA was especially helpful.

Curtis Whiteway, who has been doing his own tireless research on World War II, was exceedingly generous in sharing information.

Perhaps most important, however, were the survivors who shared their stories with me. In particular, I want to thank Daniel Steckler, Bernie Melnick, Marty Vogel, Park Chapman, Arthur Kinnis and Pete House.

M.G.B.

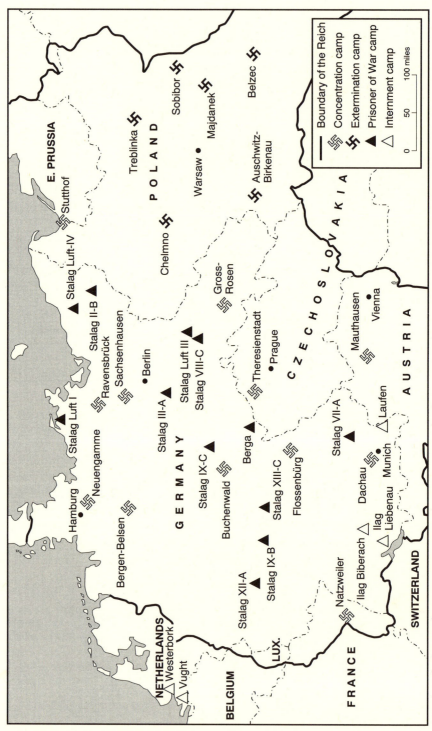

Location of prisoner of war camps, concentration camps, extermination camps, and internment camps mentioned in text

1

The Tragic Untold Story

I T WAS THE LATTER PART OF 1944. The war was turning in the Allies' favor:

The fact that Pfc. Morton Goldstein was an American did not save him when he was sent to the slave labor camp at Berga. He was a Jew and that was all that mattered to the Nazis at Stalag IX-B who segregated the Jewish POWs. When Goldstein attempted to escape, he was shot. The other American Jews who died at Berga were shown no more consideration. Looking at the pictures of American POWs liberated from Berga, you could not distinguish them from other Holocaust survivors.

Park Chapman was on his 54th mission when his B-26 was shot down over Paris. He parachuted to safety and contacted the French underground. A man posing as a British intelligence agent betrayed him to the Gestapo. He was taken to Fresnes Prison in Paris where he found 167 other Allied airmen. They were loaded into boxcars and taken to Buchenwald concentration camp where they experienced what it was like to be a European Jew. Before they were to be executed, the men were taken to a POW camp, but by then a British and American officer had died.

Lt. Jack Taylor led a team of OSS agents into Austria to collect intelligence. Taylor was captured and taken to the Mauthausen concentration camp. His job was to help build a crematorium. He and the other prisoners tried to work as slowly as possible because they knew the Nazis' ability to murder Jews would increase exponentially with the new oven. When the SS guards told them they would be the first to test the crematorium if they did not finish their work, Taylor and the others completed the task.

Sixteen-year-old Mary Berg was also an American citizen. But when the Germans decided to confine all Jews in Warsaw to a ghetto, her family was not exempt. Though her citizenship ultimately saved her life, it did not spare her from living in the hell of that ghetto for three years.

Goldstein, Chapman, Taylor and Berg were American victims of the Nazis.

Goldstein, Chapman and Taylor were soldiers who knew they faced risks when they confronted the enemy, though none of them could have anticipated they would fall prey to the Nazis' campaign to exterminate the Jewish people. But Mary Berg did not go to Europe to fight. Like thousands of other Americans visiting or living in Europe during the war years, she was in the wrong place at the wrong time. Berg became subject to the "Final Solution," and though her American citizenship ultimately saved her, other American Jews were less fortunate.

One explanation given for the world's failure to prevent the Holocaust is that the information about the Nazi extermination program was too incredible to believe. Now, fifty years later, Americans also may find it difficult to believe U.S. citizens were among the 12 million people murdered by the Nazis.

In his book, *The Abandonment of the Jews,* David Wyman documents how the U.S. government failed to save European Jewry. He concludes with a quotation from the Committee for a Jewish Army:

> We, on our part, refuse to resign ourselves to the idea that our brains are powerless to find any solution. . . . In order to visualize the possibility of such a solution, imagine that the British people and the American nation had millions of residents in Europe. . . . Let us imagine that Hitler would start a process of annihilation and would slaughter not two million Englishmen or Americans, not hundreds of thousands, but, let us say, only tens of thousands. . . . It is clear that the governments of Great Britain [and] the United States would certainly find ways and means to act instantly and to act effectively.[1]

The assumption was understandable, but this book will show it was also incorrect. Tens of thousands of Americans were in peril, but their government *did not* act instantly or effectively. Consequently, many suffered, some died.

Hundreds of books have been written about the Holocaust, yet none have examined the fate of Americans who for one reason or another fell into Nazi hands. Remarkably, virtually no mention of Americans is made in any of the major or even minor works concerning the Holocaust. One of the few references appears in Martin Gilbert's *Atlas of the Holocaust,* which lists 17 American-born people who were deported to Auschwitz, 10 of whom he says were United States citizens. Apparently, none survived. The Berga slave labor camp, which figures prominently in the story of American Jews caught up in the Holocaust, does not appear in any of his 245 pages of maps.

One reason for the lack of attention is that the number of American victims—probably a few thousand—was relatively small when compared to the total number that perished. Another is the perception of the Holocaust as a European phenomenon; most people assume Americans could not become victims. But the main reason so little has been written is that much of the evidence has been kept quiet. This should no longer come as a surprise after the revelations that the Pentagon did not disclose all the information it had about POWs in the Vietnam War or the mistreatment of those taken in the war with Iraq.[2]

The U.S. government has had good reason to cover up the story of what happened during World War II, because revealing that Americans were mistreated would raise new questions about what this country did to rescue the targets of the Nazis. Sufficient documentary evidence exists, however, to prove American officials knew U.S. citizens were in danger, were being mistreated (including being placed in concentration camps) and were murdered but were willing to do little and, in some cases, nothing to protect them.

Americans who became victims fall into two general categories: civilians and soldiers. Neither had to be Jewish, though the victimization is clearer for those who were.

Concerning civilians, this book will show that the United States government knew:

1. Anti-Jewish laws in territories occupied by Germany applied to Americans;
2. The public would be outraged and blame the government if news of the mistreatment of Americans was disclosed;
3. More than 30,000 Americans were in Europe during the war;
4. American Jews in Hungary were being mistreated;
5. American Jews were in the Bergen-Belsen concentration camp and the Warsaw Ghetto;
6. An American Jewish citizen was paraded through Frankfurt with a sign reading: "I am a member of the race which started the war."

Despite this knowledge, the government refused to take many steps that could have saved American lives. Specifically, the book will show that U.S. officials:

1. Would not check records of passports to find Americans trapped in Europe;
2. Exchange Germans for Americans because of a fear that repatriates might be spies when, in fact, returning Americans were valuable intelligence assets;
3. Were inflexible in verifying citizenship claims. In some instances, the U.S. government expected Americans in concentration camps to have proof of citizenship, though officials refused to send documents to help them establish citizenship;
4. Declined German terms to save Americans because of the fear the Nazis would try to force the United States to recognize their occupation of Europe;
5. Failed to show sympathy toward Americans who failed to take advantage of earlier opportunities to leave when conditions worsened.

American soldiers were also deserted by their government. These victims expected to be treated according to international conventions on prisoners of war and were not—but their government did nothing to help them. Moreover, given the government's knowledge of the "Final Solution," U.S. officials should have known Jewish soldiers in the American armed forces were at risk if captured. Nevertheless, Jewish GIs were sent into battle with an "H" on their dog tags to identify them as "Hebrews."

One crucial source of information about the treatment of both civilians and POWs was the Red Cross. Much has been written about the failure of the Red Cross to take steps to save European Jewry. Officials said they were afraid to jeopardize their access to POW camps where they could help save prisoners' lives. But when the Red Cross learned of Jewish POWs being segregated, it accepted as legitimate German explanations that this was consistent with Geneva Convention provisions allowing prisoners to be separated by nationality and race. Furthermore, little was done to pressure the Germans to investigate allegations of mistreatment of POWs. Thus, the U.S. government's "eyes" in German-occupied territory often proved myopic. Abuses went unreported or were minimized. American officials still received sufficient information to know POWs were being mistreated, but neither the Red Cross nor the government was prepared to do more than lodge occasional weak protests.

In the case of civilians, the U.S. government usually had contemporaneous knowledge of their mistreatment. By contrast, American officials generally did not know POWs were abused and sent to concentration camps until after the fact. Upon liberation, hundreds of former POWs were debriefed about their experiences. Despite this, war crimes trials were prosecuted without much of the available evidence from those investigations. The accused were subsequently either acquitted, given minimal sentences or convicted and, upon review, given substantially reduced sentences due to "lack of evidence"—proof that was lacking only because of government inaction in the first place.

Unwilling to face what happened to servicemen overseas, the American government refused to believe the former POWs. In some cases, American soldiers who said they were in concentration camps or slave labor camps were sent to psychiatrists. As with the Holocaust in general, most people inside and outside the military found claims that Americans had been in concentration camps—and had experienced the horrors that took place therein—just too incredible to accept.

This book examines what the United States government knew about the treatment of its citizens, when it knew it, what it did to help and what it could have done. Using original documents and interviews with survivors and experts, I will show the government could have saved hundreds, perhaps thousands of lives but chose not to.

Chapter 2 focuses on the plight of thousands of American civilians trapped in Europe by the outbreak of war. The following chapter focuses on one dramatic case, that of Mary Berg, the American teenager who spent more than three years in the Warsaw Ghetto. Chapters 4 through 10 examine the treatment of American POWs. The disproportionate amount of space devoted to POWs is a function of the available information. Chapter 4 provides a general overview of the treatment of the prisoners. The next two chapters tell the story of the POWs who were sent to Buchenwald, Mauthausen and other concentration camps. Chapter 7 discusses the conditions at Stalag IX-B, considered the worst of all the POW camps, and the segregation of American Jewish prisoners. Chapters 8 and 9 recount what happened to these Jewish prisoners and the others sent to the Berga slave labor camp. Chapter 10 offers insight into the impact being a POW had on some survivors. Chapter 11 reviews the war crimes trials and the failure of the government to bring many perpetrators of crimes against Americans to justice. The final chapter details how the U.S. government has covered up its failure to protect American citizens during the war and what might still be done to make amends for this inaction.

We must remember the Holocaust to honor the memories of the victims and to see that such a crime against humanity never happens again. But we cannot honor American victims whom we do not know. Nor can we learn the lessons contained in their tragic experiences. For their sakes, and our own, their story must be told.

2

Sorry, You Missed the Boat: Americans in Europe

AMERICANS *WERE KILLED* in concentration camps. American Jews were subject to the same anti-Semitic regulations and dangers as any other Jews who came under the control of the Nazis. Non-Jews did not face the same peril; however, thousands were sent to internment camps.

Hundreds, perhaps thousands of lives could have been saved had the United States government taken action to rescue people claiming American citizenship. Often it did just the opposite, creating obstacles that impeded Americans from obtaining the necessary documents to escape from the Nazis.

The Roosevelt Administration knew Americans were trapped behind enemy lines. In 1939, more than 80,000 American citizens were believed to be living abroad.[1] That year, the State Department established a little-known "Special Division" for handling matters related to the whereabouts and welfare of Americans abroad, including civilian internees and POWs—evidence that the United States anticipated the problems that would later arise.[2]

The State Department's initial position was that every effort should be made to get Americans out of Europe, but that no money should be spent paying citizens' expenses to return home. The United States did provide some financial assistance through the Swiss government and the Red Cross, but this was primarily for meeting basic needs of food, clothing and shelter in Europe. It was not for repatriation.[3]

On November 25, 1939, Assistant Secretary of State George Messersmith wrote that Americans in danger zones were given the opportunity to return home but for business or private reasons did not do so. State Department officials held that citizens who chose to live abroad without any apparent intention of returning to the United States could not expect their government to feel any obligation to protect them. An even deeper prejudice lay behind this viewpoint: the belief that citizens returning from abroad would become "welfare" cases. "Their real status," Messersmith wrote, "does not differ very much from that of the many thousands of unfortunate persons deserving of our sympathy, and having no claim to American citizenship, who would desire to come to this country in order to escape from danger zones or for other reasons and who seek immigration visas and passport visas to that end." The attitude that would condemn hundreds of Americans to death was expressed in the same letter:

> This government considers that by reason of having already met this particular responsibility, no situation should arise, even if conditions should become more aggravated in certain places, that would warrant it in providing further special facilities to enable Americans to return to this country.[4]

The State Department was not sympathetic to Americans who were caught in the Nazi net. Although it acknowledged the U.S. obligation "to facilitate in every way possible the return" of U.S. nationals during an emergency "from places where danger may exist," State also maintained that Americans who failed to take advantage of the opportunity for repatriation did so knowing the risks involved. The Department sent five ships in 1939 and four more in 1940 to bring home United States citizens from the European war zone, and they returned with space available. "It therefore seems safe to draw the conclusion," a Special Division policy paper written four years later says, "that those United States nationals who remained in threatened areas did so, for the most part, voluntarily, and with full realization of the occupational risks they were taking."

Thus, U.S. officials took the position that Americans who, in their eyes, missed the boat home were on their own. But this view was to have tragic consequences. Few people in places like France could imagine in 1939 or 1940 what would happen two or three years later. In the case of Americans especially, the thought that they, U.S. citizens, would not be protected must have seemed unimaginable. In fact, it *was* unimaginable to State Department officials.

At the beginning of 1941, for example, Secretary of State Cordell Hull said the Department had learned anti-Jewish laws were being imposed in France, but he expected Americans to be exempted. A couple of months later, the U.S. Ambassador to France informed Hull he was mistaken. The Germans said that measures taken against Jews "do not admit of any exceptions and must be applied to all persons residing in France, regardless of their nationality."[5] Despite being specifically told Americans would not be exempted from the anti-Jewish decrees, Hull still said he expected this to happen in a subsequent message to his Chargé in Germany.[6]

American Jews in France began to express their fears to the U.S. embassy and consulates. They wanted to know whether they should comply with the anti-Jewish laws and register as Jews before the July 14, 1941, deadline. Failure to do so could result in fines up to 10,000 francs and imprisonment in Leipzig for up to one year or both. The prefect also had the authority to order internment in a "special camp."[7]

Undersecretary of State Sumner Welles informed the Ambassador to France,

William Leahy, that the United States assumed the laws would not be applied to Americans and that the government rejected any such discriminatory policy. He said he could not understand how a Jew could be penalized by imprisonment in Germany. Welles instructed Leahy to protest any effort to deport an American from unoccupied France to a German prison. The German response was that the new laws were instituted to "ensure the recovery of the country" and vaguely stated that American Jews would be treated as "liberally as is compatible with the letter and spirit of the laws in question."[8]

American Jews were perhaps in the greatest peril in Hungary. At the end of January 1941, the Hungarian authorities began to impose new measures on Jews, including depriving them of their real estate. The U.S. government could have taken action at this point. Hull did instruct the U.S. minister in Hungary to help Americans but not to make any financial commitments. Herbert Pell responded that the probability was small that Americans in Hungary or Yugoslavia would get visas without the United States exerting pressure on Germany.[9]

By the summer of 1941, it had become extremely difficult for Americans in the occupied territories to travel and communicate; they needed special permits to leave and those were rarely given.[10] The situation was exacerbated when German consular offices in the United States were ordered closed by July 10, 1941, and the Germans retaliated by closing U.S. offices in Germany and the occupied territories.[11] All American business was subsequently conducted by the Swiss Legation.[12] To give an example of the attitude prevalent among the Swiss, which went unchallenged by the State Department, one can look at a memo written more than a year later, when the persecution of Hungarian Jews was still in its early stages. The Swiss said the Hungarians were suspending the expropriation of Jewish property after receiving assurances from the Legation that inquiries were being made regarding the American citizenship of the persons concerned. "However, to avoid extension of protection to non-American Jews, allegedly residing in the U.S., this Legation refuses protective letters in property expropriating cases to persons who could not have acquired American citizenship on account of the short period of residence in the U.S. or for other reasons."[13] It is clear from the documents that a Raoul Wallenberg-type of individual in the Swiss Legation in Budapest could have saved many Jews by testifying that they were Americans.

Another place where Americans were in jeopardy was Rumania. Franklin Mott Gunther, the U.S. minister, reported to Hull in January 1941 that hundreds of Jews had been slaughtered in the "Iron Guard Insurrection" in Bucharest. "It makes one sick at heart to be accredited to a country where such things can happen," he said.[14] Gunther later warned that Jewish property was being confiscated, but he did not know yet whether Americans would be included, though the Rumanians were asking for proof that an owner of REF Oil was not a Jew. "Whatever the cause, 1941 thus far proved to be a black year for the Jews in Rumania," Gunther wrote to Hull.[15]

He was subsequently told by the wife of a naturalized citizen that her husband suffocated in a freight car with other Jews in connection with the pogrom at Iasi where 500 Jews were killed. Another woman said a similar fate befell her husband. A third American from Iasi was missing.[16] Shortly thereafter, he reported: "The program of systematic extermination is continuing . . . and I see little hope for the Rumanian Jews as long as the present German controlled regime continues in power."[17] Gunther also learned Americans were subject to this program, informing Hull that U.S. citizens had been deported to Mhilev in the Ukraine where their fate was uncertain.[18]

Even after being informed of the seriousness of the plight of Jews in Rumania, Hull's response was bureaucratic. When an American is molested because of race or religion, he said, "you should exercise your discretion in the matter of extending unofficial good offices to him with a view to discontinuance of the molestation. . . . Person whose status as native-born American citizen has been established should in present situation be given protection and if necessary issued passports limited to short periods. Necessity for deviation from policy followed in normal times required out of humanitarian considerations."[19]

The reluctance to assist Jews in Rumania was evident in a statement by Cavendish Cannon of the State Department's Division of European Affairs, who objected to a proposal two years later to move 300,000 Jews out of Rumania to Syria or Palestine. He said, "Endorsement of such a plan [was] likely to bring about new pressure for an asylum in the western hemisphere" and that, because atrocities were also underway in Hungary, "a migration of Rumanian Jews would therefore open the question of similar treatment for Jews in Hungary and, by extension, all countries where there has been intense persecution."[20] The view that rescuing Jews somehow posed a danger to the Allies or would "take the burden or the curse off Hitler"[21] was held by several State Department officials (and was a particularly prevalent feeling in the British Foreign Office).

This was not the only excuse used to make life difficult for both Americans and non-Americans trying to escape from Europe. At the beginning of 1941, Breckinridge Long, the head of the Special Division, had told Roosevelt that consuls had been instructed to be "as liberal as the law allows" and to expedite action, but because of reports of Nazi agents pretending to be refugees, "it has been considered essential in the national interest to scrutinize all applications carefully." In another letter to the President, Long said he was proposing new regulations for travel to and from the United States for all persons, *including* U.S. citizens, because the laxity of the current law allowed subversives to enter the United States.[22]

There is no record of Roosevelt objecting to Long's proposals. The fact that the President could have made a difference, however, was apparent early in the war when Roosevelt sent a list of 200 names to the State Department in January 1940 with instructions that they be given emergency visas.[23] Despite repeated requests to take similar action to bypass State Department obstacles, the President refused throughout the war to intervene.

U.S. officials were subsequently reluctant to make exchanges because of the fear that Americans who were repatriated might be spies. "As Americans received in the recent exchange were found to include some Nazi agents, we might very well expect to receive many subversive agents among aliens who have long been exposed to Nazi methods of indoctrination," wrote James Keeley, assistant chief of the Special Division. "It would be almost an impossible task to separate the bona fide from the mala fide in such a conglomerate assemblage of people as would in the circumstances seek to come to the United States."[24]

In fact, the FBI reported consistently throughout the war that enemy espionage and sabotage efforts were unsuccessful.[25] The possibility of enemy infiltration existed, but it was more likely that Americans returning from occupied territories would be valuable intelligence resources. For example, a group of American correspondents exchanged for Axis nationals in the United States in mid-1942 relayed the news to American officials that hundreds of thousands of Jews had been killed.

Besides fear of Nazi sympathizers infiltrating, the State Department adopted the policy that it could not save any one group if it could not save everyone. "If we once open our doors to one class of refugee," Keeley wrote in December 1942, "we must expect on the basis of our experience in extending relief in occupied territories, that all other sufferers from Nazi (including Japanese) oppression (the Belgians, Dutch, Poles, Greeks, Yugoslavs, Norwegians, Czechs, Chinese, et cetera) will likewise wish to avail themselves of our hospitality. . . . Even the most optimistic dispenser of largess could scarcely expect us to become an unrestricted haven of refuge for all suffering peoples. Furthermore, to accede to the request of one group, while refusing similar refuge to other oppressed peoples, might well give rise to bad feeling and engender disunity among the happy family of the United Nations."[26]

The general sentiment in the State Department and the White House was that the Nazi discrimination of Jews should not be highlighted, nor should Jews be given special consideration. As Long said in a letter to Rep. Emanuel Celler, Jewish refugees were being taken in "not as Jews but as human beings in distress who have had our very deep sympathy." He added that "all questions which may affect individual groups are subservient" to the objective of defeating Hitler. In an ironic choice of words, he concluded: *"The final solution can be more speedily and more easily arrived at if the special interests of any group can be merged in the common interest to support the war"* (emphasis added).[27]

All of this concern referred to saving fewer than 2,000 Americans in German internment camps in 1942, not the millions of European Jews whose lives were threatened. And despite the small number of Americans, the State Department cast doubt on the authenticity of those claiming United States citizenship.[28] This was perhaps necessary to justify lumping Americans in with everyone else.

The attitude in the State Department toward anyone trapped in Europe was typified by two memos in the papers of Breckinridge Long. In response to a request for help in getting a man's sister-in-law out of Austria, A.M. Warren, chief of the Visa Division, wrote that nothing could be done unless "the alien or aliens in whom you are interested" reach an American consulate. Until then, "It is not believed that any useful purpose will be served by further correspondence in this matter."[29] In another answer to a woman asking for help, Long himself replied: "Since the recent developments in the world there would seem to be nothing further that can be done in regard to Miss Weil. Sorry—but it's a sad world."[30] Had Long said the bombing of Pearl Harbor and America's entrance in the war made it difficult to help Miss Weil, the answer would have been understandable, but the lack of sensitivity reflected in the last remark suggested a callousness unrelated to the political and military issues.

After Pearl Harbor, it became more difficult for refugees who had been born in enemy countries, or had been longtime residents there, to receive U.S. visas. Again, the procedural change was aimed at Europeans but ended up being applied to Americans as well. For example, one woman, whose Austrian-born husband was fighting with the Allies, was stranded in Vichy, France, with her twelve-year-old daughter. The mother was an American citizen but could not get a visa for her daughter because she had been born in Austria and was considered an enemy alien.[31]

The State Department did not display much greater concern for its own personnel early in the war. In his memoirs, George Kennan described how he and other American embassy personnel in Berlin were taken prisoner by the Gestapo in December 1941 and placed in solitary confinement for five months in Bad Nauheim, near Frankfurt. "Not until the end of April 1942 did the United States government bother to communicate with us, which it could easily have done through the Swiss," he wrote. A total of 130 American officials and journalists was imprisoned. In mid-May, the group was sent to Lisbon for an exchange.

> When the [State] department did finally take cognizance of our plight and consent to communicate with us by telegram for the first time, which was shortly before our departure and exchange, it did so only for the purpose of informing us that by decision of the comptroller general . . . none of us were to be paid for the months we had been in confinement: we had not, you see, been working.[32]

Ironically, a second telegram said that half his group had to be left behind to make room for Jewish refugees. Kennan complained that "individual Congressmen, anxious to please individual constituents, were interested in bringing these refugees to the United States, and this—although the refugees were not citizens—was more important than what happened to us."

He was further angered when he reached Lisbon and discovered that several foreign service officers were being sent on new assignments the following day. "The department obviously had not the faintest idea of the condition, nervous and physical, in which these people found themselves, and had not bothered to use its imagination," he wrote. "Neither those particular orders nor the reception the rest of us received upon arrival in the United States were accompanied, as far as I can recall, with any expression of appreciation on the government's part either for the services we had performed in wartime Germany or for the rigors of confinement to which this service had led."

On January 20, 1942, Reinhard Heydrich held a conference at Wannsee where he outlined the "Final Solution." In the following months, deportations to the death camp at Chelmno were eliminating the Jews of western Poland. Gas chambers were being built at Belzec and Sobibor and were soon in daily operation. The first deportations to Auschwitz were in March.

The situation in Europe had deteriorated to the point where the State Department finally recognized the danger to American citizens and made some effort to help. By this time, however, the United States was at war with Germany and its options were constrained. Going to war, in itself, was the most dramatic measure the government could take to save people from Hitler, but in the time it would take to achieve an Allied victory, thousands of Americans were imperiled. On March 19, Undersecretary Welles gave his Department the following instruction:

> It is essential to get all Americans out of enemy and enemy-occupied territory in Europe who wish to leave and negotiations necessary to attain that end are to be immediately initiated.[33]

The problem, Special Division's Joseph Green noted, was the absence of any means of informing Americans in Axis territory of the opportunity for repatriation. Green suggested that the Passport Division provide a list of passports issued in Europe during 1941, as well as a list of Americans whose passports were validated in 1940 or 1941 for continued stay in Europe, so the Department could check for Americans in Europe who might be entitled to repatriation.[34] Long argued it was impracticable to search lists of thousands of passports.[35] He left it to Swiss officials in charge of American affairs to identify U.S. citizens but refused to permit the Swiss to have access to American files, which, Green said, was contrary to the usual practice.[36] Even a limited search would have provided a list of Americans in Europe, but the records were never checked. Thus, the Undersecretary's orders to be proactive were subverted and the burden was placed on U.S. citizens to contact American officials or their representatives and request assistance.

The State Department correspondence indicates, moreover, the opportunity for repatriation would not have been open to all American citizens even if they had been found. In fact, officials planned to decide whom they wanted to allow to return to the United States. Americans in Germany awaiting repatriation, Long said in June 1942, "ought to be examined and *only those we want* should be accepted" (emphasis in the original).[37]

Long's attitude reflected the public opposition to immigration that was prevalent at the time. Having just come out of the Great Depression, David Wyman noted, Americans were concerned about unemployment. They were also xenophobic and anti-Semitic.[38] The irony, of course, was that Long was not referring to hundreds of thousands of European Jews; he was speaking about *Americans* who were being treated like foreigners because they had chosen to live abroad.

This policy was adopted despite knowledge of the growing danger in Europe. By May 1941, the Department was receiving information the Germans were pursuing a methodical policy. As Leland Morris, the Chargé in Germany, told the Secretary: "It has been apparent for some time that a systematic plan is being directed from Berlin to establish in all countries under its control the German discrimination against Jews as rapidly as the local situation permits. The first step is in each case exclusion from political activity followed by social ostracism and economic despoliation leading ultimately to compulsory labor, forced emigration and ghettoization."[39]

One of the earliest reports of Americans being arrested came in a letter from the Swiss Consulate in Amsterdam dated January 26, 1942. The report said that approximately 18–25 American men were arrested in Holland immediately after the German declaration of war. All were in a police prison. Several months later, a telegram from Secretary of State Hull to the American Interests office in Norway said that 200 Americans had been arrested there. A representative of the American Red Cross subsequently wrote to the Secretary of the American Legation in Bern that 30–40 Americans, mostly merchant seamen, had been interned in Norway and then transferred to Germany.[40]

In March 1942, the State Department learned that "only 236" Americans in territory occupied by German troops, including Poland, have been "provisionally arrested for police and safety reasons." This information may have come from the Germans, who claimed to have 236 Americans interned.[41] A memo written by Joseph Green, however, said 5,111 Americans were interned then in Germany, of whom 1,191 had passports.[42]

The Germans assured the United States that American civilians would be treated like POWs according to the Convention of July 24, 1929. When the Nazis began arresting more Americans in Berlin and the Eastern territories, they claimed their actions were a response to similar measures taken by the United States with respect to German citizens. Hull admitted that individuals were arrested on national security grounds but denied interning Germans on any mass scale "had occurred or was contemplated."[43]

While logistical excuses were given for the failure to help Americans in Hungary, people in Slovakia were abandoned primarily for political reasons. In 1942, the State Department determined it was impossible to assist 35 American Jews threatened with deportation from Slovakia and another 70 Americans seeking repatriation. The Department refused to help them because it believed Slovak authorities were trying to use the Americans to pressure the United States to recognize Slovakia.[44]

Once the decision was made not to aid Americans, the State Department was forced to cover up its failure to act out of fear of public reaction. The Special Division's Joseph Green admitted that *"if the Axis propaganda mill should give publicity to the proposed ill treatment of American citizens of Jewish race in Slovakia there may be considerable criticism of the Department by Jewish circles in the United States* (emphasis added)."[45] This is perhaps the clearest statement that the State Department was aware of the seriousness of the plight of Jews in Eastern Europe, was sensitive to public opinion and still was unwilling to act.

When U.S. officials learned in January 1943 that American Jews residing in Germany were subject to the same regulations applied to German Jews, they warned that U.S. policy toward Germans interned in the States might be reconsidered if Americans were discriminated against.[46] But that is all the United States did—hardly enough to persuade Germany that America was seriously concerned about the treatment of its citizens.

That same year, the French Department of Alpes Maritimes began to apply the same laws to foreign Jews as those used against the French. "The normal method of Aryanization of Jewish enterprises being their sale, all enterprises belonging to foreign Jews should therefore be sold in the same way and under the same conditions as those owned by French Jews."[47]

In one case, the Commissariat for Jewish Questions in Vichy began to liquidate the Société Mavest S.H., which was largely owned by a non-Jewish American citizen. When the American Legation protested, it did not take issue with the law enabling Jewish property to be taken; instead, a protest was made "that a majority of Society officials aren't Jews."[48]

The expropriation of property was only the beginning. In June 1943, the Bern Legation provided the State Department with a list of nine Americans, including two Jews, interned in six different camps. "It seems the competent authorities have decided to separate 'Aryans' and 'non-Aryans,'" the report said.[49] The United States took no action.

A year later, the American minister to Switzerland, Leland Harrison, reported that in application of the so-called "Jewish decree," Americans had been interned by the Hungarians. When the Hungarian government learned it had mistakenly arrested Americans, he said, limitations on their personal liberty were removed. Harrison said that American Jews who were interned were treated the same way as non-Jews. Later in the memo, however, he says that 65 Americans, most with Jewish names, were interned in six Hungarian camps. He then says the Swiss Legation knows of only one non-Jewish American who had been arrested and that individual had been released.

In the provinces, Hungarian Jews were sent to ghettos, but the Swiss managed to have the Americans moved to various prisons where they were said to be under "protective custody." The Swiss were unable, however, to protect American Jews' property. Hull asked the Swiss to visit the Americans.[50]

The failure of the Swiss or Americans to act on behalf of the Americans in Hungarian camps proved tragic. On July 4, 1944, an Allied raid scored a direct hit on a camp where American and English citizens were interned, killing more than 100.

The U.S. government knew the Hungarians were using people as human shields. Originally, Hungary said the internees and Jews would be concentrated in areas exposed to Allied air raids. Late in June, the Hungarian authorities changed their minds and decided to scatter the people throughout the city so the Allies could not avoid bombing concentrations of Jews.[51]

Two months after the tragedy in Budapest, word of Jews being deported from Slovakia and Hungary reached the State Department. Hull instructed Roswell McClelland, the War Refugee Board representative in Switzerland, to lodge an "emphatic protest" and make clear that the United States has "unflinching determination" to see that those responsible are apprehended and punished. Hull added that Germans will be held accountable if American citizens are transferred from internment camps.[52]

A few weeks later, Hull learned that Heinrich Himmler had personally ordered the extermination of as many as 65,000 Jews at Auschwitz. By this time, the magnitude of Hitler's plan was clear. Reports indicated about 45,000 Jews were in Theresienstadt, 100,000 were in camps and ghettos in Poland and only about 60,000 of the 130,000 Rumanians deported to Transnistria were still alive.[53] Hull said the Germans should be told that direct responsibility would be fixed and "appropriate consequences will follow" if Himmler's order is carried out.[54]

By the end of 1944, it was too late for the Jews of Hungary. The opportunity for either the Americans or Swiss to provide the means of escape had slipped away. Harrison reported that an October 17 Hungarian radio announcement declared "that the Jewish problem would be liquidated mercilessly and that there would be strict and ruthless enforcement of all anti-Jewish laws, and that no foreign passports or protective documents would be honored."[55]

As late as September 1944, more than 30,000 Americans were in Europe.[56] Hull reported that approximately 500 Americans were in Hungary and needed protection. In fact, 800 were in Budapest alone.[57]

Most American citizens who were arrested were imprisoned in internment camps. There were more than a dozen such camps, including Compiegne (northeast of Paris), Vittel (southern France), Laufen (upper Bavaria), Liebenau (near Stuttgart), Tittmoning (branch camp of Laufen), Tost (at Tost in Silesia) and Biberach (east of Munich). In 1942–44, these camps held more than two thousand Americans.[58]

Some Americans spent years in such camps. For example, Henry Kloczynski was born in Camden, New Jersey, in 1915. His parents decided to return to Poland in 1915. Kloczynski said he was treated better than most people in Golub, Poland, from 1939 to 1941, because he was an American citizen. After the United States entered the war, however, he was no longer special. In August 1942, he decided to try to contact the Swiss Consul in Berlin in an effort to get back to America. While in Berlin, he was arrested by the Gestapo because he looked suspicious. The Nazis thought he was a spy and sent him to prison where he was severely beaten. He spent about a month in each of three separate Gestapo prisons before being sent to Laufen, Bavaria. He was repatriated to the United States on February 22, 1945.[59]

Though they placed severe restrictions on the inmates' freedom, the internment camps were in no way like concentration camps. In an article in the Red Cross "POW Bulletin," the publication designed to alleviate fears about the treatment of Americans captured abroad, Russell Singleton described Ilag VII in Laufen.

> When I was in Ilag VII, internees lived some 30 to 60 in a room, and slept in two or three-tiered bunks with excelsior-filled bed sacks. Two blankets, and one sheet and pillow case, these latter being changed monthly, were allowed by the German authorities. From the same source the internees each received a clean hand towel weekly, a four-ounce piece of "ersatz" soap and about one and a half ounces of soap powder monthly. There was a hot shower-bath weekly, otherwise washing facilities were poor and there was no hot water for daily use. Heating by means of pot-bellied stoves was fairly adequate, although coal was rationed almost to a piece.
>
> Cooking was done by internees under a skeleton German supervision. For breakfast we had a weak, imitation, peppermint tea. Dinner consisted of potatoes and a soup generally made of more potatoes, carrots and cabbage. Supper—soup and potatoes, with two ounces of skimmed-milk cheese on Sundays. The weekly meat ration was about 14 ounces, including bones. To stretch this, we usually ground it up and put it into the soup. By saving it, we sometimes had two spoonfuls of watery goulash on Sundays. We were given about 10 ounces of black bread daily (substance unknown) and about five ounces of poor quality margarine weekly. There were no fresh fruits. Meals were carried to the rooms in large pails and eaten there.
>
> The Red Cross packages, while the fare became monotonous, changed all this, and, because of them, we could live fairly comfortably.

The internees did not have to do much work, at most some gardening and field labor. To occupy their time, the prisoners held educational classes and lectures. Internees deposited their money but could draw against it to purchase goods in the canteen. "Summing up, with Red Cross packages an internee could get along fairly well—if he had the will to do so."[60]

Despite such sanguine accounts, information *was* available about the mistreatment of American Jews in German internment camps as early as October 1944. A State Department report issued a couple of months later said 17 American Jews were discriminated against by being given harder work and more severe punishment than other Americans in 1942–43. "In view of the absence of war crimes," another document said, no action was taken.[61]

The Americans interned in camps in France and Germany were generally treated well, though concern was expressed for their safety. McClelland reported in February 1945, for example, that the Americans in Laufen were "still in grave danger" because a group of violently anti-American Nazis had warned 10 months earlier that if Germany were defeated they would do away with the Americans at Laufen.[62]

The attitude toward Jews in the internment camps was not one of concern, however, according to memos written by American officials after conversations with Fred Auckenthaler, the Swiss inspector of POW camps based in Berlin.[63] Auckenthaler filed many reports about POW camps and stated that "in general he found the prison camps in Germany well run and the prisoners well treated" and that a "very good spirit" existed between the Germans and the prisoners.

Auckenthaler also inspected civilian internment camps. He said that approximately 10 percent of the internees were of the "Jewish race." Echoing the sentiments associated with Nazi propaganda, Auckenthaler reported these Jews sold their Red Cross parcels to the Germans at black market prices and then wanted to share parcels distributed to other prisoners. Out of the 2,000 internees in Vittel, he said, "there were about 200 Jews who were hated and despised by all the balance" and that "their presence there constituted a serious menace to harmony in the camp." Auckenthaler recommended the Jews be sent to exclusively Jewish camps or "since they were almost without exception Jews from Poland who probably had no claim to American citizenship and who were unable to speak English, they be no longer furnished with Red Cross parcels."

Another report, written after a February 9, 1945, visit to Ilag Biberach near Munich, said only 28 Americans were found in the camp. The camp captain said that Jews transferred from Bergen-Belsen concentration camp to Biberach had vermin. Since the delousing plant was out of use, American and British internees had to disinfect the Jews, which, he complained, took a heavy toll on the carefully built-up stocks of soap and other cleaning material from the International Red Cross.[64]

Little publicity was given to the plight of Americans in internment camps. Even less attention was paid to whether Americans were in concentration camps. When the issue was raised, the government denied any Americans were in the camps and, in fact, officials investigating reports of U.S. citizens in concentration camps came back with negative answers.[65] But the U.S. government did know at least some Americans were in concentration camps. For example, the State Department had reliable information that about 200 people claiming U.S. citizenship were in Bergen-Belsen in July 1944.

In September 1944, Secretary Hull wrote to McClelland regarding the son of an American citizen believed to be in Bergen-Belsen. A few days later, the State Department received information that Jews deported from Vittel never left France. The Gestapo maintained they never went to Belsen. The Swiss subsequently forwarded a report of two Americans in the concentration camp. The Swiss were asked to find out the details and insure that "all persons claiming United States citizenship at Bergen-Belsen to be transferred to camps where Americans are primarily detained and where they are accorded all of the rights to which they are entitled."[66] Another request for information was made before a message came back with a list of eight families in Belsen. In December 1944, the State Department was informed 45 Americans were in Bergen-Belsen.[67]

This was a rare instance where the public was informed American civilians were held by the Nazis, albeit without much fanfare. A November 17, 1944, Associated Press dispatch that appeared the next day in the *New York Herald Tribune* had the headline: "Nazis Hold 200 Claiming to Be Citizens of U.S." The State Department told AP it was trying to learn the names of the Americans and arrange for them to be transferred to an internment camp. The story ended with a request that anyone having information that American citizens were being held at Belsen provide it to the Department. The story did not contain any description of Bergen-Belsen. No further information about the fate of these Americans could be found, though I did find evidence that a few survived Belsen. One was Barry Spanjaard.[68]

Spanjaard was born in America, but his parents were Dutch and had taken him back to Holland. He had an American birth certificate but not a passport. This later proved costly.

In 1940, at the age of 10, Barry had been advised by the American consul to return to the United States but was told he would have to go without his parents. He refused. Three years later, after the Nazis had overrun Holland, his family was deported to a transit camp at Westerbork, 30 miles from the German border.

One day the Spanjaards were called into the registration building. Barry described what happened:

> As we entered, I was shocked by the ugliest woman I had ever seen sitting behind a large desk. There were no chairs where we could sit, so we stood and listened to her talk with a voice like her face. . . . She then asked us for our papers, so we gave them to her assistant, who handed them to her. She did not want any direct contact with Jews. She asked us for my passport, and my mother had to tell her that I didn't have one and explained why. Frau Slottke then said: "Well, that's too bad, because now I will have to send you to Poland, instead of an internment hotel in the South of France."[69]

The next day, he learned a group of 15 people with English or American passports were being sent to the Vittel internment camp in southern France. They left in a passenger train. "If my parents had just spent that five dollars back in 1932, in New York, for my American passport, we too would have been on that train," wrote Spanjaard.

At the end of 1943, the Spanjaards were told they were being sent to another camp, one with heated barracks and kosher food. "She made it all sound like the Catskills," Barry recalled.

On January 31, 1944, seven cattle cars pulled up outside the camp. "A terrible fear came over us as we approached these horrible vehicles, and we began to understand how all those unfortunate people felt on the regular Tuesday morning transports to Auschwitz. If we were going to such a wonderful camp, why were we being taken there in these ugly boxcars?" Then 14-year-old Barry and his parents boarded the train. They were taken to Bergen-Belsen, where they spent the next year. On January 21, 1945, while his father was in the hospital, Barry and his mother were called into the commandant's office and asked if they wanted to go to the United States. Though skeptical, they accepted the offer. Spanjaard then carried his 41-year-old father, who weighed only 65 pounds, out the gate to a truck, starting their journey to the Swiss border. Barry's father had survived for two years in concentration camps, but he died in Switzerland after just three days of freedom.[70]

Spanjaard subsequently learned the Germans had wanted to make a trade for him from the beginning, but the United States government had refused. Ironically, eight years later, during the Korean War, Spanjaard was sent back to Germany by the United States Army. "If I had known then that the American government had done nothing to save me," he says today bitterly, "I would never have fought for this country."

To this day, Spanjaard maintains he was the only American placed in a concentration camp. He may not have known, however, that his mother wrote an article about the family's experience in a newspaper 37 years earlier.[71] She recalled other Americans.

In Mrs. Spanjaard's version, the family was taken out of their barracks in Westerbork on November 16, 1943, and asked for their papers. The Americans and British were told they would be sent to the internment camp at Vittel, France. The Spanjaards were told they were being sent to Bergen-Belsen. "When I showed the commandant our son's American citizenship papers and asked why we, too, were not to be interned," she recalled that he shouted: "It's none of your business!"

Whether an individual was physically abused is not the sole criterion for assessing the impact of what the Nazis did to them. Perhaps the worst thing for many survivors were the horrors they witnessed. Mrs. Spanjaard, for example, explained how many Dutch Jews went underground and left their children with Christian friends. The Nazis knew this and tortured people to reveal the Jewish children they were shielding. The kids were then shipped off to Poland. "The 7- and 8-year-olds would carry the 6-month-old babies in their arms and try to hush their crying. The 'little mothers' rarely cried. They just stared, big-eyed, uncomprehending, wondering. The sight of them drove some of us out of our minds."

One of the most traumatic experiences for many prisoners occurred when they were forced to watch other members of the family humiliated, beaten or killed. Mrs. Spanjaard remembered how the men in Bergen-Belsen were given 20 lashes a day. When the 18-year-old guards grew tired or decided to have some fun, they would force the Jews to lash each other. "Our son would see his father beaten. As an American citizen he had the privilege of not being forced to beat anyone." She said her husband never complained, and she did not know he was beaten until one day she tried to massage his back and discovered it was full of welts.

Emil Weiss, who had become a naturalized U.S. citizen before returning to Czechoslovakia, was held with 167 Americans by the Slovak puppet government at Marianka, Czechoslovakia. "We were told that we had been brought there by the Slovak government for protection against the Germans," he testified. "My wife Lena, my son Isadore and I were taken from there to Bergen-Belsen concentration camp, 90 miles from Hannover, Germany, with the explanation that we were going to await repatriation."

Three other Americans were arrested as Jews in Slovakia in early 1942, according to Isidore. He later received letters from them that came from Lublin and Auschwitz.

The Weiss family was in the concentration camp for almost two months (November 25, 1944–January 22, 1945) before Emil was repatriated. During that time, he said, American citizens were beaten by the German guards many times, "always for no reason at all." Weiss recalled standing in the middle of the barracks near the stove warming his hands one day with a group of other elderly people. An SS guard nicknamed "Red" came in and began to hit Weiss and the others with a heavy stick. "He just came into the barracks calling us 'dogs' and started swinging the stick. . . . This guard was always coming into the barracks and would hit whoever happened to be in his way." At the time Weiss was close to 70 years old and was forced to run and hide under a bunk to escape the guard.

Although the SS guard may not have known who the Americans were, the Germans in charge of the camp could have had no doubt. Weiss testified that the Americans' passports were taken away when they arrived and they were sent to a section of the camp where the Germans said all the prisoners to be exchanged were kept. They were repatriated on the *SS Gripsholm* on February 22, 1945.[72]

Most Americans who survived the concentration camps never made their stories public. Consequently, the evidence of their presence in them is often unclear or restricted to a single reference in a memoir or unrelated report. For example:

- Moscow radio quoted an American civilian who had been in the concentration camp at Bunzlau, Germany.[73]
- In May 1944, the American Legation learned that Marcel Cadet, "allegedly" an American, was in Buchenwald. The Germans responded that Cadet was a French citizen and therefore considered the matter closed.[74]
- Martin Gilbert said 17 U.S.-born people were deported to Auschwitz, at least 10 of whom were American citizens. But he does not footnote the information.[75]
- According to the Jewish Historical Institute in Poland, five Americans were in the Auschwitz camp hospital on March 7, 1945: Julius Schiller (age 57), Vittoris Benbossa (age 21), Albert Wenger (age 46), Friedrich Lewinson (age 46) and Franz Striefel (age 29).[76]
- The State Museum of Auschwitz found references to a number of Americans who spent time in the concentration camp. Ralph de Leon

was transferred from Auschwitz to Buchenwald on May 15, 1944. Wilhelm Pasternak was transferred to Dachau on October 27, 1944. Johann Kokoszynki, a New Yorker, was listed in a book about prisoners in Block 11 of Auschwitz. The Museum also listed the five men cited by the Jewish Historical Institute in Poland as having been among 700 people liberated from Auschwitz on January 27, 1945.

- The Museum also had copies of two reports written by Albert Wenger, an American lawyer and economist who was in Vienna when Hitler declared war. Wenger said he was arrested on February 24, 1943, by the Gestapo for sheltering a Jewish woman and was deported to Auschwitz. In January 1944, two New Yorkers, Herbert Kohn and Burger Mayers, were killed in the gas chambers. He said he could cite other cases but could not remember the victims' names.[77]

- In the files of the prisoners of the Police Prison in the Small Fortress in Terezin, one American is listed. According to *Terezin Ghetto 1945*, a book published by the Czechoslovakian Ministry of Protection of Labour and Social Welfare, 17 American citizens were among the more than 30,000 prisoners liberated from Ghetto Terezin on May 21, 1945. In all likelihood, these people were not Jewish.[78]

- According to death certificates, no Americans died in Dachau. Polish sources reported, however, that 11 Americans were in the camp on April 26, 1945. The OSS Section of the Seventh Army found a total of 31,432 internees when the camp was liberated April 29, 1945. Six of the total were Americans. A document listing the nationalities of the prisoners in April 1945 indicates 10 Americans were in Dachau.[79]

- An American citizen named Charles Negrin, who claimed he was a former employee of the American Consul in Budapest before the war, said he was imprisoned in Mauthausen from 1939 until its liberation.[80]

- According to Evelyn Le Chene, eight Americans, four of whom were Jews, were among the 63,000 prisoners in Mauthausen on May 1, 1945.[81]

As we shall see in succeeding chapters, other Americans, POWs, were in several camps, including Mauthausen, Flossenbürg and Buchenwald.

The National Archives' records of investigations into the plight of certain individuals usually are incomplete. They document the disappearance of someone but do not say what happened to them. For example, a memo dated November 10, 1942, says that an American named Mary Frankel, believed to be over 60 years of age, was living in a Jewish pension in Hamburg when the SS took her passport away and sent her to "the assembly point" in Theresienstadt. The Swiss Consul in Hamburg said he could do nothing unless he received instructions. No other documents could be found explaining whether any further effort had been made to find Frankel or to report her ultimate fate.[82]

A November 1944 memo says nine Americans were sent to an unknown destination and the State Department had "every reason to believe that they have been victims of the German exterminating policy of Jews." The memo goes on to say, "If we are going to attempt to save our nationals from a similar fate, we must have an opportunity to pass upon their claims to citizenship." It also states that the Germans were not allowing people at Bergen-Belsen to present their claims of citizenship.[83]

In another case, a memo reports that an American in Belgium named Armand van Allemeersch was imprisoned for violating the laws prohibiting the harboring of Jews.[84] Nothing more was in the files about this "righteous gentile."

Another American disappeared in 1942. Two years later, the State Department was trying to find the woman. The assumption was that she was taken by the Gestapo in an anti-Jewish action. She must have been sent to Auschwitz at one point because the Germans said she was "no longer at Birkenau working camp." No further mention of the case could be found in the files. Acting Secretary of State Edward Stettinius nevertheless had instructed that such cases be pursued "with the utmost vigor . . . until the German government either establishes the whereabouts and welfare of our nationals to our satisfaction or admits that it is unable to do so." He added parenthetically that failure to provide this information would confirm the Germans' guilt in killing U.S. citizens and establish a basis for war crimes.[85]

In the spring of 1944, the State Department learned that an American named Betty Trompetter was removed from her home in Nantes in July 1942. The Swiss had begun looking for her at the end of 1942 but were told by the Germans that Betty and her mother Marcelle were evacuated to an unknown destination after refusing to leave their home in a Zone Interdite.

In one of the more forceful communiqués found in the Archives, Hull wrote to the American Interests section in France that the United States "can't understand the attitude of the German government" in failing to provide information about the Trompetters. "The United States government expects an explanation of [the] German government's action in this matter, including reasons for the arrest of the two American citizens, and information concerning their present whereabouts and welfare," Hull wrote.

The most the Germans would say about the Trompetters was that they were "foreign Jews" who did not follow orders to evacuate. The German Minister of Interior said he did not know where they had been taken.[86] Hull continued to insist on an answer, writing in September 1944:

> The United States government is shocked to learn that the German government is unable to find Marcelle and Betty Trompetter, two American women who were forcibly removed from their home at Nantes, France, by duly constituted authorities of the German government. It is known that these women informed the German authorities who took action against them of their American nationality. Furthermore, representations on their behalf were made to the German authorities as early as November 1942. Since the German government is after all this time unable

to account for them, the United States government has no alternative but to presume that they have been treated by the German government as other Jewish persons who were forcibly removed from their homes and transferred to unknown destinations and like most of those unfortunate individuals have either been put to death or relegated to a state of untold terror and misery which has generally led to death.

The message goes on to assert the Germans have violated their obligation to treat Americans according to the Geneva Convention. "The United States government reiterates its publicly stated intention of leaving no stone unturned in its effort to bring to justice the perpetrators of such crimes."[87]

Not surprisingly, the Nazis did not appreciate American or British requests for information about their citizens. What is shocking is the hypocrisy of their replies. Responding to the September message Hull had transmitted through the Swiss, the German Foreign Office wrote—nearly two months later—that the contents represent "an expression of calumny of the worst nature, worded in a way contradictory to all established relations between civilized nations." The Germans said they would no longer accept notes from the enemy powers unless "their wording corresponds to the customs established in the relations between civilized nations."[88] The Swiss response was to cave in to the Germans and to tell the Americans that they preferred not to forward "offensive" notes for fear that it would jeopardize their position as a protective power.[89]

In March 1945, the State Department released a list of 27 Americans deported to Germany from occupied territories in Europe, who were still listed as having disappeared. The Trompetters were among the missing.[90]

How many American Jews could have been saved had the United States taken steps to protect its citizens? Obviously, it is impossible to say. As noted earlier, the records of people claiming American citizenship are incomplete, but the State Department acknowledged more than 30,000 American civilians were still in Europe in 1944. If only a tiny fraction of these had been Jews, the State Department's failure to act would have been that much more inexcusable. Would it have been so difficult to help those few people, especially given the information available by that time of Hitler's extermination campaign?

Even when the Germans wanted to exchange Americans, the United States frequently demonstrated an unwillingness to act on its citizens' behalf. In early 1943, for example, the German government believed the U.S. had agreed to exchange Germans in the United States for Americans in Germany. The Nazis said the United States government would determine how long Americans would be interned in Germany.[91] The State Department's response was that the United States "does not deem it in the public interest to reply to the German government" and therefore "Americans must continue to remain under German control."[92] To show how many people might have been affected, a year earlier, nearly 2,500 Americans had been on a list to be considered for exchange.[93] Ultimately, several exchanges were made to repatriate Americans held in Germany and Germans held in the United States, but thousands of people remained trapped in Europe.[94]

At the very least, U.S. officials could have shown flexibility and leniency in the evaluation of claims of American citizenship. Instead, the Department adhered to a strict policy that required claimants to prove their citizenship. Simultaneously, the Department adopted an equally inflexible policy to obstruct Americans from obtaining the necessary documentation, prohibiting the transfer from the United States to enemy territory of any documents, including those that could substantiate claims to American nationality.[95] On top of this, bureaucrats in the Department were fighting turf battles over who would authenticate citizenship.[96]

The absurdity of this position was to place the burden on the Jew in Nazi hands, as occurred when the government demanded proof of citizenship from a man held in Auschwitz.[97] Many Jews may not have had legitimate claims, but the State Department knew that rejecting applicants effectively condemned them, initially to persecution and later to death.

State modified its policy somewhat in 1944. It still would not send documents to enemy territory but said it "is always prepared to protect American interests in enemy territory by furnishing information concerning the American nationality of the American nationals involved."[98] The government also took steps to protect its employees. Secretary of War Henry Stimson assigned military ranks to diplomats, trying to insure they would be treated as POWs if they were captured.[99]

Throughout the war, two major obstacles to the rescue of European Jewry were xenophobia and anti-Semitism. Had the news of Americans being mistreated been publicized, however, greater public sympathy might have been aroused for saving Jews, bombing the concentration camps and relaxing immigration quotas.

3

Americans in the Warsaw Ghetto: The Diary of Mary Berg

T HE DIARY OF ANNE FRANK has become world famous. The little Dutch girl left a remarkable record of her family's life in the attic in Amsterdam. But Anne Frank could not describe the horrors perpetrated by the Nazis. She did not observe them from that attic. An American girl did bear witness, however, and she too kept a diary. That American, Mary Berg, survived the Warsaw ghetto.[1]

In 1939, the head of the SS Intelligence Service, Reinhard Heydrich, issued instructions that Jews in the occupied areas of Poland be transferred to the ghettos that were to be established in large cities. Anti-Jewish measures were instituted requiring the wearing of a special Jewish badge, imposing forced labor and condoning the looting of Jewish property.

By the end of 1940, the largest ghetto had been established in Warsaw. Ultimately, nearly half a million Jews would be imprisoned there. Two years later, 70 percent of the Jews of Poland had been exterminated and most of the ghettos liquidated. Before the war was over, almost three million Polish Jews perished.

Few people are aware that any Americans were in the Warsaw ghetto. The only mention of an American survivor of the Warsaw ghetto I could find in the press was a small item in the *New York Times* about Mrs. Stella Wegtman of Chatham, N.J. According to the report, she "lived through the siege of Warsaw, while her Polish husband was killed and all their possessions destroyed." The Germans took her and other civilians into the countryside one day, but she escaped before learning what her fate was to be. She walked to Cracow and hid until the Red Army liberated her.[2]

But Mary Berg's diary makes clear many Americans were in the ghetto. Other than a record of a meeting in which the head of the Special Division, Breckinridge Long, was told this, the U.S. government seems to have no records of these victims of the Holocaust.

Mary was only 16 when she was sent to the ghetto. As the daughter of an American citizen, she was a member of a tiny privileged group. She wore an American flag pinned to her lapel and another flag attached to the door of her apartment to protect her from the Nazis. She was fortunate because she did not suffer the same fate as most of the Poles, but she lived with those who fought daily to survive.

On October 10, 1939, Mary's family learned the Germans had broken through the Polish front lines and were moving toward Lodz. They did not know where to flee—toward Warsaw or Brzeziny. Most chose Warsaw. Those who went to Brzeziny were massacred.

In December, two drunken Gestapo men broke into Mary's house and demanded certain objects they did not have. Her mother showed them her American citizenship papers, but they were not mollified. One drunk pulled out his gun and shouted: "Swear on Hitler's health that you're an American citizen or I'll shoot you on the spot!" Jews had been forbidden to say the Führer's name so Mary's mother asked if an exception could be made. The Nazi smiled and put his revolver away. The men left, "clicking their heels and saluting the American flag that hung in the hallway."

A few weeks later, Mary's mother received a letter from the American consulate summoning her to Warsaw. Mary was already there living with a gentile friend who, at the risk of his life, pretended she was his daughter. Later her sister arrived and the two girls used to go for walks in front of the American Embassy. "Somehow, we feel more secure in its shadows," Mary wrote.

The situation deteriorated as spring arrived in 1940. Mary stayed off the streets where men, women and children were being taken by the Nazis to do hard labor. "Better-dressed Jewish women have been forced to scrub the Nazis' headquarters. They are ordered to remove their underclothes and use them as rags for the floors and windows. It goes without saying that often the tormentors use these occasions to have some fun of their own."

One American woman underwent this treatment. Generally, foreigners were spared, but on this occasion the woman was forced to scrub floors in her fur coat. The woman complained to the American consul, who demanded that the German Governor pay her damages. The woman received 3,000 marks. "But Polish citizens of Jewish origin have no one to protect them, except themselves," Mary wrote.

In late April 1940, Mary moved into an apartment. Her mother tacked a card saying "American citizen" on the door. "This inscription is a wonderful talisman against the German bandits who freely visit all Jewish apartments. As soon as German uniforms come into view at the outer door of our building, our neighbors come begging us to let them in so that they too can benefit from our miraculous sign. Our two little rooms are filled to the brim—for how could we refuse anyone? All of the neighbors tremble with fear and with a silent prayer on their lips gaze at the two small American flags on the wall."

By the end of May, all the American consulates in Poland were closed. Mary's mother received word from the American consulate in Berlin her passport would be ready at a certain date. It no longer mattered. A new decree had been issued forbidding Jews from Warsaw to leave.

Jews also were prohibited from attending schools. Illegal classes were held in Mary's home, which was considered relatively safe because of her mother's American citizenship. "The illegal character of the teaching, the danger that threatens us every minute, fills us all with a strange earnestness," Mary wrote. "The old distance between teachers and pupils has vanished, we feel like comrades-in-arms responsible for each other."

This was still before the ghetto was constructed. On November 15, 1940, she described the change: "Today, the Jewish ghetto was officially established. Jews are forbidden to move outside the boundaries formed by certain streets . . . . Work on the walls—which will be three yards high—has already begun. Jewish masons, supervised by Nazi soldiers, are laying bricks upon bricks. Those who do not work fast enough are lashed by the overseers. It makes me think of the Biblical description of our slavery in Egypt. But where is the Moses who will release us from our new bondage?"

As an American, Mary's mother was allowed to leave the ghetto. Once a month, American citizens could pick up a package of foodstuffs from the American colony relief office in Warsaw. Friends gave Mary's mother letters to post, which had to bear Mrs. Berg's name, because the addresses had to match the name on the passport holder mailing them.

By the summer of 1941, the situation in the ghetto had deteriorated. Mary wrote a plaintive entry in her diary that reflected the feeling of Jews after the war: "Where are you, foreign correspondents? Why don't you come here and describe the sensational scenes in the ghetto? No doubt you don't want to spoil your appetite. Or are you satisfied with what the Nazis tell you—that they locked up the Jews in the ghetto in order to protect the Aryan population from epidemics and dirt?"

Mary described the scene the correspondents missed: "Komitetowa Street is a living graveyard of children devoured by scurvy. The inhabitants of this street live in long cellar-caves into which no ray of the sun ever reaches. Through the small dirty windowpanes one can see emaciated faces and disheveled heads. These are the older people, who have not even the strength to rise from their cots. With dying eyes they gaze at the thousands of shoes that pass by in the street. Sometimes a bony hand stretches out from one of these little windows, begging for a piece of bread."

In mid-September, Mary was out with a friend and wandered into an empty neighborhood. She said she wanted to go home, but it was too late. A German guard spotted them and aimed his rifle. "Everything died in me; I felt a stinging sensation in my shoulders, as though a bullet had hit me." She escaped unhurt.

Mary celebrated her 17th birthday on October 10. She thought it frivolous, given the unhappiness and misery surrounding her. She said her uncle had taken ill with typhus. The day before Mary found a louse on herself and knew that it would only be two weeks before she, too, would be infected if the louse had been contaminated.

A month later, her uncle was skin and bones. Only 27, he had once been strong and handsome. "At every step in the ghetto one encounters such human wrecks, and these are the lucky ones who succeeded in escaping the Angel of Death," Mary wrote. "In the streets, frozen human corpses are an increasingly frequent sight."

In another entry, Mary says that 60 people were executed the night before. A few lines later, she talks about her garden. "The greens and sun remind us of the beauty of nature that we are forbidden to enjoy."

In June 1942, Mary learned that an American woman was allowed to take her child to an internment camp. Meanwhile, three other American women, who had husbands and children who were born in Poland, remained in the ghetto.

Adam Czerniakow, the leader of the Jewish community in the ghetto, was told by the authorities that all foreign Jews would be allowed to leave provided their documents were in order. More than 80 were taken to Pawiak Prison in mid-July.[3]

The Bergs believed they would be among those to be exchanged. They were then deluged with people who expected them to get help the minute they reached the United States. But at that point it did not look as though Mary or her father would be allowed to leave. They were told that Mrs. Berg would be exchanged because she was an American, but she could only take children under 16. By then Mary was older, but her sister Ann was still 15 and would be permitted to leave. The Gestapo later told Mrs. Berg the whole family could go with her. "Today, I boldly removed my armband," Mary wrote. "After all, officially I am now an American citizen." But her ordeal was not yet over.

The Bergs and other Americans were transferred to Pawiak Prison. Mary anticipated freedom but was guilt-ridden. "Have I the right to save myself and leave my closest friends to their bitter fate?" she asked herself.

It was Mary's impression that the Germans needed people they could trade for Germans held in the United States. She was in a prison cell with a total of 11 Americans. When she was sent to register with the Germans once, 21 Americans were in the group.

At this time, Dr. Gaither Warfield, a missionary from Warsaw, brought a list of Americans still in Warsaw to Breckinridge Long. Warfield said they had been caught accidentally and had been unable to get out. He also brought a list of 83 Americans in the internment camp at Laufen. Long told him, "The German government had prevented our efforts to return Americans to the United States in any quantity and it would depend largely upon the ability of each one to arrange for exit permits." He added he would be happy to do whatever he could to help.[4] Of course, it was virtually impossible for anyone in Warsaw to obtain an exit permit on their own. No records of any effort by Long to assist them could be found in the Archives.

Meanwhile, the foreigners living in the prison were isolated but not mistreated. The internees composed an "anthem" in honor of the different nationalities in the prison:

There is in the Pawiak a brand-new nation
From every country and every city.
They live together in great unity
In great cold and great starvation.

Most of them are from the land
Which lies near the Paraguay;
There the life is especially gay
For the fowl and flies in the sand.

The most aristocratic group
Comes from Costa Rica;
Among them there is the black beard
Who is the leader of our troupe.

There is the prospective wife
Of a citizen of Bolivia.
Little she knows what to expect
From her future married life.

And our only Mexican
Has proposals without number.
All the girls are raving mad
To get hold of this rare man.

Two brunettes from Nicaragua—
One is quiet and one is loud,
One is modest and one proud,
But both fighting mad pro domo sua.

Three Carmens and a toreador,
An old woman and granddaughter
With lots of bags and heavy bundles
Dream of their "native" Ecuador.

Those whose flag has stars and stripes
Are the proudest of them all;
Though locked up behind these walls
They are the lords and masters.

Despite their relative seclusion, the inmates were aware of what was taking place in the ghetto, and it was driving them mad. "We are here as on an island amidst an ocean of blood," Mary wrote. "The whole ghetto is drowning in blood.

We literally see fresh human blood, we can smell it. Does the outside world know anything about it? Why does no one come to our aid? I cannot go on living; my strength is exhausted. How long are we going to be kept here to witness all this?" She considered the waiting "worse than death."

The Germans did not believe the exchanges would allow American Jews to escape the "Final Solution." Mary remembered the deputy commandant of Pawiak rapping his riding crop against his shiny boots while he boasted: "The Germans will conquer America too; we will be there before you have been exchanged."

Outside the prison, shootings continued. Inside, the "fortunate" Jews were slowly starving to death. They received four ounces of bread in the morning and ersatz coffee. At noon, they were given a dish of hot water the Germans called soup and some kasha. In the evening, they received another bowl of soup with a potato or beet in it. This diet left Mary's mother too weak to move.

While many Jews were killed within earshot of the prison, others were deported. It was not until late September 1942 that Mary learned the deportees were sent to Treblinka where they were exterminated.

On October 23, 150 "Americans" (including citizens from Latin America) were assembled in the prison yard to leave. The commandant then ordered all the men to report to the gate. He said the trains did not have room for the women; they would have to wait until tomorrow. Mary managed to kiss her father goodbye before he was taken to the train. She was relieved to see him go because he was a Polish citizen and therefore had no American papers. Once he was in an internment camp, however, he would not have to live under the threat of being sent to Treblinka. Nevertheless, Mary could not help asking herself: "Shall we ever see him again?"

Mary, her mother and sister did not leave the next day. Nor were they allowed to leave in the following days or weeks.

In December, a new group of Americans from Radom arrived in Pawiak. Mary also received two letters from her father, who was now interned in Tittmoning. He wrote that he felt as if he were in "paradise" after what he had gone through the last few years.

On January 17, 1943, Mary and her mother and sister were taken to the "Aryan" side of the ghetto so they could say goodbye to some of their friends. When they left the prison, the streets were empty. "In many houses the windows were wide open despite the cold, and the curtains fluttered in the wind. Inside one could see the overturned furniture, broken cupboard doors, clothes and linen lying on the floor. The looters and murderers had left their mark."

After they said goodbye to their friends they were returned to Pawiak. Mary watched transports being loaded with people bound for Auschwitz. "Is that where the Nazis intend to send us, too?" she said to herself.

Finally, at two A.M. the next day, Mary and her family left Pawiak prison for the last time. They were taken by train to the internment camp at Vittel. "Of course, I was glad to be rescued from this valley of death, but I could not help reproaching myself and wondering whether I really had the right to run away like this, leaving my friends and relatives to their fate."

Like her father, Mary also felt the internment camp was paradise compared to the three years she spent in the ghetto. Each person had their own bed and the camp was clean. "What more could one ask for?" For the first three days, Mary said she did not leave her bed because she "couldn't get enough of the pleasure of lying in the clean sheets."

One day Mary saw some American nuns in the park. They began to ask her about Poland and she told them about starving for six months in prison. They gave her some chocolate, but she was afraid to eat it. A nun broke off a piece and put it in her mouth. It was the first chocolate Mary had eaten in four years.

At the beginning of February 1943, Mary saw her first Red Cross parcel. Her mother cried. "All of us admired the care with which some unknown American had packed everything. Every little item reflected human warmth."

Mary continued to feel conflicted by her escape from the ghetto. On one day she would rejoice in her freedom and on another she would lapse into feelings of guilt. Of course, she was not the only one who felt this way. Survivors of the concentration camps would later experience similar emotions. "We, who have been rescued from the ghetto, are ashamed to look at each other," she wrote in June. "Had we the right to save ourselves? Why is it so beautiful in this part of the world? Here everything smells of sun and flowers, and there—there is only blood, the blood of my own people. God, why must there be all this cruelty? I am ashamed. Here I am, breathing fresh air, and there my people are suffocating in gas and perishing in flames, burned alive. Why?"

On August 6, 1943, almost 10 months after she last saw him, Mary was reunited with her father when a transport with all the men from Tittmoning arrived. A couple of months later she celebrated her 19th birthday.

Strangely, the Nazis allowed a travelogue about New York to be shown in the camp cinema. Mary saw the Statue of Liberty and Broadway. The film ended with a ship entering the port and the crowd applauded wildly.

Shortly thereafter, the mood of the camp again swung as the Germans ordered Jews to register. No one knew the reason for the order, but rumors flourished. Nothing happened.

Still more weeks passed. After more than a year in Vittel, Mary learned the first exchanges were to take place. Her mother was desperately trying to arrange for her family to be in the first group. The inmates' nerves were being frayed by the Nazis' vacillation. At one point, Mary learned her family would not be allowed to leave because her father was of military age and the commandant did not want to separate families. Of course, such a rule would have meant almost no family could have left. "This reminds me of the Nazi tactics in Pawiak," Mary wrote. "There, too, they changed their minds every minute, apparently for the sole purpose of torturing us."

The torture continued for a few more days. Then, on March 1, 1944, nearly three-and-a-half years after being sent to the Warsaw ghetto, the Berg family boarded a train for Lisbon. They arrived in New York on the *SS Gripsholm* two weeks later.

The Bergs had survived, but Mary could not forget those she left behind. She wrote to one of her friends in Warsaw: "My Rutka, tell all of those who are still alive that I shall never forget them. I shall do everything I can to save those who can still be saved and to avenge those who were so bitterly humiliated in their last moments. And those who were ground into ash, I shall always see them alive. I will tell, I will tell everything, about our sufferings and our struggles and the slaughter of our dearest, and I will demand punishment for the German murderers and their Gretchens in Berlin, Munich and Nuremberg who enjoyed the fruits of murder and are still wearing the clothes and shoes of our martyred people. Be patient, Rutka, have courage, hold out. A little more patience, and all of us will win freedom!"

4

The Meaning of Fear: Soldiers in Captivity

THE IMAGE MANY AMERICANS HAVE of German prisoner of war camps was probably shaped by *Hogan's Heroes,* the television show where prisoners made fools of bumbling Nazis. In truth, most POW camps were run by competent Germans who maintained tight control over prisoner behavior. In some cases, guards were ruthless. Many POWs were murdered, but most suffered because of conditions in the camps, that is, a lack of food, medicine and hygiene. American Jewish soldiers, meanwhile, faced the added danger of being mistreated because of their religion and also faced the ultimate threat of being deported to a concentration camp.

"From my vantage point as one of the senior POW officers who dealt with German guards and administrators all the way from the lowly camp unteroffizier to Himmler's G-2 and Hitler's four-star General in charge of all POWs in Germany," wrote Maj. Gen. Delmar Spivey, "I can categorically state that the life of a POW was a sorry one. It was one of fear, apprehension, deprivations, danger and frustration which have taken their toll on all of us."[1]

Spivey added that many Germans "honestly tried to live by the spirit and letter of the Geneva Convention. Unfortunately, they were few and far between and all too frequently were prevented by their superiors from carrying out their good intentions."[2]

The first American POW in Germany in World War II was captured on April 14, 1942. A total of 93,941 Army and Air Corps personnel were POWs in more than 50 permanent camps in the European and Mediterranean theaters.[3] Almost 99 percent survived. Of the 1,121 who died, approximately 6 percent were in one virtually unknown camp where the fatality rate was 20 percent. That camp, Berga, is the subject of Chapter 8.

Approximately 600,000 Jews served in the United States armed forces in World War II. More than 35,000 were killed, wounded, captured or missing. Approximately 8,000 died in combat.[4] Those soldiers were casualties of war, but there were others among those who were captured who became victims of the Holocaust.

POWs who are defined as Holocaust victims were discriminated against specifically because they were Jewish; they were not abused simply because they were prisoners. Many non-Jewish POWs were sent to concentration or labor camps where POW conventions were not observed and soldiers were treated like political prisoners. These men were not under military control; rather, they came under the supervision of the Nazis responsible for carrying out the "Final Solution."[5]

The mistreatment of captured soldiers should have come as no surprise to the U.S. government given what it knew of Nazi atrocities committed against civilians. The U.S. Counsel at Nuremberg, Thomas Dodd, explained:

> The transition from the mistreatment of political opponents, of racial and religious groups, to the abuse and the killing of prisoners of war in violation of the rules of warfare was not difficult for the members of the indicted organizations. . . . Reichsleiter Goebbels and Bormann, speaking for the Leadership Corps of the Nazi Party, were those who instituted the policy of lynching Allied airmen by the German populace . . . while at the same time military units of the SS wantonly executed prisoners of war on every battlefield. To the Gestapo and the SD [the SS Security Service] was given the first responsibility for carrying out the barbaric Hitler order of October 18, 1942, and its subsequent amendments calling for the summary execution of Allied commandos and paratroopers. Nor should it be forgotten that throughout the war the Gestapo screened prisoners of war for Jews and those of the Communist political faith, who were then deliberately murdered.[6]

"The attitude of the Wehrmacht to Jewish war prisoners was an extension of the general policy of the Third Reich to the Jewish problem as a whole," Szymon Datner observed. "The 'aryanization' of the army was begun on March 12, 1934, by the Reich Minister of War. An order of May 21, 1935, stated that an indispensable condition of recruitment was 'Aryan' origin and that only 'Aryans' could hold superior rank. It also forbade those in active service to marry 'non-Aryans.' Later, Jews were prohibited from being drafted into active service and persons of mixed blood could not hold commands."[7]

The fears of Jewish soldiers stemmed from the knowledge of what was happening to Jewish civilians and what had happened to other POWs, notably Soviet Jewish POWs. In his 1941 "Commissar Order," Hitler ordered the elimination of political representatives and commissars whom the Führer considered the "driving forces of Bolshevism." That July, all Jewish POWs from the eastern front were ordered to be killed. Unlike the Americans, the Russians did not have dog tags identifying their religion, so the Germans made their determinations based on appearances. In 1942, 4,000 Jewish Soviet POWs were sent to Majdanek; only a few survived. From May 1, 1940, to December 1, 1943, 20,000 Russian POWs were murdered at Auschwitz.[8]

No similar order was ever made concerning Jewish POWs from Britain, France or the United States. Although Nazi propaganda claimed the Allies did not care about Jews, the Germans thought those nations would care very much if Jews from their armies became victims. Moreover, the Nazis were concerned that the 370,000 German POWs would be mistreated if the Western nations learned Jewish prisoners were being abused.[9]

In fact, the U.S. military increased the probability of captured Jews being identified by stamping their dog tags with an "H" for Hebrew. This was ostensibly done so the correct chaplain could be called if a soldier was wounded or killed. One former POW said this religious identification system was useless since each battalion only had one minister and the one in his was a Catholic. "In my three years overseas, I never saw a rabbi," Arnold Krochmal said.[10] The consequence of this practice was to place unnecessarily at risk 600,000 American Jewish soldiers.

The most dangerous time for any soldier was immediately following his capture, particularly after Hitler began to encourage the lynching of airmen and other summary executions of the enemy. Often, the fate of a GI depended on who captured him and how disciplined they were. Generally, when prisoners were taken by the regular German military, they were not mistreated. The SS was another matter, of course.

Still, Jewish soldiers never knew what to expect. During the Battle of the Bulge in December 1944, for example, long columns of Americans were being marched to German rear areas. The SS ordered POWs to expose their dog tags. Sgt. George Golman said to Cpl. Billy Heroman: "My God, what am I going to do?" Heroman was wearing a rosary and he handed it to Golman. When the SS made their inspection, they saw the rosary and didn't bother to check Golman's dog tags. Then Billy Heroman had a narrow escape, as Golman tells it: "Billy has a hook nose and the Germans began questioning him pretty hard. The evil eyes of the SS were upon Heroman until—again, quick thinking—he pulled out a Bible and challenged the Germans to turn to any page and he would quote passages to them. Then he started reciting the doxology to them in Latin and finally convinced them that he was Catholic."[11] Other Jews were also shielded by comrades who swapped dog tags or gave them bibles.

Several soldiers said Jews were sometimes executed after being captured. Arnold Krochmal said a Jew from his company was shot. "The GIs, in turn, caught the German captain whose troops had done this, tied his legs together, tied him to a jeep and dragged him."[12] Like many such stories, it is almost impossible to verify this account.

We do know that most POWs were taken for interrogation after their capture. Arthur Durand described the process at Dulag Luft, the transit camp of the air force located near Oberursel:

> If the prisoner was able to withhold the desired information throughout extended friendly conversations, threats of violence abruptly followed. The primary threat,

that the captive would be turned over to the Gestapo, was employed most effectively when the prisoner refused to identify his unit. The interrogator repeatedly insisted that this information was needed to prove the subject's claim that he was an aviator. Until such proof was given, he reminded the prisoner, no word would be sent out regarding his capture. . . . Furthermore, they [prisoners] knew that until the Red Cross received information about their captivity, the Germans could kill or otherwise keep them hidden away for years, all the while claiming they had never been captured. Jews were told they might be subjected to persecution, and whenever the Germans learned a prisoner had relations in German-held territory, they suggested what might happen if they did not talk.[13]

Second Lieutenant Edgar Denton testified after the war that he and his crew had been forced to bail out of their plane in November 1944. They were captured and taken to headquarters. The Germans asked which of the men was Weissman. They had his name because the men had all given their name, rank and serial number. Weissman was being interrogated when an air raid began. The crew thought they heard pistol shots during the raid and suspected Weissman had been killed because he was not sent away with the other men after the air raid. He was never on any POW lists and was listed as missing in action after the men returned to the States.[14]

It was in the initial period after surrendering that all POWs, but especially Jews, were at greatest risk of mistreatment or worse. When they were captured, Jews had to make a choice whether to hide their identities or risk an uncertain fate. Leonard Winograd was taken to a prison at Zagreb where he was slapped by a German noncommissioned officer because he had refused to tell him his religion. Winograd's friend told the prison commander he did not know if Winograd was Jewish. The NCO was subsequently ordered to apologize for slapping Winograd. He refused "because he was a German and I was a Jew and, he told me, he could *see* that I was a Jew because of my face."[15]

Later Winograd was taken to an air force interrogation center near Frankfurt. The interrogator said he had nothing against Jews, but the Gestapo was responsible for all suspected terrorists, and unless Winograd talked he would be turned over to the Gestapo. "He advised me that they would not be as considerate of my feelings or my safety as the German Air Force would be."

Winograd refused to talk. "The interrogator's last words to me were that he felt very sorry for me. He really did not think that I was an underground bandit, but I had been very foolish and had not helped him at all."

Winograd was sent to Stalag VII-A in Moosburg. A British POW responsible for filling out informational forms on new arrivals told him he would not write down that he was a Jew because after five years as a prisoner he had seen too many Jews disappear. "I answered that I would not lie about my Jewishness. He suggested that he write down Protestant for my religion. I refused. He told me that I was signing my own death warrant. I told him that I had not come halfway around the world to lie about my religion; *that* was what the war was all about, and if I did what he asked and we won the war, I would still be the loser. He wrote it down and told me that he was sorry for me." Winograd was lucky; he suffered some abuse but survived to talk about it. Even so, he felt "the ever-present horror of being a Jew in prison in Germany."[16]

One POW camp where the possibility of deportation to a concentration camp nearly became a reality was in Stalag Luft I, an air force officer camp in Barth, near the Black Sea. After the massive Allied bombing of Dresden in early 1945, Jews in the camp were segregated by the Nazis. The decision to accept the German order was made by the ranking Allied officer, Colonel Hubert Zemke.[17]

Zemke said he received a list of Jewish POWs from the commandant but did not know why they were to be segregated. He insisted that religion was irrelevant to the prosecution of the war. The Germans went ahead and separated the men. Zemke says he requested that they be placed in a barracks next to his so he could keep an eye on them, and the Germans consented. He was also responsible for the distribution of Red Cross parcels, clothing, food, blankets, and other items, which Zemke said were evenly disbursed to all prisoners, including the Jews who had been segregated.[18]

Earlier, the Nazis convinced the American barracks leader to go along with a separation of British and American POWs despite protests by junior officers who presciently warned that allowing such segregation would set a bad precedent. According to former prisoner Ed Neft, when Jews were ordered segregated, the POWs understood the action was taken on orders from Berlin under a clause of the Geneva Convention permitting segregation according to race and religion.[19] "To point out how discriminatory this 'segregation' was," Eugene Hayes, another ex-POW noted, "there were American POWs of black, Hispanic, oriental and Arabic descent being held in the same camp but they were not segregated!"[20]

Irving Lifson remembered the camp being stunned in January when another senior officer, Col. Einar Malmstrom, was presented with two lists, one of "Jewish" prisoners and another "Probably Jewish." Lifson was on the probable list. "My fear from the time I bailed out finally came to pass," he wrote. When the Germans were asked the purpose of the lists, they said the Jews did not belong in Barth and were being sent to an all-Jewish camp. "At that point in time, we didn't know about the extermination camps, but we had a gut feeling that we were going to be killed."[21] Another former prisoner, Sam Kalman, explained that the block captain used the excuse that the approximately 120 Jewish officers were to be sent to a "central" camp, but there was little doubt in the minds of the prisoners that this meant a concentration camp.[22]

Some Jews threw away their dog tags or tried to hide their identity, but the Germans had their own methods of distinguishing prisoners. According to John Vietor: "The goons posted a list of names in each barracks, supposedly the names of the Jewish officers concerned. Vaunted German thoroughness was noticeably lacking in the capricious manner in which they had decided who was Jewish and who wasn't. Kellys and O'Briens were included and a few Cohens left out, much to the bafflement and concern of the kriegies [prisoners] involved."[23]

One Jewish POW who did not come forward said he eventually learned that he had been put on the probable list because he had refused to disclose his mother's maiden name during the initial interrogation when he arrived at the camp. Maurice Fridrich's block captain told him he was on the list and asked if he was Jewish. The man said no and the captain believed him because he had never seen him at services. Later, the captain told him the Germans were going to further interrogate the "probables." Fridrich was never questioned. He thinks the Germans gave up because one of the first POWs they interviewed was an American Indian who convinced them he was not Jewish by dropping his pants and showing them he still had a foreskin.[24]

While in the camp, the Jews were not mistreated. In fact, Neft said they were permitted to conduct religious services, which they did at least initially "to piss the Nazis off."

Kalman said prior to the segregation order, High Holy Day services were held in a tent facing the center of the compound and the ever-present Nazi guards. The Nazis gave permission for the tent to be used for Christian worship. Unbeknownst to the Germans, it was made available without Nazi approval to Jewish POWs by Father Michael Charlton, a Roman Catholic priest. Charlton was a captain in the British Forces and served as the POWs' Catholic chaplain. Kalman said an American lieutenant led the services in Hebrew from memory. "Fasting was hardly a problem," he added.

Kalman said the 40 Jews who attended these services did so not only as a religious observance but also as an act of defiance. Once they were segregated, moreover, the Jewish POWs stood together proudly during the twice-daily roll calls.[25]

In the end, the Jews were never transferred from the POW camp. "The camp we were supposed to go to must have been overrun by the Russians in Poland," Lifson believes, "because they kept postponing it, and on May 1, 1945, the Russians overran Stalag Luft I."[26] Kalman thinks the deportation order would have been carried out if the Germans had won the Battle of the Bulge.[27]

In other POW camps, American Jewish soldiers were victims of "special treatment" that ranged from various types of discrimination to physical abuse.[28] For example, at Stalag II-B, the Germans refused to negotiate with Pvt. Harry Goller, the "Man of Confidence" (MOC) elected by his comrades to represent them to the commandant, when they learned he was Jewish. They had dealt with him for nearly a year before that. Also at Stalag II-B, American Jews were singled out for kickings, cuffings and blows from rifle butts.[29] At Luft III (Luft camps were for air force officers), the Germans relieved the cook of his duties after they discovered he was Jewish. At Luft IV, one Jewish POW was treated worse than the rest of the Americans. Also at Luft IV, a German guard called "Big Stoop" picked up a belt and beat an American Jewish prisoner during a strip search.[30] At Stalag IV-B, Jews were told by other prisoners not to admit their identity. The POWs told newcomers Jews were sent out to collect bombs that did not go off but that when moved usually exploded.[31]

During a Red Cross visit to Stalag VII-A in January 1945, British, American and French spokesmen protested that Jewish prisoners had been segregated. Nearly a year later, an intelligence report prepared by the War Department repeated that Jewish POWs in the camp had been segregated for a time and were not offered any religious services.[32]

At Stalag XIII-C, the German guards ordered all Jews to step forward. The non-Jews said not to move. Some stepped forward and were taken away. They were never seen again. One former POW at XIII-C recalled having a friend who did not step forward. Instead, Al Goldstein was sent out with other POWs to work in a warehouse. Apparently, someone tipped off the Germans that he was Jewish. "Al's punishment for being a Jew was he went to work with the group but when he got to the warehouse they would put him down in the bottom of an elevator shaft and he wouldn't get out of that shaft until nightfall. His punishment was that he was not able to associate with anybody and had to stay in the elevator shaft."[33]

Jewish POWs could usually count on their comrades for help. For example, there was a concerted effort to help the Jews conceal their identities in Luft III. Durand said it was either successful or else the Germans decided not to bother the Jews in that camp. The only Jews he knew who died were a man who suffered fatal injuries trying to escape from a train and a soldier who had pneumonia in the camp. After 1943 Hitler had ordered that military honors should not be given to POWs who died in the camps. Nevertheless, the commandant of Luft III decided to go ahead with such a funeral for the man who jumped the train. When he learned that the GI was a Jew, he concealed the man's identity and had a Catholic priest administer last rites.[34]

In at least one instance, the POW camp commandant refused to obey the order to segregate Jewish prisoners. One Jewish air force officer who ended up in Stalag III-A in Luckenwald said Hitler had issued an order to segregate Jewish prisoners so they could be terminated. The camp commandant came to Jerome Katzman, knowing he was Jewish, to ask him to identify the Jewish prisoners. The commandant said: "We do not have any Jewish prisoners, do we?" Katzman replied: "Nope." And that was the end of the incident.[35]

The casualty figures cited at the beginning of the chapter probably do not include POWs who died in concentration camps. Investigators during the war said no POWs were in the death camps. In April 1945, at the request of General Eisenhower, a Congressional committee visited Buchenwald, Nordhausen and Dachau. They submitted a detailed report of the shocking conditions.[36] "In the first place," the report noted, "the concentration camps for political prisoners must not be confused with prisoner of war camps. No prisoners of war are confined in any of these political-prisoner camps, and there is no relationship whatever between a concentration camp for political prisoners and a camp for prisoners of war."

There were indeed distinctions between the types of camps, but many POWs *were* sent to concentration camps—including those visited by the committee— where the prisoners were tortured and killed. And the United States government knew it. Besides those incidents, a handful of other cases can be cited where Americans were reported in concentration camps: One American major who had been captured behind enemy lines on a mission for the OSS was found in Dachau when the camp was liberated.[37] In September 1944, Hallett Johnson of the American Legation in Stockholm wired to the Secretary of State that he had been told by an informant that some American fliers shot down in Munich, some of whom were black, had been sent to Dachau. Between December 1942 and April 1943, several dozen American and British captured airmen were machine-gunned at Sachsenhausen.[38]

War crimes investigators described Flossenbürg as "a factory dealing in death." According to several reports, 13 American *or* British parachutists were hung there after being captured trying to blow up bridges in March or April 1945.[39] One account said a Serbian medical student claimed he helped cut down 13 Americans and carried their bodies to the crematorium.[40] He could have mistaken the Americans for Englishmen.

Regardless, a report of the U.S. Third Army, Judge Advocate Section, introduced at Nuremberg, concluded American POWs were killed at Flossenbürg concentration camp. In the war crimes trial against the Nazis specifically responsible for Flossenbürg, the prosecutor said: "English and American POWs were placed in dark isolated cells. Some of these inmates remained in these cells from their arrival until April 1945, a few as long as 11 months. . . . An American second lieutenant who was confined in this prison was hanged the day before Good Friday in April 1945." The SS medic at the camp testified he had treated an American who was later executed.[41]

The most horrifying stories concern American POWs sent to Buchenwald and Mauthausen. They are detailed in the next two chapters.

5

Bodies in the Mirror:
POWs in Buchenwald

Six months before the Congressional delegation requested by Eisenhower arrived in Buchenwald, a group of Americans learned firsthand what Eugen Kogon called the "Theory and Practice of Hell."[1] For a nine-week period that most felt was an eternity, 82 United States Air Force personnel, along with 86 other Allied fliers, experienced what had become the lives of European Jews. The stories of the Allied airmen who ended up in Buchenwald are similar. Most were shot down over France during the summer of 1944, taken in by the resistance and eventually betrayed.

When Bill Gibson's plane was hit by cannon fire, for example, he bailed out. Only then did he discover that he had only clipped on one side of his parachute. He began spinning around and landed on the roof of a little farmhouse. The pilot of his plane noisily landed nearby on a box of empty wine bottles. The two men ran off until they found somewhere to sleep. They woke up to a tremendous roar and saw three Focke-Wulf 190s no more than 50 feet above their heads. "We'd fallen asleep at the end of a main runway of a German fighter base," Gibson recalled.[2]

A farmer picked Gibson and the pilot up and hid them in a one-horse cart and took them to his home. He turned them over to the resistance, which eventually put them in a hotel in Paris to be transferred to Spain.

One day a man who claimed to be an American came and asked suspicious-sounding questions that they refused to answer. He then met them in a large black car. The pilot and Gibson sat in the front. Two other airmen sat in the back with another man. "They drove us down the Champs Elysées," Gibson said. "I saw a building ahead with two swastikas. Then I felt something in my side, and looked down and saw it was a .45 automatic. The driver said: 'Sorry boys, German police. You're our prisoners.'"[3]

Sometimes fate took a hand.

Ed Carte was on his 22nd bombing raid. It was an easy target, a marshaling yard outside Paris. His plane was hit by antiaircraft fire and became engulfed in flames. He clamped on a parachute but hesitated when he got to the escape hatch. His navigator kicked him out.

When Carte landed, he gathered up his chute and ran. He found another member of the crew and the two of them fled the scene of the crash. They were running one in front of the other to avoid ambushes. Carte was behind when he came to a fork in the road. The other crewman was out of sight. Carte called out to him but received no answer.

Carte then had two choices: the road to the right or to the left. He chose to go to the right. Later, Carte learned his comrade had gone to the left, hid with the French underground for three months and was liberated by the Americans. Carte was less fortunate. He was captured by the Gestapo.[4]

Many Allied airmen were captured in civilian clothes, but others were either in uniform or still in possession of their dog tags. The Nazis had no doubt as to their identities. But their military status had by then ceased to be relevant.

In May 1944, Hitler decided that enemy airmen who were shot down should be executed without court martial if they had attacked downed German airmen, public transport trains or civilians. Airmen found guilty of the above offenses were considered "Terrorfliegers" (terror fliers). German civilians were also encouraged to lynch captured pilots. Those airmen who were turned over to the authorities were subject to "special treatment" at the hands of the SD (the intelligence service of the SS), that is, to be killed.

The German Foreign Office objected that the shooting of prisoners of war was contrary to international law. It suggested that enemy airmen be informed on capture that they were not regarded as prisoners of war but as criminals and would therefore not be handed over to the authorities responsible for POWs but to prosecutors.[5] Hitler's decree was subsequently enforced inconsistently. Nazi Party fanatics and local police carried out sporadic lynchings, but the Luftwaffe did not pass the order down the chain of command.[6]

The Allied airmen captured around Paris were taken to Fresnes Prison in the city, where they were incarcerated with other "criminals." Most of the POWs were not severely mistreated in prison, though some were beaten or placed in solitary confinement.

Around midnight on August 15, all the prisoners in Fresnes—including 168 Allied airmen—were put in old 40 and 8 boxcars (so named because they were designed for 40 men or 8 horses) that were originally used in World War I to carry troops to the front. The prisoners had no idea where they were going beyond that they were heading for Germany.

"We were packed so thickly on the train that there was no possibility of lying down to sleep or rest," recalled Staff Sergeant Thomas Richey. About 80–90 people were packed in cars that could fit no more than 35 comfortably. It was unbearably hot, with little ventilation. Only 10 or 15 could sit at once. None of the soldiers had wounds, but some civilians were sick, including some who had typhus. A few of the women were pregnant. The latrine consisted of a pail that was emptied no more than twice during the entire trip. The only food was a half loaf of bread and some jam and an occasional drink of water.

Many people passed out from sheer exhaustion and the trauma of having SS guards shooting over them. The guards would throw "heavy missiles in our midst and use every device and method to keep us terrified and awake," said Richey.[7]

At one point the prisoners were taken out of the boxcars because a bridge was blown out. Most cars were stuck in a tunnel, the smoke and lack of fresh air making many men feel faint. The prisoners spent the day marching around the bridge to take another train. Officers and NCOs were forced to carry the Germans' kits and supplies about three miles. Several men were beaten along the way.[8]

Later in the trip, several men escaped. The Germans had threatened to shoot five people for every one that escaped. They ordered 35 men out of a boxcar.

A French boy, about 17 years old, was near the window. One guard shot him through the hand. The Germans took him out of the car and ordered him to walk toward the river. While he was walking, they opened fire and killed him. They stepped up and pumped several more shots into his body. Five of the 35 men were ordered to dig a grave. The prisoners were allowed to return to the train, but the Germans stripped everyone in the boxcar from which the men had escaped. They were kept naked for 24 hours.[9]

The train ride was wretched. Some people died in the suffocating conditions. "All of us were glad to get out at Buchenwald," Park Chapman recalls. "Of course, we didn't know it was a civilian concentration camp."[10]

The transport that left Paris carried 1,650 prisoners, including the 168 POWs. About 850 of the passengers were women who were sent to Ravensbrück; some eventually came to Buchenwald as "volunteers" for the brothel. The rest arrived at Buchenwald around noon on August 20, 1944. Fewer than 300 would go home to France.[11]

The POWs were classified as *Polizeihiftling*—political prisoners—and their orders said they were not to be transferred to another camp. Of the 82 Americans, 40 were officers and 42 enlisted men. At least one of these men was Jewish, but no effort was made to identify Jews, and the prisoners never discussed it among themselves.

When the prisoners left the train, they walked through the camp gate and saw naked people coming out of the building to which they were being led. "We thought that won't happen to us," Jim Hastin recalled.[12] Inside the building, the prisoners were shaved from head to toe. "If a guy had a big moustache, the clippers went right across his mouth. There were no disinfecting or sanitary measures. After five days on the train, you can imagine the condition of us, with diarrhea and the other problems we had."[13]

The men were then stripped, and their clothes and personal effects were taken from them. They were given about a two-minute shower and then handed a dish-size towel for every two men. Prisoners then marched up a few steps and were told to straddle a bucket while a man hit them with a mop under each arm and in the crack of their behinds to disinfect them. "You walked two or three steps," Hastin recalled, "and it felt like someone had put turpentine on you or really lit you up." The Germans then issued each man a thin pongee shirt and light denim pants, which were taken from Jewish prisoners who had been exterminated. The shirt had a red triangle with the letter "A" over their hearts to signify they were political prisoners. A black number was stenciled on a piece of white tape stuck to their pants. The survivors remember their numbers to this day.

The POWs' shoes were taken away. They were not returned until about two weeks before they were released. When they left the camp, their clothes were also returned but not their other personal possessions like wedding rings and cigarette lighters.

The Germans had originally told the men they were being sent to a labor camp. The POWs did not know anything about Buchenwald. "When we first saw the condition of prisoners, we started worrying," said Hastin.

Hastin had injured his foot when he landed in his parachute, and he walked with a cane. An SS officer took the cane away and hit him across the back. "There are no cripples here," he said.[14]

Initially, the men were forced to sleep outside in a yard paved with large granite stones. It was freezing, but the POWs had only one blanket for every five men. They slept belly to butt to keep warm. One guy would say "turn over" and everyone would reverse positions. "The guy on the end whose butt was exposed had to be the first one to turn, and we had to turn one at a time. You rolled from your right side to your left side. And the next guy did the same so he could keep his belly warm and your butt warm. It was like a large sleeping bag," recalled Hastin.[15]

At first, the weather was relatively warm, but it later rained for nine straight days. This meant the men had to sleep in wet clothes on the damp ground. Since they had no shoes, many men cut their feet, which then became infected. "Feet and legs swelled up to where you could not distinguish an ankle from the rest of the leg," François Deuteuil recalled. "They had to be assisted to the urinals and the roll calls."

During the last week it snowed and the temperature dropped to five or ten degrees above zero. Sometimes the men had to stand outdoors for up to seven hours, barefoot, at attention, while the entire camp was counted during the roll calls conducted at 5 A.M. and 6 P.M.

Some POWs found or stole shoes of some sort. The value of such things became clear to Arthur Kinnis when he gave a Frenchman who had been a millionaire the extra pair of clogs he had. The man broke into tears.[16]

The latrine was about fifty feet away. It had no seats, just a railing. The pit was not screened or covered on the sides. It had only a roof. This trench, with room for no more than 15 people, was used by all the prisoners—numbering in the thousands—in the compound. It was a source of filth and disease, which drained into some barracks. The POWs, when they were barefoot, had to wade through mud and urine to use it.

According to one POW, Frederick Carr, dead bodies were put in the latrine until they could be carted away and cremated. "Dead bodies were in the latrine all the time," he said.[17] A faucet outside the latrine provided drinking water.

After about two weeks, the soldiers were moved to the Kleinelager, Block 58, an old horse barn that served as a barracks. It had been formerly occupied by 500 gypsy children, ages two to twelve, who disappeared one day. Later, the POWs were told they had been exterminated.[18]

About 68 Americans slept in a space 20 feet by 7 feet. When Congressional investigators toured Buchenwald, they figured out the space in the bunks was about 35 cubic feet per man, whereas the minimum prescribed for health by U.S. Army regulations was 600 cubic feet. "It was impossible for everyone to lay straight on their backs."[19] Five men slept in a four-tier bunk that was large enough for only two.

The barracks had no mattresses, only one thin blanket full of vermin. They also had no heat. Initially, two blankets were available for every three men, but they stole additional ones until each man had one blanket.

"If you had to go to the john, which was 9–10 times per night, you'd slide out and run like hell and then slip back in."[20] Most of the men had lost control of their bladders and wet themselves. Park Chapman remembers suffering from dysentery and having to pull his shirt between his legs to make a kind of bag and then duck-waddling to the latrine. "I just released my shirt tail and then tore it off up to my navel and dropped it. I didn't poop on the barracks floor. I was scared they'd run me out of the barracks."[21]

Breakfast consisted of about one-third loaf of black bread and one-twentieth of a pound of margarine issued at 5 A.M. Arthur Kinnis said he could not stomach the bread at first and would light a fire to burn the wood out of it. The Nazis stopped that practice.

At 11 A.M., the POWs had to pick up their lunch. Only about two-thirds of the men were fit enough to carry soup, which was served in a barrel that took four men to haul. Each man was given one liter of soup made of dehydrated vegetables that were always wormy. The prisoners called this the "green death." At about 4 P.M. ersatz coffee was served. It was usually cold because it came from the kitchen on the other side of the camp. Twice a week, they were given a small ration of potatoes and once a week a small piece of bologna. Some days the men got three or four glasses of water, others only one glass.

The men had to make their own wooden spoons. At first, they did not have enough bowls and had to share. Two or three men would eat out of the same wooden pot, which was seldom washed.

Most of the time, Hastin said, they spent picking fleas and killing lice. Since they were always hungry, their conversations tended to revolve around food. Someone made a deck of cards, but the Germans would beat the prisoners if the guards caught them playing.[22]

The senior officers protested more than once about their imprisonment. Each time, however, Stratton Appleman said, they were told that "we were Luftwaffe gangsters and were lucky to be treated as well as we were."[23]

The POWs tried to behave like an army unit. This gave them a degree of security. Also, they kept to themselves and did their best to block out what they saw around them. But they could not. Even today, 47 years later, survivors break down when they recall the horrors they witnessed. "I'm like an old Jew who cries when he talks about the concentration camps," said West Virginia survivor Park Chapman.

These American soldiers were in no way prepared for what they were to see. "When we first arrived," recalled Frederick Carr, "we noticed one group being given a few loaves of bread and they would fight, actually chew one another, to get their ration of bread."[24] The POWs saw other inmates kicked and beaten. Some prisoners were blind, others could not speak, still others were missing limbs. They were all scrawny with gaunt eyes. The flesh was rotting away. "It was a shock to see so many emaciated forms," Arthur Kinnis said in an interview. "We were told by a Frenchman the only way out was up the chimney."

The POWs did not see anyone go into the crematoria, but they knew the ovens were working day and night. "The foul smell got into your nostrils, but you got used to it," Chapman recalled.[25] The only people who were witnesses were those who worked in the ovens, but after four months they too went "up the chimney."[26]

At one point, 1,700 Polish Jews were brought into the camp. They were walking skeletons. The POWs took up a collection for them when they heard they were being sent to Auschwitz. Another time, a Polish Jew was hung and his body kept dangling for four days outside their barracks.[27]

On October 5, 300 Jews arrived from salt mines where they had been doing forced labor. They were being sent to Auschwitz. "They appeared utterly devoid of hope. Their faces bore signs of the deepest sorrow. Many had tears in their eyes. They were packed into the same boxcars in which they had arrived, so many in each boxcar, they must stand for the duration of their trip—probably their last."[28]

"People you knew disappeared regularly," Chapman said. "I met a husband and brother who were with me in Paris. They disappeared. Another man, a Frenchman who had worked in the American Embassy in Paris, was designated for a transport. He gave me his gold wedding ring and told me to give it to his wife if I survived."[29]

Bill Gibson recalled seeing the guards let their dogs loose on a prisoner whom they chewed to pieces. Another former prisoner said the guards used to give a command and their dogs would snarl and leap for your face. The guard would pull them away at the last minute and then laugh like a maniac. "They were sadists, absolutely brutish," he said.[30]

On another occasion, a Pole who had collaborated with the guards was beaten to death by the prisoners and thrown into the latrine. Chapman did not want to look. "I didn't want to see anyone kicked to death. I was also afraid the Germans would kill those involved. They did nothing. I think they wanted to let the man die."[31]

The POWs who survived Buchenwald swear they saw shrunken heads and lamp shades with human tattoos in the camp "museum." Russian POWs had eagles tattooed on their chests. One Russian told William Powell that the commandant's wife, Ilse Koch, thought that they made good decorations for lamp shades and had the tattoos cut off their chests.[32]

Some POWs were beaten, but, by and large, they were not physically abused by the guards. The man in charge of the Allies' barracks, a man named Bach, roughed the men up a bit but "didn't treat us Allied prisoners nearly as bad as he did the regular civilian political prisoners," Carr testified.[33] Another guard, known to be particularly vicious, was called "Big Stoop." He carried around a two-by-four that he used to beat prisoners. The POWs made a point of avoiding him.

One grotesque feature of the camp was a brothel. Women from Ravensbrück—a concentration camp for women—and elsewhere in Europe "volunteered" for this duty to stay alive. The Germans also used the girls for experiments.[34] Even more bizarre was the movie theater. Chapman remembers seeing a film while he was in Buchenwald. Other men remember an orchestra that played "while some of these hideous goddamn tortures were going on."[35]

Many POWs' lives were undoubtedly saved because they managed to avoid working. At one point, the Germans lined up the Allied prisoners and asked if any were plumbers, electricians or carpenters. No one said anything. A German officer walked up to one POW and asked: "What is your occupation?" He said: "I'm an officer in the U.S. Air Force." He went to the next man and asked the same question and got the same answer. As he went down the line, he grew increasingly angry and began yelling. He started to reach for his weapon when he was called away by another German. When he came back, he said: "I never saw such a bunch of hobos, nobody with an occupation." Earlier, Phil Lamason, the senior officer, had instructed the men not to say anything about what they did before the war.[36]

The Germans wanted the POWs to work breaking up stones in the quarry. They threatened to take the POWs' rations away and later to execute them. But the Allies refused to work and the Germans never carried out their threats.

One of the worst aspects of captivity was that the POWs knew their families were suffering. The U.S. Air Force had no idea where they were. To cite one example, Mrs. Robert Chalot received a letter on March 30, 1944, from the Commander of the Eighth Fighter Command saying that her son John had died. He suggested she take solace in knowing that "he went as a red blooded man, his colors flying in honor; with his eyes fixed on a great ideal." Four months later, Mrs. Chalot received a letter from the Adjutant General in the War Department to say that her son was missing. Then, in early October, the Adjutant General wrote again to say no further information had been received. On December 3, almost 9 months after she had been told her son had been killed, Mrs. Chalot received a telegram informing her that the International Red Cross had reported John as a POW. But that was not the end of the correspondence. A chaplain from the 355th Fighter Group wrote to the Chalots on March 6, 1945, almost exactly a year after he had first been reported missing, reaffirming that John was a POW and ingenuously adding that "we have every reason to believe our men, held prisoners, are receiving reasonable fair treatment."[37] No official ever told the Chalots their son had been in Buchenwald.

It would be misleading to suggest that the POWs were all heroic figures. They were not singing patriotic songs or defying the Germans (beyond their refusal to work). And, after several weeks in the camp, it was evident no one could be trusted. No POW dared leave anything around for fear it would be taken. On the other hand, other prisoners occasionally helped the POWs. A group of Danish priests, for example, shared food from their parcels. But the POWs quickly learned they were fighting for survival and few rules applied.

Among the dangers of the camp were the Allied forces, which bombed and strafed the area. A munitions factory was located near the camp and was frequently bombed. The POWs' barracks was about a half mile from the factory, but others were as near as 200 yards.[38]

When the Americans flew over, the SS ordered the POWs to lie on their stomachs and said if they raised their heads they would be shot. "The bomber pilots were trying to dig deeper into the ground," Hastin said. "Later, we all dug in."[39]

The Americans dropped leaflets and the prisoners were told if they so much as tried to take one they would be killed. One leaflet showed a picture of a POW camp in the States and said in German that this was the way prisoners were treated in America.[40]

No Americans were killed or injured during the raid. As punishment, the appell (roll call) that usually took two hours was dragged out for six.[41] And men had to be out of the barracks whether they were dead or alive. The latter would sometimes have to drag out the former to insure the count was correct.

On August 24, between 1218 and 1234 hours, 129 B-17s from the Eighth Air Force bombed the Gustloff Munitions Works and the DAS Factory.[42] The larger of the SS barracks was smashed and the place was still burning the next day. Two prisoners' barracks and half of another in the other compound and the crematorium were burned by incendiary bombs.

In the rush to get out of the buildings as the bombs exploded, many people were trampled to death. When the majority got outside, they rushed the gates to seek safety in the forest; SS guards machine-gunned and killed about 300.

Approximately 150 SS guards and their dependents were killed and approximately 250 more were wounded; 315 prisoners (perhaps as many as 500) were killed and more than 1400 wounded in the raid.[43]

One Englishman was lying on the ground. He said: "My god, I've been hit." Another prisoner asked him where and he said in the back. The SS had their guns trained on the prisoners. The unhurt man ran his hand along the downed prisoner's back and found a piece of shrapnel about an inch and a half thick sticking out of his shoulder blade. He grabbed the scorching hot metal and yanked it out.

After the raid, the SS ordered all the POWs out of the barracks and told them to leave their possessions because they would not need them. "This was when the prisoners shook hands and said: 'I guess this is it because they're going to take us up and say we were killed in the bombing,'" Hastin recalled. "We gave what food we had away. Then as we were going out the gate, they said leave one man to watch your stuff. I don't know who it was, but it was like a load was taken off."

The prisoners were then ordered to extinguish the flames. One recalled a German saying: "You started the fire; you put it out."[44] The POWs were forced to fight the fires in their bare feet under the constant threat of detonating explosives. Many prisoners got burns on their feet from this duty.

The POWs were told to take care of the prisoners who were injured in the factory, but the Germans gave them only crepe paper bandages and some iodine. "I don't know how many were killed," one POW testified. "We were told we have to look after these guys. There was no way we could do anything for them."[45]

The principal threats to the POWs were malnutrition and disease. Some civilians had been in the camp since 1936. All of them were unhealthy, many were unable to stand. The Allied prisoners had to mingle with the sick prisoners. Not surprisingly, at least 30 men were sick, the majority with pneumonia and pleurisy. Most of the other men had dysentery. They all lost 10–60 pounds. For the most part, sick POWs could expect no more than to have their scabs cut off with an unsterile pocket knife and to have their sores swabbed. The dentist claimed to have pulled out more teeth than anyone in the world. Before the war, the man had been a carpenter.[46]

The men resisted medical treatment until they were so sick they could not get off the ground or had such a high fever they became delirious. The POWs did not want to go to the hospital because they believed they would never survive if they did. "We saw bodies stacked like cordwood from the hospital," Kinnis recalled, "so we didn't want to go to the hospital." One POW who was in the hospital said he saw as many as a dozen people die every night. "I can still see the faces of these men lying there dying—skin and bones, their eyes glassy, mouths open. They were trying to cry out the names of their loved ones."[47]

Although most POWs avoided the hospital, they could not escape Nazi experimentation. None of the men know why, but they all received an inoculation of some "green stuff" in the left breast. The same needle was used until it broke off. At first the POWs thought the shots were for TB, but they began to have doubts when they learned about other experiments. The only immediate reaction was for the area where they were injected to turn black and blue, though some men now say their left breasts became larger afterward.[48]

Two Allied soldiers died in Buchenwald, one British and one American. RAF officer Philip Hemmens died first, around September 14, of rheumatic fever. He had received practically no medical attention for seven days before he was put in the hospital. The next day he died. The Germans returned the body so the prisoners could conduct a funeral service for him, then he was cremated.[49]

The American, Lt. Levitt Beck, died of pneumonia, which may have been contracted during the first couple of weeks when they slept outside in the rain. He, too, was sick for about a week. A Harvard-educated Austrian doctor, a fellow prisoner, came down to the POWs' barracks every day. He gave Beck some aspirin, which was about all the medicine he had to dispense, and took his temperature. The doctor said not to take Beck to the hospital because they were going to be transferred in a week. His condition worsened, however, and he was taken to the infirmary.

Hastin remembered going to see Beck in the hospital. Beck told him: "Jim, I'm never going to get out of here alive. They piled seven corpses at the foot of my bed this morning."[50]

The fact that so few men died was probably because they were young and in good shape. Nevertheless, most felt they barely survived two months in a camp where some inmates lived, incredibly, for years.

The senior Allied officer, Phil Lamason, worked with two British spies, Yeo-Thomas and Christopher Burney, and the Communist Underground Committee to smuggle out a list of the Allied prisoners through a trusted Russian prisoner who worked at a nearby airfield. The Russian told a Luftwaffe officer that Allied airmen were at Buchenwald. Not long afterward, two officers from the Luftwaffe came to interrogate the POWs. They said they'd heard a rumor the Allies were there and had come to verify it. He said their transfer to the concentration camp was "all a mistake," that they had lost track of the POWs after they left Paris.

The German officers brought in a Red Cross form with blanks for their name, squadron, rank, serial number, religion and marital status. They were also asked where they were stationed, whether they owned a dog, their dog's name, the type of aircraft they were flying, their mother's name and whether they had siblings. "We were told we would be left in Buchenwald if we did not fill out the forms," said Chapman.

Most POWs recognized the Germans were trying to elicit information they were not supposed to divulge. Hastin remembered filling out the form but leaving everything blank except his name, rank and serial number. He said one POW had reminded him he could be court-martialed for filling out the entire form.

The German said: "You didn't answer all the questions."
I said: "I can't."

He said if I didn't fill out the form they couldn't verify who I was.
I said: "No, if I don't fill it out, then it will prove I am what I say I am."
He said: "Do you want to stay in Buchenwald?"
I said: "I guess I'll take my chances."
He said: "There'll be no chances. If you don't fill out this form, you stay in
Buchenwald."

Chapman also refused to fill out the form. "It had nothing to do with morality," Chapman said of his decision. "It was just that I had done this once
before—when the bogus British intelligence agent convinced me to fill out a
form in Paris—and I was not about to make the same mistake twice."[51]

Afterward, Hastin and Chapman were taken to another building where more
than a dozen other men who had refused to fill out the form were being held.
Kirby Cowen understood German and said one Feldwebel had remarked: "These
are the only soldiers in the whole bunch."[52]

Some men were frightened into giving the Germans what they wanted. After
witnessing the horrors of concentration camp life, they undoubtedly took seriously the threat of remaining there. As it turned out, no one was punished and all
of the POWs were later reunited.[53] The POWs did not know if the Red Cross
forms were genuine or merely a ruse. Apparently, the answer is the former, since
several ex-POWs were able to obtain confirmation of their imprisonment in
Buchenwald from the International Red Cross Tracing Service—more than forty
years later.

Apparently, many political prisoners believed the POWs were in a special protected category. Eugene Weinstock wrote that when the Allies began to close in, it
became clear the prisoners would be destroyed with the camp itself. "Only American and British war prisoners could hope for life," he said, "since they were under
the jurisdiction of the regular German Army rather than the SS murderers."[54]

The SS may have been reluctant to kill prisoners who were technically the responsibility of the army, but the POWs had no way of knowing this. Most had
doubts they would ever get out of Buchenwald. No one knew where they were
and the winter was approaching. In addition, the Germans had already murdered
37 British secret agents. Still, they did not realize how lucky they had been until
nearly 40 years after the war. Then they learned their execution was scheduled for
October 26. Lamason was the only one who knew. He did not tell his surviving
comrades until the mid-80's.[55]

Chapman said he was not afraid to die but did not want to do so in Buchenwald. "I had too many things left undone." Nevertheless, he believes it was a mir-
acle he survived.[56]

On October 19, at 4 P.M., all but 13 (seven Americans) of the soldiers were removed from Buchenwald. Those who remained were hospitalized but were bitter
they had been left behind. Later, the 11 survivors were brought to the POW camp
for airmen at Sagan, Luft III.

Those who left in the original group were in poor physical condition. "I left Buchenwald wrapped in crepe paper bandages from ankles to hips," Chapman recalled. "I had hives from nerves and fleas and got infections from itching. The infection bored in and created holes so you could see the bone."[57]

Another POW remembered that SS troops lined the road with Schmeiser automatics as they left. "I don't know where they thought we were going," he said. "As if it was not obvious enough, they made a point of saying: 'You're still our prisoners.' One Feldwebel from the Luftwaffe said in English that according to the Geneva Convention if we tried to escape, we'd be shot. It was so ludicrous because the Geneva Convention never applied inside that gate, but he was staring inside that gate saying it. I couldn't believe it."[58]

When the POWs from Buchenwald arrived at Luft III on October 21, 1944, they were surprised to find the Allied officers there took great interest in their experiences. Earlier, 50 of the Sagan prisoners had been murdered following their "Great Escape." This, combined with the revelations about the concentration camps, convinced the senior Allied officers they had to be prepared for anything.[59]

According to records in the National Archives, the 82 airmen were not the only American soldiers to be sent to Buchenwald. Sgt. William Lee told war crimes investigators that he and about 60 other Medical Corps personnel were transferred from Stalag V at Frankfurt to the German Army Hospital at Buchenwald on October 1, 1944—less than three weeks before the group of Allied airmen departed. The Corpsmen were later sent to Bastogne.

Lee said the men were sent to treat wounded German military personnel, but that was not all that was expected of them.

A German Sergeant on October 20 pulled a can of American shoe polish out of his jacket and tried to get me to shine his shoes. I refused, but he insisted. I finally cursed him out in English. This guard then aimed his Luger pistol at my head, from approximately four feet away, and pulled the trigger. The weapon either was not loaded or it missed fire. So in anger the guard threw the weapon at me and hit me in the stomach. I was doubled up in pain and another guard raised his rifle to strike me with the butt and I threw my forearms over my head to ward off the blow. My left arm was fractured and I was knocked out.[60]

According to records from the war crimes trial of the Germans responsible for Buchenwald, other Allied prisoners also spent time in Buchenwald. A man from Washington, D.C., named Karl Berthold is mentioned. On September 10, 1944, 16 Allied prisoners were called to the main gate and never seen again. The Polish underground intelligence service in the camp said they were strangled a day or two later.

Hauptscharfüehrer Gustav Heigel, administrator of the bunker at Buchenwald, told investigators he thought 12 Americans were brought to Buchenwald in August. Heigel's answers were confused, but he said he was told: "They have to be especially watched." He said the men were young, about 30, and he thought they had been sent for "special treatment." Heigel treated the Americans as he did other prisoners he held who were to be executed, for example, taking their property. He said they were gone the next day so he did not know what happened to them. The man in charge of the crematory said he did not cremate any Americans.[61]

In a letter protesting the reduction of sentences given to Germans convicted of war crimes at Buchenwald, one of the original prosecutors wrote that "there were at least 300 Americans at Buchenwald: medics from infantry, airmen from Bomber and Fighter commands, those who fell into the Nazi dragnet when France was occupied and others."[62]

In his book on his experience as a prisoner in Buchenwald, Eugen Kogon mentions not only the Allied airmen but also two other Americans. According to Kogon, the prisoners learned that 18 Englishmen and the two Americans were to be killed in April 1945. The men were hidden by fellow prisoners and escaped execution.[63]

How can any reader appreciate the level of degradation the POWs encountered in Buchenwald? Many books have been written to describe the horrors that occurred there and, though the Allies were spared the worst treatment most Buchenwald inmates experienced, it is nevertheless important to get a sense of the conditions they endured. The best description may be that of Edward R. Murrow when he entered the camp after liberation.[64]

There surged around me an evil-smelling stink, men and boys reached out to touch me. They were in rags and the remnants of uniforms. Death already had marked many of them, but they were smiling with their eyes. I looked out over the mass of men to the green fields beyond, where well-fed Germans were ploughing. . . .

[I] asked to see one of the barracks. It happened to be occupied by Czechoslovaks. When I entered, men crowded around, tried to lift me to their shoulders. They were too weak. Many of them could not get out of bed. I was told that this building had once stabled 80 horses. There were 1200 men in it, five to a bunk. The stink was beyond all description.

They called the doctor. We inspected his records. There were only names in the little black book—nothing more—nothing about who had been where, what he had done or hoped. Behind the names of those who had died, there was a cross. I counted them. They totaled 242—242 out of 1200, in one month.

As we walked out into the courtyard, a man fell dead. Two others, they must have been over 60, were crawling toward the latrine. I saw it, but will not describe it.

In another part of the camp they showed me the children, hundreds of them. Some were only 6 years old. One rolled up his sleeves, showed me his number. It was tattooed on his arm. B-6030, it was. The others showed me their numbers. They will carry them till they die. An elderly man standing beside me said: "The children— enemies of the state!" I could see their ribs through their thin shirts. . . .

We went to the hospital. It was full. The doctor told me that 200 had died the day before. I asked the cause of death. He shrugged and said: "Tuberculosis, starvation, fatigue and there are many who have no desire to live. It is very difficult." He pulled back the blanket from a man's feet to show me how swollen they were. The man was dead. Most of the patients could not move.

I asked to see the kitchen. It was clean. The German in charge . . . showed me the daily ration. One piece of brown bread about as thick as your thumb, on top of it a piece of margarine as big as three sticks of chewing gum. That, and a little stew, was what they received every 24 hours. He had a chart on the wall. Very complicated it was. There were little red tabs scattered through it. He said that was to indicate each 10 men who died. He had to account for the rations and he added: "We're very efficient here."

We proceeded to the small courtyard. The wall adjoined what had been a stable or garage. We entered. It was floored with concrete. There were two rows of bodies stacked up like cordwood. They were thin and very white. Some of the bodies were terribly bruised; though there seemed to be little flesh to bruise. Some had been shot through the head, but they bled but little.

I arrived at the conclusion that all that was mortal of more than 500 men and boys lay there in two neat piles. There was a German trailer, which must have contained another 50, but it wasn't possible to count them. The clothing was piled in a heap against the wall. It appeared that most of the men and boys had died of starvation; they had not been executed.

But the manner of death seemed unimportant. Murder had been done at Buchenwald. God alone knows how many men and boys have died there during the last 12 years. Thursday, I was told that there were more than 20,000 in the camp. There had been as many as 60,000. Where are they now?

Perhaps as many as 300 Americans spent time in Buchenwald. Of the 82 American POWs sent to the camp in August 1944, 81 survived. But neither the Americans nor the other Allied POWs returned home unscarred. The ordeal changed their lives. "For forty years," said Dave High, "when I shaved in the morning, I could see the pile of bodies in the mirror."[65]

6

End of the Line for Spies—
Mauthausen

ALTHOUGH AUSCHWITZ is better known, Mauthausen may have been the worst concentration camp of them all, and that is where many POWs were sent to be executed. In fact, more American military personnel were sent to this camp and killed than to any other except Berga. Moreover, U.S. officials were aware that Americans were sent to Mauthausen, but little was done either to secure their release or hold the perpetrators of crimes against them responsible.

In early September 1944, a group of American paratroopers, perhaps as many as 48, were brought to Mauthausen. A former prisoner, who worked in the stone quarry behind the camp, told war crimes investigators these men were forced to carry rocks up 148 steps to a dump near the camp entrance. The prisoners then had to run back down and carry another 100-pound load back to the top. Some collapsed under the whip of SS Kommandoführer Kisch.

One man was forced to carry a stone that the witness estimated weighed 140 pounds:

> He staggered and dropped it a number of times. He was bleeding and perspiring profusely. Kisch screamed at him and lashed him continually. At the top of the stairs, the man dropped the stone again, slumped on all fours as Kisch whipped him unmercifully. He waved his hand and said: "All right, all right," then staggered toward a barbed wire charged fence. By prearrangement with a sentry in a nearby tower, Kisch gave a sign and the sentry shot the American three times. He groped for the fence, straightened out as he hit it and died without a sound.

The source learned later that three other Americans were shot in a similar manner. A few days later, he heard shots in the pit. Kisch was emptying his gun. When the witness reached the top of the stairs with his first load, he saw the bodies of 10 Americans lying in a heap. He said the rest of the Americans were killed the same way and their bodies cremated.[1]

Other Americans were sent to Mauthausen to meet a similar fate. On September 5, 1944, for example, a prisoner transport of 47 Dutch, English and American officers was brought into Mauthausen. The men arrived in civilian clothing. They were given baths and sent to a barracks. The next morning, the number of each prisoner was written on his chest with an indelible pencil. Later that day, they were sent to carry stones. According to the orderly who wrote the numbers on their chests, all 47 were shot that same day. A roster of the prisoners identified two as Americans.[2]

In her book on Mauthausen, Evelyn Le Chene mentions several instances in which soldiers were brought to the camp. During the summer of 1944, for example, she says 36 airmen were brought to the camp and interrogated. They were taken away by Wehrmacht officers, but at least five were brought back to Mauthausen and cremated.

In early 1945, Le Chene says, six American airmen arrived in the camp. One was already dead and another badly wounded. "They were savagely beaten and their heads were repeatedly cracked against the stone wall. The injured airman died under this battering, and he and the other dead man were taken off to the crematorium." The other men were taken away from the camp and never seen again. In April, nine Americans were shot down. Four were brought to the camp and interrogated. One fell dead during the questioning; the others were shot at the entrance of the crematorium. The bodies of two other airmen were later brought to the camp, but the remaining three were never seen.[3] U.S. officials learned about the 47 POWs several months after their deaths. They had more immediate information, however, about a group of secret agents they sent behind enemy lines in August 1944.

Shortly after the Slovak uprising that month, the Czech Intelligence Service in London learned several British and American flyers recently liberated from German POW camps in Slovakia were at Banska Bystrica and Tri Duby. This was where the Czech Forces of the Interior (CFI)—a group of partisans—was defending a liberated area against enemy troops. The information was forwarded to the Office of Strategic Services (OSS—the forerunner of the CIA) in London. A decision was made to send teams of agents into Slovakia to evacuate downed airmen, provide supplies to the partisans and gather intelligence. These were to be the first OSS units to operate in central Europe.

OSS Bari arranged for the 15th Air Force to send an evacuation flight on September 17. Two B-17s with fighter cover landed at a secret air base established at Tri Duby. They stayed on the ground for less than an hour, picking up 17 flyers and dropping two OSS teams.

The first group of agents, known as the "Dawes" team, consisted of intelligence officers, weapons and demolitions experts and a radio operator. A 35-year-old textile worker from Charleston, South Carolina, Lt. J. Holt Green, was in command of Jerry Mican, Joseph Horvath and Robert Brown. They were later joined by a second team, code named "Houseboat," composed of John Schwartz and Charles Heller.

The Dawes team was dispatched as a liaison group to the CFI headquarters at

Banska Bystrica with the assignment of transmitting to Bari intelligence and situation reports on the progress of the campaign, as well as estimating arms, ammunition and demolition requirements for further resupply of the CFI.

Three additional OSS teams were sent in on October 7. The "Day" team comprised E.V. Baranski and two civilians, Anton Novak and Daniel Pavletich. Their mission was to work close to combat lines west of Banska Bystrica for frontline tactical intelligence.[4]

The "Bowery" team comprised Tibor Keszthelyi, Steve Catlos, and civilians using the code names Francis Moly and Stephen Cora. They were to arrange with the CFI underground to infiltrate two civilian agents across the Hungarian border to the vicinity of Budapest and were then to return to Dawes HQ for evacuation. The infiltration of Moly and Cora was successfully accomplished on Oct. 11, and Keszthelyi and Catlos rejoined the Dawes group.

Francis Perry was sent in under code name "Dare." He was to represent the German Austrian desk, collecting information on Slovak headquarters and exploring the possibility of courier routes over the frontier.[5]

Two other civilians also were dropped. Emil Tomes, an American who lived in Slovakia, was sent in to work independently on counterintelligence; the other was Associated Press correspondent Joseph Morton.

Despite the covert nature of the operation, the OSS gave Morton permission to report on the evacuation of fliers. He sent a message to AP saying he was off to cover the "greatest story of his life." When he arrived in Slovakia, Morton immediately sent back a story with the plane that had carried him there, but the dispatch was snatched up by censors. He was never heard from again.[6]

On October 17, six Flying Forts landed with arms, ammunition and demolitions equipment. Six additional agents were sent to join the Dawes team: James Gaul, Lane Miller, William McGregor, Kenneth Lain, J. Dunlevy and photographer Nelson Paris. Gaul, a Harvard Ph.D. who spoke six languages, became Green's deputy.

By the end of October, the situation began to deteriorate as organized resistance began to fade. Green had said he wanted to fly out a group of airmen, as well as several members of his team, including correspondent Morton. This flight was scheduled for October 18 but had to be postponed. Constant weather problems, either in Slovakia or at the point of origination, prevented the flights from ever being made.[7] This proved to be a death sentence for those who were to be evacuated.

OSS Bari's concern for the teams was evident in the message to Green on October 25 stressing that their security was "vital" and urging him to do everything possible to insure the safety of the party.[8] Green's options were running out, however, after Banska Bystrica was bombed by the Germans and the Tri Duby airstrip was lost.

Green decided to evacuate the camp. He divided his group of 37 (agents and downed fliers) into four units, headed by Lain, McGregor, Perry and himself. The group retreated with the CFI in the direction of the Russian lines. On the long, arduous march, many Czech soldiers and Americans became ill from lack of food and exposure.

On November 6, a patrol consisting of one OSS Army enlisted man, Pvt. Schwartz, and five Air Force personnel was captured by the Germans. Shortly thereafter, the Czechs and Americans fought off a German attack.

A week later, Green's group, after almost nine days of marching in the bitter cold through the mountains, stopped at a farmhouse on the outskirts of the village of Doolnia Lehota. On the following day they traveled to a nearby mine camp where partisan nurses dressed their feet. It was learned later that the Germans captured and killed these nurses.

Green and his men lived on the mountainside not far from the Czech Brigade's headquarters from November 18–30. During that time, Green contacted Major Sehmer of the British mission and went to Polomka to send a message to Bari over the British wireless.

In Green's absence, on the 30th, the Czech Brigade was attacked by the Germans. Perry and one Slovak soldier had gone down to the village for food and were captured. The rest of the Americans narrowly escaped.[9]

Bari had not received any messages from any of the teams since the end of October. In early December, Green finally contacted headquarters. The next and last message from the Dawes team, although badly garbled, was interpreted as follows:

> Thirty of our groups and wilsh (sic) now in estate near Dalnialsheta [illegible] southeast Brezno. No news Baranski, Novak and Pavletich. McGregor, Lain and John Krizan [cover name of John Schwartz] with flyers whereabouts unknown since separation Nov. 10th. All equipment lost. Majority in bad condition because exposure, frozen feet, exhaustion from long mountain marches and starvation diet. Drop soonest to Sehmer complete extra heavy clo . . . [10]

By then, the net had begun to close around the agents. On December 9, Baranski and Pavletich were arrested. Three days later, Keszthelyi and Mican were captured.

The rest of the group stayed in the mountains for the next three weeks, most of them living in a shack about three hours north of Polomka and the remainder at a winter resort hotel at a place known as "Velky Bok." On Christmas Eve, the British and Americans held a party at the shack. Religious services were conducted by Lt. Gaul. The next morning the men were washing their clothes when they came under attack and were surrounded by Germans. The partisans guarding the house resisted for three hours but were driven away by artillery fire from Polomka. According to a Czech soldier, 14 persons fully dressed and in complete uniform were marched out of the shack and taken away.[11] Only one man escaped—Anton Novak, a 25-year-old Czech who was part of the "Day" team. He eventually made his way through the Russian lines to Belgrade.[12]

This was the end of the Anglo-American mission. Between November 6 and December 26, 1944, 15 agents were captured along with 2 American civilians, 2 British officers and one private, and a Czech officer who had joined the group. Five people escaped capture because they were away from the shack at the time of the attack: two OSS Army enlisted personnel (Catlos and Dunlevy), a British officer, a British enlisted man and a Czechoslovakian girl working with the OSS unit.[13] Lain and McGregor, who separated from the Dawes team to escort the group of Air Force personnel, were captured by the Germans and imprisoned in a POW camp. The camp was subsequently overrun and they were repatriated. The same was true for Schwartz.[14]

Unaware of what had happened to the agents, a final attempt was made to re-supply the OSS teams on December 27. The pilot flew off course, however, and missed the target.[15]

In early January, Werner Mueller, one of Berlin's best linguists, and Dr. Hans Wilhelm Thost, an interpreter for the Reichssicherheitshauptamt (RSHA–Reich Security Main Office), were ordered to go to Mauthausen to interrogate a group of English and American officers who were taken prisoner in the sector held by the Slovak rebels.

Thost testified after the war that he saw one POW in a room with Frank Ziereis, a balding 43-year-old Bavarian who was Mauthausen's Commandant. Ziereis slapped the man across the face. He continually demanded that his subordinate, a cigar-smoking, World War I U-boat sailor named Habecker, hang the prisoner by his wrists.[16]

Meanwhile, in another room, two SS officers were interrogating another POW. The American was in a crouching position with his hands bound beneath his thighs behind his knees. One SS man was holding a heavy whip in his hand, and Thost could see the American's forehead and buttocks were bloody from where he had been lashed. The second German seemed to think the mark on the POW's face was funny. He called it a "Jesus halo."

Thost said he was overcome watching this torture and went back to the room where Habecker was still trying to coerce information from the first POW about the Allied service in Bari that had sent him to Slovakia. Ziereis took out three or four wooden rings, about the shape and size of a pencil, which he put between the prisoner's fingers. He then pressed them together hard. "This 'Tibetan Prayer Mill' causes intolerable pain," Thost said. "Ziereis got an intense pleasure out of that torture."

Later, Ziereis had Sehmer, the British agent, hung by his wrists in another room. Thost heard him scream. Afterward, Sehmer was brought back to sign a confession, but he could barely write "because all the blood was drawn from his hands."

The worst treatment was given to Baranski. When he refused to reveal details of his mission, the Commandant tied his wrists behind his back and fastened them to a chain hanging from the ceiling. Ziereis kicked the table Baranski was standing on out from under him, leaving the American dangling. After seven or eight minutes, Baranski said he would tell all, "but the Commandant let him hang a few more minutes."

During the next four or five days, the British and American POWs continued to be tortured. Thost said these interrogations were carried out so the prisoners had no permanent injury. "These Gestapo men did not torture the prisoners in fits of anger but, on the contrary, with all composure. . . . The pleasure experienced by Ziereis and Habecker was apparent."[17]

When the Germans were satisfied they had elicited all the information they could, the POWs were told to remove their uniforms and put on prisoners' uniforms. Then they were marched out.

Mueller sensed something was wrong and asked an SS officer why they were not being transferred to a POW camp. He was told a teletype message from Berlin, signed by Ernst Kaltenbrunner, Chief of the RSHA, had come in ordering their immediate execution. The order directly contradicted his earlier instruction that Americans and Englishmen were to be exempted from the "bullet order" directing that escaped prisoners be taken to Mauthausen and eliminated.[18]

Mueller asked how the prisoners were to be killed. He was told: "Don't be excited; they will have a very easy death."[19]

The Americans were unaware they were going to be executed, according to a Polish prisoner who was in Mauthausen at the time. The signs on the door they entered said they were going to the bath. "After they undressed," Wilhelm Ornstein testified, "they went to another room with a camera where Ziereis was yelling: 'photograph, photograph.' Baranski, Green, Gaul, Perry, Keszthelyi, Mican, Horvath, Haller, Paris, Pavletich, Sehmer, Willis and Wilson were shot by SS Hauptsturmfuhrer Georg Bachmayer." Ornstein took Nelson Paris's dog tag off his neck after he was killed and later gave it to investigators. He said the Americans were executed on January 26 and cremated.[20]

The OSS canceled its operation in Slovakia at the end of January, long after contact with the Dawes team had been lost. By this time, the agents were all believed to be dead.[21] In fact, on January 24, 1945, Allied Force Headquarters intercepted a broadcast from Berlin that said 18 members of an Anglo-American group of agents were captured and executed.[22] Additional reports to this effect were picked up a couple of weeks later.[23]

Meanwhile, the need to obtain information from Austria prompted the OSS to send in a new team of agents made up of volunteer Austrian corporal POWs (Perkins, Grant and Underwood), who had homes or contacts in the Vienna area. All were in their early 20s, single, in excellent condition and eager to participate.

The mission, code named "Dupont," was led by Lt. Jack Taylor, an experienced agent who had one of the most outstanding records in the European Theater. He had been the Chief of the Maritime Unit in Cairo and made over a dozen clandestine landings on the coasts of Crete and Albania. He was the Operations Officer at Bari.

The Dupont team was dropped about 25 miles south of Vienna near the Hungarian border. They quickly discovered their radio equipment was lost.[24] "Our mission seemed doomed to failure from the start," said Taylor.

The agents found the people were friendly but reluctant to allow them to stay in any one place for more than a night. As they moved around, they collected intelligence on bomb damage and targets in and around Vienna. They decided the quality and quantity of information warranted taking extreme risks in getting it through to Italy. Two men were to try to cross the border to Yugoslavia where they would join the partisans and contact an Allied mission to be evacuated to Italy. They then planned to return with radio equipment.

As the days passed, the Austrians began to get nervous that the Russians would overrun the area and that they would be captured and sent to prison. Taylor decided all four men would go to Italy, with him and Underwood going as planned through Yugoslavia and Perkins and Grant traveling via Udine.

The temperature was well below freezing each night so the men slept in their clothes and buried themselves in hay. On December 1, 1944, they climbed down from their loft for supper in a tiny room next to the manger.

> I had just finished shaving and unfortunately had shirt, tie and coat on, but not my field jacket. The watchdog barked; we snapped the light off as usual and remained quiet. We heard the front gate open, followed by the door to the house. In a few minutes we heard someone come to our door but as it was usual for one of the family to come and tell us when the "coast was clear," we thought nothing of it. Suddenly, the door was thrown open and eight plain-clothesmen rushed in; we grappled for a few seconds but I was forced back in the corner, beat over the head with a blackjack and, while groggy, had my arms pinioned behind my back. My left arm was then twisted backwards until the elbow joint was torn loose, much as you would the joint of a chicken leg. Four men were on each of us and I realized the futility of further struggle. Blackjack taps on my head continued while my wrists were chained together behind my back, painfully tight, and locked with a padlock. The same had been done to Underwood who was held down under the table. He was bleeding profusely from several cuts on his head. Outside were two more men with tommy-guns.

Taylor was taken to Gestapo Headquarters in Wiener Neustadt, stripped and given an examination. His money belt was found, as were gold coins he had sewn into his trousers. They also found his signal plan, cipher pads and other evidence of his involvement in intelligence-gathering.[25]

The Gestapo wanted him to put on civilian clothes, but he refused for fear of being photographed in them to show he had been captured out of uniform. He was later taken in his underwear to Mortzinplatz IV Gestapo Headquarters in the old Hotel Metropole in the center of Vienna. Taylor saw his team in other rooms of the building. He never saw them again.

Initially, Taylor was not allowed to lie down or sleep, nor was he given any food or water. His injured arm was turning green and blue and swollen, but the

Gestapo would not bring in a doctor to examine it. Taylor was not tortured, but he was slapped around and intimidated. Each morning he awoke expecting to be executed.

Taylor was held in solitary confinement for about two months, seeing and speaking to other people only during air raids. He had severe dysentery and lost a lot of blood. By the middle of February, he had to stop exercising because he had lost too much weight and the exertion made him too hungry. Taylor then contracted pneumonia. He believed he survived only because a friendly guard smuggled in a package of sulfanilamide from one of the other prisoners who had stolen it from Taylor's medical kit.

The Russians began to close in and Taylor hoped Vienna would be overrun before he could be executed or evacuated. Instead, he and 37 other prisoners were put on a train. Taylor had no idea where he was being taken. When the train stopped, he and the other prisoners were marched five miles to a camp. It was Mauthausen. Taylor climbed the hill past the rock quarry and described what he saw:

> Several prisoner work parties under heavy SS guard passed by on their way to the quarries. They were the most terrible looking half-dead creatures in filthy ragged stripes and heavy wooden shoes, and as they clanked and shuffled along the cobblestones, they reminded me of a group of Frankensteins. We kidded ourselves saying we would look the same in a few days, but we were all struck with cold dread terror.

Taylor and the other prisoners were marched through the main gate and lined up outside the shower room where they were individually questioned, slapped, slugged and beaten with a stick by three SS men in relays for approximately three hours. Unterscharführer Hans Bruckner screamed "You American swine" every time he struck Taylor.

The prisoners were told the rules of the camp. Violation of most was punishable by death. The penalty for failure to stand at attention and remove one's cap whenever an SS man passed, or when speaking to an SS man, was merely hanging the victim by his wrists chained behind his back.

When the next group of new prisoners was having the same rules and regulations announced to them, Taylor heard the speaker say: "'And if you attempt to escape and are recaptured, you will be shot immediately, like this,' and [he] simultaneously pulled his pistol and shot an old prisoner standing near, who had just been recaptured after an attempted escape."

Taylor and the other prisoners were marched to the bath, stripped and all their belongings confiscated, except three wristwatches and a wedding ring, which they slipped to a Polish kapo. They were shaved, given a hot shower and handed an old suit of ragged underwear. The men never saw their clothes again. They were then led out barefoot and forced to stand at attention for more than an hour before being marched to the barracks.

"We received our first food in 48 hours and later were assigned prison numbers, two of which were stamped on cloth with the appropriate colored triangle indicating political or criminal prisoner and citizenship and one stamped in metal for a wrist bracelet. The cloth numbers were sewn on the left breast of the coat and the outer side of the left trouser halfway to the knee," recalled Taylor.

"After two days, we began by devious means to get wooden shoes and old trousers or shirts," Taylor said. "Stealing was practiced on a scale which cannot be imagined and one had to carry with him at all times his total belongings. . . . Stealing was a matter of life and death for most and [was] practiced almost continuously."

The prisoners had to sleep in their clothes to keep them from being stolen. "Prisoners who could 'organize' a topcoat or raincoat and at night slept on it for a pillow would invariably wake to find it missing and rarely were able to recover it. I had two pair of shoes stolen from under my mattress at different times while sleeping and recovered one pair. Modess, my bunkmate, slept in his boots and actually caught a man trying to pull them off."

Taylor heard rumors of Americans in the camp but discovered most were Europeans. He did locate three other Americans. One was a woman who had been captured in France, interned in Ravensbrück and evacuated to Mauthausen in February 1945 when the Russians approached. Through friendly Czechs, she was assigned to the laundry where she could get extra food, but her health deteriorated and she was sent to the Viener Graben women's hospital outside the camp.

Sgt. Louis Biagioni, a radio operator for an OSS team captured in northern Italy in the summer of 1944, was held for several months by the Gestapo before being transferred to Mauthausen. On December 26, he was taken to Linz, tried, condemned to death and returned to Mauthausen. He split wood in the garage while awaiting his execution, which never took place. After liberation, he learned an effort was made to exchange him for a German sentenced to death in the United States. When the plan fell through, the same Czech who saved Taylor destroyed Biagioni's records.[26]

A black fireman named Lionel Romney had been with the Merchant Marine and was captured by the Italians after his ship, the *SS Makis,* sunk June 17, 1940. He was eventually sent to Mauthausen and did lumberjack work in the forest, for which he received extra food.

Taylor was not eligible for work outside the outer chain of guards because, as he learned later, he was supposed to be executed. He was assigned to help build a new crematorium. He carried sand, cement and water-mixed cement for the Spanish tile layers. "We dawdled at our work to delay completion of the crematorium," Taylor said, "because we knew that the number of executions would double when cremation facilities were available."

As it was, Taylor estimated 250–300 people died each day of starvation. By the end of April, the figure had climbed to 400–500. Twice a day, 120 people would be gassed.

One morning, two SS officers informed the kapo overseeing the project that it had to be finished and ready for operation on the following day or the workers would be the first occupants of the new ovens. "Needless to say," recalled Taylor, "we finished the job in the allotted time."

The next day, April 10, 1945, 367 new prisoners, including 40 women, arrived from Czechoslovakia and were marched through the gate straight to the gas chamber. They christened the new ovens.

"Black oily smoke and flames shot out of the top of the stacks as healthy flesh and fat was burned as compared to the normal pale yellow smoke from old emaciated prisoners," recalled Taylor. "This yellow smoke and heavy sickening smell of flesh and hair was blown over our barrack 24 hours a day and as hungry as we were, we could not always eat."

Taylor had dysentery but worked so he would not be sent to the hospital where five sick people were forced to share a single bunk and rations were half "normal" and infinitesimal amounts of medicine were supplied. Few people returned alive from this "hospital." The dead were dumped in a mass grave on a hill already containing 15,000 corpses.

Taylor's next job was carrying large soup kettles (110 pounds each) about one-half mile within the outer cordon of guard posts and barbed wire to the neighboring Hungarian camp. It was populated by nearly 20,000 Jews, mostly Hungarians, who had been marched to Mauthausen. "The Jews were so weak from their walk, none could carry the soup so we had to." Two wagons carried the dead out each morning.

Each kettle was carried by two men. "I received several bad beatings because I could not support the weight on my injured left arm. We were beaten severely and often with sticks by the SS and camp firemen while staggering along under the weight. When afforded an opportunity, we dipped our ever-handy spoons under the lids and managed several mouthfuls of extra soup."

About the middle of April, Taylor was transferred to another barracks, Block 10, which was occupied mainly by Czechs and Poles, with a few Russians, Germans and Austrians. Prisoners slept only two to a single bed there. Taylor's next job was to carry stones from Block 13 to the front of the hospital where a road was being built. He then worked with a Polish gardener, digging up the space next to the barracks and making a garden. By then he was so sick with dysentery and fever he could hardly walk to the dispensary. He had lost more than 50 pounds. On a couple of occasions, he fainted and had to be dragged out for roll calls.

Most of the Block 10 prisoners were old-timers and consequently had good positions through which they could obtain extra food. Bread, margarine, potatoes and occasionally horsemeat, cereal and schnapps were obtainable through the black market. Czechs, Austrians and Hungarians were allowed a few packages from home. "I had received bread and margarine in exchange for our watches and ring at the rate of two loaves of bread and 1/2 kilo margarine for each Swiss watch. Divided four ways this food lasted a week." Prior to this, the typical meals consisted of ersatz coffee for breakfast, beet soup for lunch and soup and a slice of bread for dinner.

Taylor met Poles, Czechs, Slovaks, Yugoslavs, Hungarians, Austrians, French, Belgians, Dutch, Spaniards and even a few Germans who had been leading members of the government, the military, art, culture and science. "Many of these men said to me: 'We're sorry you're here but, if you live, it will be a very fortunate thing; for you can tell Americans and they will believe you, but if we try to tell them, they will say it is propaganda.'"

As an American, Taylor was trusted, whereas they could not trust their own people because of stool pigeons. Consequently, he was told hundreds of eyewitness atrocity stories. "It was too dangerous to take notes, but I tried to keep mental account of the teller and enough of the story to remind him later when and if the opportunity came to set down the details. . . . I had seen only a small percentage of the torture, brutality and murder that these men had seen and suffered, but on this basis I was prepared to believe their stories 100%, in most cases. After all, the acts were themselves so terrible that anything worse could hardly be imagined."

The examples Taylor gathered were themselves virtually unimaginable. He learned prisoners had been executed by gassing, shooting and hanging; clubbed with wooden or iron sticks, shovels, pickaxes, or hammers; torn to pieces by dogs trained especially for this purpose; injected with magnesium-chlorate, benzine and other chemicals; left naked in subzero weather after a hot shower; given scalding showers followed by whipping to break blisters and tear flesh away; mashed in a concrete mixer; drowned; forced over a 150-foot cliff; driven into the electric fence or guarded limits where they were shot; forced to drink a great quantity of water then to lie down and allow a guard to jump on their stomach; buried alive; had their eyes gouged out with a stick; had their teeth knocked out and genitals kicked and had a red-hot poker shoved down their throat.

The head doctor, Dr. Podlaha, told Taylor prisoners were also executed if they had an unusual lesion, deformity or tattoo. "A hunchback and dwarf, who had come to the notice of one of the SS doctors, were executed and their skeletons cleaned and mounted for specimens. . . . Research was carried on in which healthy prisoners were used as guinea-pigs. These experiments mainly concerned typhus and the minimum food requirements to sustain life. The former used infected lice with a celluloid cover taped over them to the patient's leg. The latter consisted of a strictly controlled diet in which the results were measured in the number of deaths."

Toward the end of April, the prisoners had their first contact with the International Red Cross. All women from the western nations, including the American, were evacuated to Switzerland.

"These times became very dangerous," Taylor said, "as certain streets were walled off with barbed wire and we feared a mass execution. At certain unpredictable times, all prisoners were isolated in their blocks and a general tenseness gripped the whole camp, SS included. We heard rumors the Commandant and other high-ranking officers were discussing our futures as a mass wherein we would all be executed or transported to another area or left in the lager, which would be defended using us for hostages."

At this point, daily rations were cut. Taylor said people in the hospital were cannibalizing their own dead comrades. Jews in the tent camp were paying a $20 gold piece for two loaves of bread and a half kilo of margarine. Two wagonloads of dead were hauled away each day to the mass grave on the hill.

Taylor said the prisoners heard that after seeing the conditions in Buchenwald, Churchill or some other prominent British statesman had given the Germans a warning that the consequences would be serious if similar conditions were found in other camps. "Whether true or not, there immediately began the gassing of those of the sick who might not die before the Allies arrived and would present evidence of starvation or mistreatment." At that point, Taylor was worried the Germans would kill everyone to eliminate proof of the camp conditions.

American bombers made their last raid on Linz toward the end of April. Two bombers were shot down. "I saw SS Hauptsturmführer Bachmayer ride out on his horse in their general direction and several hours later I heard that he had picked up two men, tied their wrists together, and attached them to the back of a car with a few feet of rope; the airmen then had to run behind the car while Bachmayer galloped alongside and whipped them."

Taylor also heard that six American airmen were lined up inside the gate by the laundry and that they were being mistreated by the SS. It was dangerous to be seen noticing such things; nevertheless, Taylor walked past the area and saw the men being beaten. Later, they were placed in jail. "When I passed by whistling Yankee Doodle, two of them climbed up and stuck their heads against the bars. It was too dangerous to talk and I passed on quickly. Apparently, they were not executed and it is thought that they were transferred to a POW camp near Linz as others had been before."

The prisoners never received any Red Cross parcels, but one day SS troops were noticed eating bars of chocolate and smoking American cigarettes. Taylor said all the packages had been stolen by the SS for themselves and their families.

After six weeks in Mauthausen, Taylor knew the Americans were approaching. He recalled his last days in the camp:

We never dreamed that Americans would ever be near, but at the end of April we heard rumors they were coming fast. The SS departed about the first of May. . . . Saturday, May 5, the guns were much louder but still some distance away and I had not hoped that they would arrive before Sunday. Late in the afternoon, however, I heard rumors that an American jeep and half-track were at the entrance, and, staggering through the frenzied crowd, I found Sgt. Albert Kosiek. I could only say "God Bless America" and hold out my dog tags with a quavering hand.

Sgt. Kosiek and the men accompanying him had no idea two large concentration camps (Mauthausen and Gusen) were in the area. They had been on routine reconnaissance.

The liberators wanted to send Taylor to a hospital, but he insisted that valuable testimony and documents were at Mauthausen and he wanted to return for them. "I hated to go back, and it was one of the hardest decisions of my life to stick to, but it was an opportunity which would not long be available." Taylor returned to Mauthausen and found the camp in the hands of the Communist prisoners. They were holding trials and had already killed about a dozen people. The next day, the Americans took over and restored order. The Army doctors began to try to save the lives of prisoners who were often beyond help. In fact, after three weeks of medical care and nourishing food, Taylor reported that prisoners were still dying at the rate of more than 50 a day.

"After the Americans had liberated us, I discovered that I should have been executed on April 28, 1945, along with 27 other prisoners from Block 13," Taylor said. "A friendly Czech, Mylos, who worked in the political department, had, unknown to me, removed my paper and destroyed it so that I was not included with the 27."[27] Despite his distinguished OSS record and the ordeal he had lived through in Mauthausen, Taylor was initially suspected of being a double agent after his liberation. It quickly became clear this was absurd.

Taylor proved to be a key witness in the subsequent trial of Nazis responsible for Mauthausen. He not only provided eyewitness testimony—for example, he saw the dog tags of two officers, Leroy Teschendorf and Halsey Nisula, after their execution—but also gathered information from other prisoners that formed the basis for much of the prosecution's case.[28]

After the liberation of Mauthausen, a dispatch dated May 11 in *Stars and Stripes* quoted an unnamed American officer who had been in the camp as saying 32 American and British POWs had been "beaten, tortured, gassed and finally cremated." He specifically mentioned a U.S. Air Force and naval officer who were gassed April 1 and 12. The officer added that "there was so little food that men ate men." In grisly detail he went on to describe the cannibalism he had witnessed:

> During the night of April 25 and the next day I personally know of two cases where new corpses were butchered. In the first instance, an arm and a thigh were cleavered off and eaten by fellow prisoners. In the second case the belly was ripped open and the heart and liver were devoured. Then they ate the chest muscles.

The American said that he did not think he could have survived another two weeks. He was one of the lucky ones. More than a dozen other Americans were not so fortunate. They were tortured and executed.

7

Jewish POWs Are Singled Out

THE WINTER OF 1944 was the coldest on record in Europe. New winter clothing arrived in Belgium and France but never reached the soldiers on the front lines.

In what became known as the Battle of the Bulge, the German Army launched a surprise attack with a more than two-to-one advantage. The 106th "Bag Lunch" Division was thrown into an indefensible position and proved it was indefensible. Many men sent to fight had little or no training. "Some guys had been in the army about six weeks and were put in the Bulge," recalled one veteran in an interview. "One guy didn't know what outfit he was in until he saw it on his discharge papers."[1] Another veteran of the Bulge had been with the topographical engineers and been given two weeks of training before being sent into combat.

As American troops were overrun, they were marched to the rear. The SS ordered the POWs to expose their dog tags. Some men were singled out, apparently for execution. To protect their Jewish comrades, some gentiles exchanged dog tags; some even passed them Bibles.[2]

Daniel Steckler had been in Luxembourg when he was captured by the Germans. "The most fearful thing to me was the fact that, as a Jew, I carried a dog tag that had a great big 'H' on it, standing for Hebrew," he said, "and I didn't think that I would last for five minutes."[3] When the Germans were not looking, Steckler ripped off his tag and threw it in the snow. "It made me feel goddamned mad," he recalled bitterly 43 years later, "because it made me feel as though I was tearing a piece of me off."

Edwin Cornell was another Jew captured at the Bulge. "My primary concern was how I, as a Jew, would be treated as a prisoner of war. Soon after capture, I found an opportunity to bury my Hebrew bible in a wooded area. My dog tags, which bore a conspicuous letter 'H,' I chose to keep, fearing that a person without identification could be shot as a spy."[4]

On December 17, 1944, 985 prisoners captured during the first two days of the German counteroffensive were marched from Belgium into Germany. During this march, they received food and water only once. The walking wounded received no attention except such first aid as American medical personnel in the column could give them. They reached Gerolstein four days later and were packed into boxcars, 60 men in each. The cars were so small the men could not lie down. On route, they were fed only once. Eight men seeking to escape jumped into a field and were killed by an exploding land mine. The German sergeant in charge, enraged that anyone had attempted to escape, began shooting wildly. Although he knew that every car was densely packed with prisoners, he fired a round through the door of a car, killing an American soldier. The day after Christmas, the men arrived at Stalag IX-B at Bad Orb, approximately 30 miles northwest of Frankfurt-on-Main.

At its peak, the camp held more than 4,000 American POWs. Later, 1,275 non-commissioned officers (NCOs) were transferred to Stalag IX-A, Ziegenhaim. This was partly made up for by the arrival of 1,000 privates from Stalag XII-A, Limburg, at the end of February 1945.

From 290 to 500 prisoners were jammed into one-story wood and tar paper barracks divided into two sections with a washroom in the middle. Washroom facilities consisted of one cold water tap and one latrine hole emptying into an adjacent cesspool that had to be shoveled out every few days. Each half of the barracks contained a stove. Throughout the winter, the fuel ration was two armloads of wood per stove per day, providing heat for only one hour a day.

Bunks, when there were bunks, were triple-deckers, arranged in groups of four. Usually two men slept per tier and stayed in bed until 8 or 9 A.M. because it was so cold. Three barracks were completely bare of bunks and two others had only half the number needed, so that 1,500 men were sleeping on the cement floors. "There were 300 men in one barracks and there was not enough room for all of us when we would lie down," Gaetano D'Angelo told investigators.[5] Fortunate POWs received one blanket each. At the camp's liberation, however, some 30 prisoners still lacked any covering whatsoever. To keep warm, men huddled together in groups of three and four.

All barracks were in a state of disrepair: roofs leaked, windows were broken and lighting was either unsatisfactory or lacking completely. Very few barracks had tables and chairs. Some bunks had mattresses and some barrack floors were covered with straw, which prisoners used instead of toilet paper. The outdoor latrines had 40 seats to accommodate the needs of 4,000 men. Every building was infested with bedbugs, fleas, lice and other vermin.[6]

A thousand men lacked eating utensils and ate with their hands out of helmets, old tin cans or pails. The meals consisted mainly of sugar beet tops and split pea soup. As many as 15 men shared a loaf of bread. Breakfast consisted only of tea or coffee that was little more than stained water, which most prisoners used for washing or shaving. The POWs received only one shipment of Red Cross parcels during their imprisonment.[7] The minimum ration an inactive man needs to survive is 1,700 calories; the POWs in Bad Orb received about 1,400. In just one month, between February 8 and April 1, 1945, 32 Americans died of malnutrition and pneumonia.

The first indication that Jewish prisoners would be treated differently came when the Germans told the barracks leaders that a Jewish barracks leader would not be tolerated because a Jew could not represent Aryans. At the time, one barracks leader was a Pfc. Goldstein. He was ordered removed.[8]

What happened next is unclear, as accounts differ. The most dramatic version of events is that all 4,000 American prisoners were assembled in a field. The commandant ordered all Jews to take one step forward. Word ran through the ranks not to move. The non-Jews told their Jewish comrades that they would stand with them. The commandant then said they would have until six the next morning to identify themselves. The prisoners were told, moreover, that any Jews in the barracks after 24 hours would be shot, as would anyone trying to hide or protect them. The American in charge of the prisoners barracks filed a Red Cross protest, which the Nazis ignored.[9]

Most POWs dispute this version. Over the years, survivors may have confused the segregation of the Jews with another incident in which all the men were assembled in front of machine guns following the discovery that two Germans had been murdered in the kitchen by starving POWs looking for food.[10]

On Thursday, January 18, 1945, Sid Goodman wrote in his diary: "All Jewish boys to be separated tonight into where the officers formerly lived. Very cold. I wonder what the future holds in store for us?" Goodman recalled that an American officer came in and said it was the policy of the German government to segregate Jewish soldiers. "He asked all Jewish soldiers to identify themselves. Only a few did. He said he didn't want to frighten us, but said, 'If some of you guys are Jewish and they find out about it, dire things could happen.' A little later, he came back with a list of names that sounded Jewish, and we were all moved to another barracks and locked in."[11]

"A shiver of fear ran along my spine as a trooper announced they were looking for Jews, or anyone with a Jewish-sounding last name," recalled Willis Carpenter. "We all thought of a GI in our barracks with a last name of Goldstein. Goldstein was a naturalized American Jew who, with that pronouncement, was about to have his whole life changed—possibly shortened." Carpenter said he and others begged Goldstein to lie about his name, but he refused to do so. "He was proud of his heritage and would not disgrace either his family or himself by hiding under an assumed name. He appeared calm and resigned as he was led out the door at gunpoint. Most of us believed his fate was sealed on that day, as were other Jewish Americans that were taken from their barracks by the troopers."[12]

Joseph Aborn said his barracks leader came back from a meeting and called out serial numbers. Afterward, he told them they had to take their blankets and move to another barracks. All those whose numbers were called were Jews. Aborn recalled 8 or 10 Jews being in his barracks and 119 altogether moving to a new barracks. The Man of Confidence, Carl Kasten, sent word to each barracks that the Germans knew which Jews had told them they were a different religion but that nothing would happen to them if they reported to the barracks. If they failed to give themselves up, however, they would be punished.[13]

Gerald Zimand came forward with the other Jews. "I was a smart-ass kid. I thought: 'What are they going to do to me?'"[14]

Reme Bottcher said the barracks leader went to a meeting every day with the Germans to discuss rations and other issues. He was told to tell all Jews in his barracks to register. Today, he says he would never have done it, and he told Jews in his barracks not to at the time. He said there were about 15–20 Jews in his barracks out of 400 POWs. Bottcher said one non-Jew in his barracks, Andy Combader, was segregated because he was an "undesirable." The German standard for determining whether a POW was undesirable was usually if he had stolen anything or "smarted off" or gotten into any trouble.[15] Bottcher said he only visited the Jewish barracks once. "It was just a concrete floor, no beds." He didn't know what happened to the Jews until he saw Combader after the war.[16]

Pete House recalled a chaplain visiting each barracks to inform the men the Germans had ordered the Jews to be segregated because that was the way it was in Germany. "It seemed sort of reasonable at the time, although there were two black artillerymen in my section and they were not segregated."[17]

Some men succeeded in avoiding the segregation by deception, others by luck. One of the latter was Leroy Erlandson who testified that he got pneumonia when the group was sent out and did not go.[18]

Another was Louis Edelman, who remembered the Germans telling all the Jews to come out and saying they would be put in a better camp. He destroyed his dog tags because he was afraid and did not volunteer.

Edwin Cornell remembered the order for Jews to come forward was a "moment of agony and decision." His first thought was: "'What right had our captors to treat us in that manner? We were there as American soldiers and only as American soldiers.' Simultaneously, I experienced both fear and anger." After much soul-searching, Cornell decided it was morally necessary for him to step forward. His two gentile buddies insisted he hide his identity, however, and ultimately convinced him to do so. One of his friends held on to his dog tags for the rest of his imprisonment. "And thus began a period of indescribable mental torture for me. I found it painfully impossible to walk even remotely near the Jewish compound. Thinking about it tore me apart. Today, over 45 years later, I still agonize over my decision," Cornell says. "I console myself with the fact that I did nothing to hurt anyone, except perhaps myself, since the trauma of this ordeal will remain with me as long as I live."[19] What Cornell does not know is that his place had to be filled by someone else.

On that fateful day in mid-January, approximately 130 Jews came forward. Perhaps as many as 50 noncommissioned officers in this group were taken out of Bad Orb with all the other NCOs. The Germans had a quota of 350 and filled the remainder with prisoners considered troublemakers, those they thought were Jewish and others chosen at random. Marcel Ouimet was segregated with the Jews, though he was a Christian. "They didn't believe me," he told investigators after his liberation. "We were told we were being sent to a better camp where we'd have a movie once a week."[20]

The other prisoners could see the Jews being forced to clean the outside latrines and perform other dirty tasks the rest of the POWs did not have to do, but they apparently were not otherwise mistreated.[21] This group left Bad Orb on February 8. They were placed in trains under conditions similar to those faced by European Jews deported to concentration camps. The POWs were packed 60 to a boxcar. Many men had dysentery, but the only toilet was a bucket in the corner. The air was foul with the stench of unwashed bodies and human waste. Some men became sick from the smell.[22] The only food available was what they had smuggled aboard.

None of the men on the trains had any idea they were being sent to a slave labor camp where conditions were little better than a concentration camp. That camp—Berga—had the highest mortality rate of any camp where POWs were held.

8

"We're Building the Pyramids Again"—Berga

WHEN COMPARED TO THE SUFFERING of the Jewish men, women and children of Europe who were sent to concentration camps, it may be difficult to imagine that hardened American soldiers could have been reduced to the kind of living skeletons one associates with Holocaust survivors. Yet this is what happened.

The 350 Americans who emerged February 13, 1945, from the boxcars that had taken them from Stalag IX-B at Bad Orb were mere boys, most still in their late teens, learning to dance and fantasizing about Rita Hayworth. When they went into the army they knew the risks, but they were still not prepared to be treated like beasts of burden, animals in the service of the Führer. They were, after all, *Americans.* But this meant little to the Nazis who knew them only as Jews who had no rights under the Geneva Convention or any other ethical code.

The POWs had been taken to Berga, a quaint German town of 7,000 people on the Elster River, whose concentration and POW camps did not appear on most World War II maps. In fact, the hamlet was the site of four camps, three holding POWs of different nationalities and a fourth for civilian political prisoners.

The POWs were interned in camps associated with Stalag IX-C (Bad Sulza), but many Americans mistakenly believed theirs was a subcamp of Buchenwald. That subcamp was actually restricted to political prisoners. The 1,800 civilians sent there in November 1944 were assigned to dig a series of tunnels for an underground armament factory. This was to be the principal job of the Americans as well.

Years after the war, the American men who survived these work camps did not tell their tale. Instead, they watched in silence John Wayne movies showing American war heroics, ashamed their experience was so much different and never acknowledged. Under different circumstances, the American camp might have been quite pleasant, a resort two miles from town on a hill along the edge of a forest with a millstream running behind it. But this was a prison—a work camp—surrounded by barbed wire with guards patrolling the gates and barracks. "The guards said if we got within five feet of the fence, they'd kill us," Dr. Myron Swack recalled.[1]

These strapping young men from places like Herrin, Illinois; Piedmont, South Carolina; Danielson, Connecticut; and Lima, Ohio, joined the army to fight the Nazis. They never imagined they could end up in a place like Berga, living like the inmates of concentration camps, sleeping two to a bed in four-tiered, lice-infested bunks in a foul-smelling, wood barracks with barred windows. The space was so cramped the prisoners had to devise a system whereby some men would stand for a certain length of time and then return to their bunks to let the others stand.

The 80 American Jews were sent to this slave labor camp because they were Jews, but once they arrived they were not treated differently from the other POWs in Berga, with a couple of exceptions. Initially, they were segregated again and placed in a separate barracks. Also, Stanley Cohen was chosen by the men to be their Man of Confidence, the man allowed to voice grievances to the camp officers. The commandant said a different man would have to be appointed because Cohen was Jewish. Besides being the subject of insults from the guards, all the Americans in Berga suffered equally.[2]

A 59-year-old school teacher from Haardt named Ludwig Merz was responsible for the Americans and about 60 other work details, comprising various nationalities, in the region of Thuringia. Initially, the commandant of the American camp was a Technical Sergeant named Kunz, an unimposing five-foot ten, one-hundred-fifty-pound man with blonde hair and a black Hitler mustache. Kunz came under fire from his superiors almost immediately because several prisoners escaped.

After Carl Kasten, Joseph Lytell and Ernest Sinner fled one night in early March, Merz replaced Kunz with Sgt. Erwin Metz, a 52-year-old manager in the food industry from Erkmannsdorf. A slightly larger man whose voice reminded Americans of Donald Duck, Metz had commanded the Slovak detail and, like his predecessor, was part of the *Landeschutz*, or National Guard.[3]

"[Metz] was strictly the Prussian military type," recalled Stephen Schweitzer. "He demanded a salute from all men in the group, and was very much put out when he didn't receive it. He had sadistic tendencies and seemed to delight in making the men uncomfortable at every opportunity."[4]

Kunz and Metz supervised 25 guards, who were under the command of Pfc. Andreas Pickart. Most of the guards were older men from the *Volksturm*—the civilian guard—with some disability that made them unable to fight. But what they lacked in strength they made up for in brutality. A typical example was Paul Hockart, a 56-year-old with stiff fingers, asthma, and a bad back, who regularly beat prisoners with a rubber hose.

The dehumanization of the prisoners began at the time of capture when most of their personal possessions were taken away, stripping the men of their connection to home. A missing ring or watch would nevertheless trigger memories of loved ones as a POW sat outside in the snow, shivering on the wooden beam that covered the trench that served as a latrine.

It was nearly as cold inside the barracks. Few of the men had warm clothes; they were wearing what they had on when they were captured. Prisoners huddled together around the single pot-bellied stove, seeking warmth more from each other than from the few pieces of coal the Germans allowed them. "We slept with our shoes on," Joseph Guigno, an Italian-American from Massachusetts, recalled, "otherwise our feet would swell so bad you couldn't put them on."[5]

The only other source of warmth was the ersatz tea—really nothing more than hot colored water—the men were given in the morning and the watery soup made from turnips or beet tops in the afternoon. "It was like garbage," Winfield Rosenberg said. "It had bugs in it sometimes."[6]

This starvation diet was supplemented only by sawdust-like bread, margarine and an occasional piece of meat that resembled sausage. The food, which was the same as that given to the political prisoners, was prepared in the slave labor compound at the foot of the hill. Several prisoners had to haul it back to the barracks in carts.

Whereas meals are usually a time for garrulousness, the enjoyment, if one could call it that, of such meager rations was a more solitary activity. It was about the only time the men were not working or sleeping, giving them the opportunity to fantasize about their families and liberation. This was the extent of their freedom. But under these conditions, their thoughts could rarely escape the hardships they were suffering.

Conditions in Stalag IX-B were the worst of any POW camp, but they were recalled fondly by the Americans transferred to Berga, who discovered that the main purpose for their imprisonment was to serve as slave laborers. Unlike POWs in most camps, who were not required to engage in forced labor, the inmates of Berga were expected to perform the kind of work used by the Nazis to kill Jews slowly.

As in concentration camps, the detail prisoners were assigned too often determined the chance of survival. About 30 of the 350 American POWs were used as craftsmen—carpenters, locksmiths, cabinetmakers, and electricians—and sent to individual construction firms. Ten men were put on a cleaning detail and stayed inside the camp. The nine medics and an interpreter tended to the sick. Another 10 men were assigned to the food detail and were responsible for picking up rations. Eight more comprised the burial detail. The rest, those who were not too ill to work, were sent to the mines.

When the first group of men was sent out to work, those who stayed behind were gripped with the fear of the unknown. "We waited with bated breath to find out what work we had to do," Steckler remembered. "When we saw, our hope was obliterated."

The men returned covered with a thick gray coat of dust. One said: "We're building the pyramids again. We're back to the days of the Pharaohs."[7]

The new Pharaoh came in a corporate guise. The mining project was supervised by a mysterious organization called Schwalbe 5. War crimes investigators never established who owned the company. Metz said it was a conglomerate of six or eight construction firms that was run by the SS—the commander was First Lieutenant Hack. This SS connection led the investigators ultimately to conclude that Schwalbe 5 must have been a military organization.[8]

Schwalbe 5 employed approximately 3,000 political prisoners, civilians and POWs. Approximately 70 American POWs worked each of the three shifts in the mines. The first one began at 6 A.M. and ended at 2 P.M. The second lasted from 2 P.M. until 11 or 12 P.M. And the last shift was from midnight to 6 A.M. By the end, the Americans were working 12 hours a day, seven days a week. The workers were not allowed any breaks and were given no food or water.

Each day, the men trudged approximately two miles through the snow to a mountainside in which 17 mine shafts were dug 100 feet apart. There, under the direction of brutal civilian overseers, the Americans were required to help the Nazis build an underground armament factory. Aiding the German war effort compounded the shame felt by the GIs.

That shame was exceeded only by the horror they felt when they first learned from the civilian political prisoners about the "Final Solution." Many of these people, still wearing their striped prison outfits with yellow triangles identifying them as Jews, had been in the Buchenwald concentration camp. Most POWs only saw the civilians when they changed shifts. They would exchange desperate glances. The Americans, who still expected the U.S. Army to deliver them from bondage, saw no such hope in the eyes of the civilians. They had already seen too much. "They told us that the Germans were killing Jews by any means," Norman Feldman recalled.[9]

Most of the time these civilians were too afraid to speak for fear that they would be killed. Many were. "When they fell over [from exhaustion and hunger]," Winfield Rosenberg recalled, "the Germans took them out and shot them."[10] As Bernie Melnick observed: "The Jews were like dead cockroaches. They just threw them in the river."[11]

The civilians worked primarily at night when temperatures sometimes plunged to –20 or –30 degrees. Some Jewish POWs were also forced to work the night shift. "Thank God it was a mild spring; otherwise, we all would have died," Steckler said.[12]

The cold was not the only hazard of the job. The men worked in shafts as deep as 150 feet that were so dusty it was impossible to see more than a few feet in front of you. The Germans would blast the slate loose with dynamite and then, before the dust settled, the prisoners would go down to break up the rock so that it could be shoveled into mining cars.

"They hitched us up like horses [to jackhammers]," Steckler recalled. "Sometimes a prisoner would not be strong enough to control the jackhammer, and two or three men would have to dig their heels into the ground and stand back to back to enable them to operate the machine."[13]

When the cars were full, three men would push them up a railroad track and tip them over to dump the rock into the Elster River. This would have been back-breaking work even if the men had been in top physical condition; for the half-starved POWs it was lethal.

"Practically everyone was affected by dampness and dust," Milton Shippee said. "We asked for masks like German civilians used in the mines, but didn't get any. We also asked for overshoes and rubbers, but the Germans said no. We had overcoats, but the Germans wouldn't let us work in them. If anyone started to go into the mines with an overcoat on, he was pulled aside and the coat torn right off him. A few men had overshoes, most had regular GI shoes. Some got so bad the Germans gave them wooden sandals to wear."[14]

The work itself was not the only threat to the Americans' well-being. If the overseers were dissatisfied with the way a prisoner was working, they would beat him with a rubber hose or other object. One foreman became known as "Rubber-Hose Charlie." Soldiers, who were naturally inclined to resist, would have had to restrain themselves under normal circumstances. But in this case, they were too weak to fight back even if they had the desire to do so.

Nevertheless, some POWs did find ways to be defiant, such as engaging in minor sabotage activities. Leo Zaccaria would collect iron during air raids and throw it in the river so the Germans would not have it. Another time he dumped one of the carts in the river. It was sticking out of the water so the Germans could see it, however, and they made him retrieve it. "The coldest day of my life was when I had to go into the river in my underwear to pull that cart out," he said.[15]

Costa Katimaris engaged in a battle of wills with his overseer. The guard would frequently beat Katimaris. "The more he whipped me, the madder I got, but I liked it because he got mad." Katimaris stole the guard's whip one day and threw it in the river. "The guard used to smoke a pipe and I decided it had to go. I stole it, too."[16]

One night, the Jewish POWs went on strike. Rosenberg recalls the German reaction: "They came into the barracks with dogs and fixed bayonets. They threw us out in the snow. We were so weak, we couldn't resist. I was hit with a rifle in the back and legs."[17]

It has sometimes been suggested that Jews in concentration camps were passive victims. In truth, many instances of resistance were recorded. The example of Berga demonstrated, moreover, that even soldiers were unable to put up much of a fight against their guards after weeks of backbreaking work and malnourishment. "I was too weak to step over the railroad tracks," said Joseph Guigno. "I crawled."[18]

According to Daniel Steckler, all the lights would be turned out during air raids and the prisoners would be placed in a circle with a machine gun in the middle. "We'd sing the *Star-Spangled Banner, America the Beautiful,* even *Hatik-vah*," he said. "Then when the lights came on, they'd go around the circle and beat us."[19]

After work, the men frequently had to struggle to return to the barracks. Some POWs collapsed during the day and had to be carried; others literally crawled. Steckler said they would carry their dead back out of fear the Germans would throw them in the river. Some men lost their minds; the rest had to cope with the horrible shrieks of those at the end of their wits. More subtle noises, like footsteps, could be menacing because they indicated the approach of a guard who might choose, on an impulse, to beat the prisoners.

None of the POWs remembered a library, but an inventory of books was found at the camp with 67 English titles, including *A Passage to India, Pride and Prejudice* and *Far from the Madding Crowd.*

The men did what they could to sustain each other. "You kept each other warm at night by huddling together," said Steckler. "We maintained each other's welfare by sharing body heat, by sharing the paper-thin blankets that were given to us, by sharing the soup, by sharing the bread, by sharing everything."[20]

Dale Patrick recalled the day he was loading rocks into the cart when it tipped over and all the rocks fell on top of him and pinned him in the river. He was still forced to work the rest of the day. When he got back to the barracks, all of the men brought their blankets and made a tent around the stove to warm Patrick and prevent him from catching pneumonia.[21]

Some men also survived on guile. William Minto, for example, managed to slip away into a stable to get oats on occasion. He also got a potato once in a while from two Serbs who were slave laborers from the town. "I got along pretty well," Minto said, "because I did a lot of conniving without getting caught."[22]

Other POWs would trade with the Germans for food. Tony Drago exchanged his watch for two packs of cigarettes. He then traded the cigarettes for food. "This ability to trade cigarettes for food gave me security," he said. He used to keep a box with a rope around his neck. Two days before he was freed, Drago discovered someone had stolen his cigarettes. "Fortunately, I didn't know."[23]

It would be nice to report that all the prisoners were indeed comrades who remained united against the common enemy, but that is not the whole truth. Actually, many POWs stole from each other. They pilfered money, food and tobacco. "If you tried to hide bread overnight, someone would steal it. They would steal your sweater," Milton Filler said.[24]

Zaccaria said he was part of a committee that didn't allow stealing. "If we caught someone, we'd beat them up." Meanwhile, Zaccaria admitted he stole more than anyone else.[25] Several POWs also suspected some of their fellow prisoners were informants or collaborated in some way with the Germans.

While the movies often portrayed Allied POWs in World War II as husky, clean-cut young warriors defiantly marching past their captors to the strains of patriotic anthems, the prisoners of Berga were scrawny, unshaven boys struggling to maintain their sanity and stay alive.

To the extent they had the energy to speak at all, the men talked mostly about food. They exchanged recipes for their favorite homemade dishes like chili or meatloaf. They also regaled each other with descriptions of where in their hometowns one could obtain the best steak or ribs. "We had seven-course conversations," recalled Milton Filler.[26]

These fantasies did not satisfy their hunger, however, and men would eat out of the garbage can or whatever was on the floor. "Guards threw potato skins in the latrine and thought it was funny to watch hungry prisoners jump in after them," recalled Sam Lubinsky.[27]

Gerald Zimand summed up the impact of their treatment: "We were dragged down to being animals."[28]

The POWs' physical, as well as their mental, states were further damaged by the Germans' withholding of Red Cross packages. In February, four of the American medics were sent to Stalag IX-C with 16 of the sick men. They told one British group leader about the plight of the men in Berga and he arranged to have two truckloads of Red Cross food parcels sent to the camp.

Some survivors described what happened next:

> We were told we would get these food packages if we washed and shaved and cut each other's hair and had the barracks clean by a certain time the next day. Lack of soap and razors and scissors made that impossible. There was only one razor and one scissor in the group. He [Metz] refused to give us the food. This kept going on for one week. He lined us up and told us through the interpreter that the toll count for the work we did at the mine was insufficient and we were causing too much trouble, breaking the shovels, losing picks, throwing dump carts in the river, etc., and for that reason we would not get the food. He grabbed at the least excuse to avoid giving us the packages.[29]

One medic, Samuel Fahrer, told Metz the sick men needed the packages. Metz responded by slapping him and making him join the other men working in the mines instead of being allowed to stay in the dispensary tending to the sick. After about a week, Metz finally handed out the parcels, one of only three they received during their stay in Berga. When someone complained to Metz that their treatment violated the Geneva Convention, he replied: "There is no Geneva Convention."[30]

The Americans understood the risk of capture but still were not psychologically equipped to become victims of Hitler's campaign to rid the world, not just Europe, of Jews. It was hard enough for a soldier to see a comrade die suddenly on the battlefield, but it was something else again to see a once vital young man worn down to the point where he expires.

In their silent moments, the Americans prayed for deliverance and survival. Few, if any, of the American Jews were religiously observant. Most never went to synagogue and did not have Jewish educations. Unlike many European Jews who were driven by their treatment to question their belief in God, the American Jews did not feel abandoned. They still had faith the U.S. Army would strike down the German Pharaoh.

The POWs knew the war effort was all-consuming, but they expected their government to try to extricate them from their predicament. But there was little that could be done short of winning the war. Many reconciled themselves to the possibility that they would never see their families again. Most of those who survived, however, refused to give in to despair.

The secret to survival varied only slightly among the men. Al Diamant told George Tabele: "We've got to get home for those kids." Tabele said that's what kept him alive.[31]

"Those of us who survived," Steckler said, "were too mean to die. Those who gave up, died. Bob Kessler died in my arms because he said he couldn't go on."[32]

"Surviving was all you thought about," Rosenberg agreed. "You were so worn down you didn't even think of all the death that was around you." He said his faith sustained him. "I knew I'd go to heaven if I died, because I was already in hell."[33]

Sadly, some men who died were victims of their own vices. These were the people who traded food for cigarettes. "Those who smoked and lived were stealing food," according to Robert Rudnick.[34]

Since the only thing most American POWs knew about the concentration camps was what the political prisoners told them about Buchenwald, they could not imagine that human beings were being treated worse than what they had to endure. These proud young men lost as much as 60 pounds and were regularly beaten. In several cases, sick men were forced to work until they expired.

One day on the way to work, a group of men broke out of the column and bolted off the road into a sugar beet patch. The guards chased them. All the POWs came back except one who was too slow. He was a big boy they called "Red." The guard caught Red and hit him on the head with the handle of a bayonet, causing a deep gash. Red felt groggy but was forced to work the rest of the day. He was not bandaged until that night. A few days later, Red began to scream that he could not see. The Germans would not do anything for him. About a week after the initial beating he was dead.[35]

Paul Arthur Van Horne recalled one American who was beaten because he was too sick to work. Van Horne and another POW then helped the semiconscious man back to the barracks. He was forced, however, to go to work the next morning. He lasted only four days.[36] Some men did not realize the extent of their injuries until they were taken to hospitals. "I received two fractured right ribs which I did not know about until an x-ray was taken when we were liberated," said Marvin Gritz.[37]

In postwar recollections, the POWs said the majority of guards did not mistreat them. Some were even singled out for their humane behavior.[38] But most guards more than made up for these individuals. Many were retaliating for Allied bombing raids on their nearby homes.

One of the most vicious guards was a civilian the prisoners called "Scarface." One of his arms was paralyzed so he could not use his hand and he always wore a black glove over it. He forced the men to try and lift heavy machinery and equipment and kicked or hit them when they were unable to do so. "Once he forced us to unload a flat-car of railroad rails after it was time for us to quit," Donald Hildenbrand recalled. "When the weight shifted and the car almost overturned, he forced us to keep on working. The car did overturn and a friend of mine suffered a broken foot when it was caught between the rails."[39]

The accounts differ, but it appears a non-Jewish English professor from Colorado named George "Buck" Rogers was the first American casualty. Rogers was too sick to go to work after passing out in the mine the day before. "The next morning, when Rogers could not get up, the Kommandofuehrer [Metz] came around to get the men out, and when Rogers did not get out of bed the Kommandofuehrer pulled him out. Rogers started to dress and then collapsed and became unconscious. In order to revive him the Kommandofuehrer threw a bucket of water over him." Afterward, Milton Shippee said, Rogers caught pneumonia. "It was close to freezing in the barracks and he was drenched. Rogers had to work that day. In the evening, he went out of his head and then died."[40]

That was March 9, 1945. Over the course of the next four weeks, at least another 23 Americans succumbed as a consequence of malnutrition, overwork and lack of medical care. Several died of pneumonia and diphtheria and almost all suffered from diarrhea or dysentery. Dr. Rudolf Miethe, a physician from Berga who visited about once a week, told Merz the prisoners got sick from drinking water from the scum-covered Elster River—something they were forced to do because the men did not have adequate drinking water—but Merz did not believe him.[41]

The day-to-day health of the POWs was in the hands of the nine American medics who had only a meager supply of medicine to treat the 70 men who were usually sick at any given time. "We had large, white cold tablets and some brown pills for diarrhea. Few dressings were available so we used paper for bandages," Gritz testified.[42]

Every day, Sgt. Metz held sick call about 8 A.M., and if he thought a prisoner was sick enough, he would let him stay in the barracks or go to the dispensary; that is, unless he really needed a prisoner, then no matter how sick a POW was, he would still have to work. "Metz fancied himself sort of a doctor," Leon Trachtman testified. "When the fellows went on sick call, he would examine them by asking them to stick out their tongues. He would say: 'Healthy tongue. Go to work.'"[43]

Stanley B. Cohen saw David Young die. Metz ordered Young to get up, but he could not, so Cohen called for two medics to help him out of bed. Metz commanded Young to stick his tongue out. Then Young collapsed to the floor. Metz threw a pail of water on him. "Young flickered his eyelashes and gave no other indication of consciousness," Cohen told war crimes investigators. "Metz bent down and touched his head. He said: 'It is warm. You can let him stay in today.'" He died a little while later.[44]

Few POWs were allowed to go to hospitals and most of them were transferred only when they were on the verge of death. Metz sent a total of four transports to hospitals, the last being forced to return. Altogether, only 25 of the 350 men were hospitalized; at least one POW died on route.[45]

POWs who died in the camp were placed outside the barracks. They would stay there until the doctor came to sign a prisoner's death certificate, frequently two or three days later. In the last few weeks at Berga, bodies were stacked as many as four high against the fence that surrounded the compound.[46]

Though the Germans kept the death certificates, the POWs kept some records themselves. A hospital log found at the camp was entered as evidence in the war crimes trial of Merz and Metz. That log listed 24 men who died at Berga from a variety of ailments, including cardiac arrest, pneumonia, grippe, dysentery, malnutrition, stomach ailments, jaundice and a hematoma.[47]

The death of a POW provided the others a reprieve since those who were selected for the burial detail were spared a few hours of work. The head of the guards would order the Americans to strip the bodies and turn the deceased's possessions over to another POW who lived near the hometown of the dead man. The clothes were given to those POWs who needed them. The detail would take the dead man into town where the casket maker would build a wooden pine box. Meanwhile, the POWs would beg for food and cigarettes from the townspeople.

Some bodies were put in individual coffins, others were simply wrapped in blankets. Although not as severe as the mass graves used for European Jews, some POWs were buried together in unmarked plots in a civilian cemetery less than a mile outside the camp. A few of the non-Jewish POWs had crosses placed on their graves with their helmets hung on them.

According to Jerome Cantor's father, his son was buried in a coffin with his name carved on the lid, the date of death and a Star of David. A buddy asked for his dog tags, but the Germans refused. When he protested to Metz that this was a violation of the Hague Convention, Metz told him: "I am the Hague Convention." Cantor's coffin was buried in a single grave with a marker. When the body was dug up later, however, no marker or coffin was found. "A number of other bodies—not American dead—were piled on top of his. The Germans could not leave even the dead sacred."[48]

Steckler recalled one morning when 12 men had to be buried. "When I woke up in the morning, the guy to the right of me was dead, the guy to the left of me was dead, the guy across from me was dead. The whole goddamn world seemed to have died overnight." Rosenberg had the same experience. "It seemed like [men were dying] one a day," he said with the numbness he developed in Berga.

"One kid from California went out of his mind one night. We quieted him down, but the next day, when I woke up, I looked over and he was dead."[49]

Many POWs did not want to wait to be overcome by exhaustion or disease. It was every American's duty to try to escape, and several healthier POWs tried. Strangely, most of the men interviewed for this book did not know these efforts were being made or that any were successful. None of the men who escaped could be located, but during the war crimes trial of Metz and Merz, the reason given for the replacement of Kunz with Metz was that three men had escaped in one night. Metz was expected to put a stop to the escapes.

Zaccaria said a few people would get together and arrange escapes. One method, he said, was to go to the latrine at night and hide in the rafters. When the coast was clear, the prisoner would climb under the electrified fence.[50] Tony Drago said it was possible to disappear into the woods on the way to work in the morning. He went with a couple of other men one day and hid in a barn. They were cooking potatoes. The next thing they knew the Germans had surrounded them. They were taken back to camp and beaten.[51]

Myron Swack recalled working beside Bob Sullivan one day. Sullivan said, "I'm leaving" and jumped off the bridge. Swack thought he had broken his neck but found out later Sullivan had survived the jump and gotten on a train before being recaptured in Dresden.[52]

Rosenberg recalled that the Germans threatened to kill 10 men if one escaped.[53] The threat was never carried out. But after prisoners were recaptured, Metz would force them to stand outside in the freezing cold all night, and in the morning they would have to go to work without any food or sleep.[54] Despite the harsh punishments, Metz did not have any more success stopping escapes than his predecessor. In fact, according to the war crimes trial record, seven men escaped in the first five days Metz was in charge. Both Metz and Merz were criticized by their superiors and were under pressure to take more drastic action. Metz did.

On March 20, two men from the food detail slipped away on the road to pick up breakfast. About two days later, the rural police station of Weildetab called and said one American POW, Morton Goldstein, had been picked up and two more were believed to be in the woods. The captured man was turned over to the Burgermeister in the town. In an unusual move, Metz himself went to the mayor's house to pick up the prisoner. When he arrived, he found the Burgermeister having breakfast with his family. Goldstein was in the kitchen. "What, you're making yourself comfortable here?" Metz said. "I'll fix you."

Metz left to look for the other men. He came back a short while later and told the mayor there had been 20 escapes, mostly at night on the way to or from work. According to his testimony, Metz then said: "If one takes off, he walks the way of death." He also told the mayor that "prisoners who ran away should be shot on sight and that there was an order to that effect."

As he was taking Goldstein back to the camp, Metz bumped into a friend of his from the construction company. While they talked, Goldstein kept walking. In Metz's version, he told him to slow down, but Goldstein jumped over an embankment and started to run into the woods. Metz yelled "Halt!" three times and then fired his pistol twice. Goldstein was hit in the chest and the back of the head. Four American medics brought Goldstein's body back on a stretcher and left it between the barracks for about a week before his comrades could get permission to bury him. This was meant to be an example for the others.[55]

In other POW camps, the Wehrmacht or Luftwaffe officers treated their prisoners with a degree of honor as fellow military men. The Americans at Berga expected similar treatment, but this was not the case. Even in death, Goldstein was not treated with the respect accorded to most prisoners of war. His fate was similar to that of his European brothers and sisters, proof that when it came to killing Jews, all laws—including international agreements regarding the treatment of POWs—were irrelevant.

Only one other American POW was shot at Berga. A few weeks after Goldstein was killed, one guard, Hans Grieshammer, shot another recaptured POW in the back while he was "trying to escape."[56]

Other POWs who attempted escapes were killed more indirectly. For example, while working at the mine during one day shift, Bernard Vogel and one of his friends decided to make the break for freedom when they heard the nightly air-raid siren. "They had the darkness to their advantage, and we all hoped and prayed their efforts would be rewarded," Alan Reyner recalled. "The lack of food, however, undermined their strength considerably and a few days later they were apprehended and brought back to Berga to stand trial for their misdeed. Their sentence was another slash in their already meager rations and hard dirty work (digging out the putrid latrine) in addition to their work at the mines. It wasn't long before this schedule brought the results the Germans had apparently hoped for."[57] Both men became seriously ill and later died.

The POWs' plight improved a little after a visit in early March by Albert Speer, chief of Nazi war production. The Americans were moved closer to the political prisoners' camp, to a new barracks on a meadow near the Elster River along a canal. Approximately 500 Russians and 150 Slovaks were also moved to this camp but were housed in their own barracks. The reason the Germans later gave for the move was to put the prisoners nearer to the work site: They were now about 30 feet away instead of half an hour distant.

After 40 days of working in the mines, with one day off, the POWs were put to work hauling lumber for 12 days. They took a train to the forest and cut trees. Some POWs worked laying rails. The heavy, frozen steel had to be lifted by at least two men in a three-step process. First, they would pick up the rail and put it on their knees, then raise it to their shoulders and finally stand up. If someone collapsed, all the weight would fall on the other man.[58]

The Americans then were supposed to work on the railroad from 7:30–11:30

A.M. and 1–5 P.M. That was not quite how it worked out. "We went to work during the day—6 to 6 with non-Jews," according to Steckler. "It was dark when we left and when we returned." When an air raid commenced, the POWs had to lie in ditches. On those occasions, they would get back to the barracks as late as 9 or 10 P.M.[59]

At his trial, Merz claimed moving the POWs out of the mines was his idea. The Slovaks, he said, were working outside the mountain and were drilling a railroad tunnel. They were better accustomed to this kind of work than the Americans, as were the Russians. Merz said he suggested replacing the Americans with Russians. Metz also took credit for the change, claiming he told Lt. Hack that the Russians who arrived March 18 were miners from Silesia. A few days later, the switch was made.[60]

German civilians frequently maintained they knew nothing about the concentration camps even when they lived close enough to smell the stench of burning flesh. The townspeople of Berga were no less aware of the demonic activities at the camps in their midst. Ernest Kinoy recalled being sent to pick up the bread ration from the center of town. "We were loading the cart in the courtyard. An army sergeant was with a kid from the concentration camp. He ordered the kid to attention. Then he hit him and knocked him down for not being at attention. He repeated this over and over. Across the street women with baby carriages watched without interest as the German beat the kid."[61]

The political prisoners had a different view of the Americans. At one point the POWs were brought to their camp to be deloused. They were shaved and soaked in kerosene. One political prisoner said he thought the Americans looked too soft to survive.[62]

But time was running out for the Germans. As the sound of the Allies' artillery and bombing got closer, the POWs began to anticipate the end of the war. One Jewish political prisoner reported the change in the mood in the Berga camps:

> Ever since the noise of the guns had first been heard in the distance, a great uneasiness had possessed the camp. Wherever I went, I heard excited discussions. When the men came back after work, they told at evening roll-call how the atmosphere had changed even at work. The German civilian workers were beginning to be friendlier. They would chat to the prisoners; they no longer swore at them as they used to do before. The American prisoners of war, who were working on the banks of the Elster, were in a better mood, too, and if a prisoner of our camp passed by they would wink at him gaily. Even those at the end of their tether found fresh strength since the guns had been heard.[63]

On April 4, Metz received an order to evacuate Berga and to begin to march the prisoners toward Politz. Metz did not want to bring the sick prisoners because they were too ill and he had no way to transport them, but Merz insisted that they had to leave. Metz requisitioned a horse cart to carry those Americans who could not walk.

Shortly thereafter, instead of hiking up to the mountain as usual, the prisoners marched in the opposite direction. When the transport left, an American interpreter and four POWs stayed behind to see to the burial of the dead prisoners.

This was but the end of a chapter of the Americans' ordeal. The human skeletons found no cause to rejoice in this flight from hell. They were leaving friends behind and returning to the unknown. The torment of the dead was over, that of the living was to continue. Fewer than 300 men survived the 50 days they had spent in Berga. Like the Israelites who escaped Egypt, however, these Jews had not yet been delivered from Pharaoh. But, instead of wandering in a desert, they were embarking on a march of death.

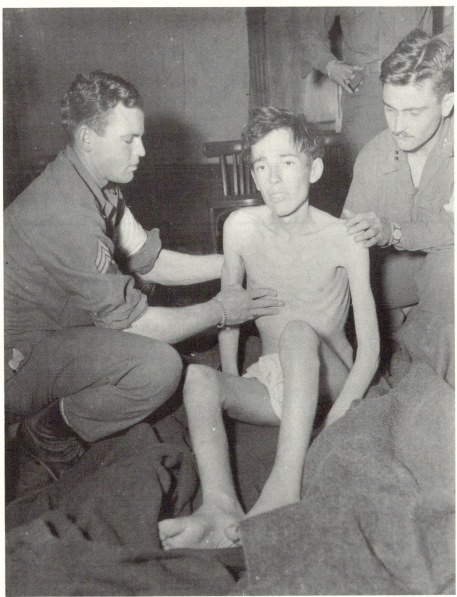

Pfc. James Watkins, 20, of Oakland, CA, was found at the prison hospital in Fuchsmuehl, Germany, by the U.S. Third Army after surviving the death march from the Berga labor camp. Source: National Archives.

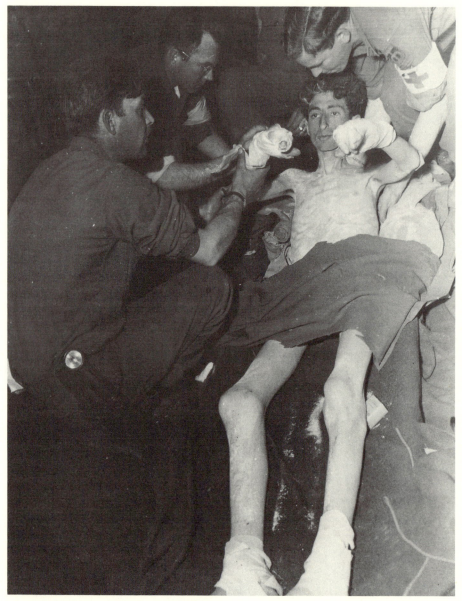

Pvt. Alvin L. Abrams, 20, of Philadelphia, PA, was one of the Jewish POWs segregated at Stalag IX-B and sent to the Berga labor camp, where he was worked to the verge of death. He barely survived the death march after the camp was evacuated in April 1945. He was found at the hospital in Fuchsmuehl, Germany. Source: National Archives.

Lying on stretchers are some of the sixty-three emaciated American POWs liberated in Fuchsmuehl, Germany. From front to rear, the Berga survivors are Pvt. Winfield Rosenberg, Lititz, PA; Pfc. Paul D. Capps, Herrin, IL; Pfc. James Watkins, Oakland, CA; Pfc. Joseph Guigno, Waltham, MA; and Pvt. Alvin L. Abrams, Philadelphia, PA. Source: National Archives.

Photo from the war crimes trial of Ludwig Merz and Erwin Metz showing German civilians exhuming the bodies of American POWs who died in the Berga labor camp. Source: National Archives.

An American soldier stands over the grave of John Simcox, one of the POWs who died in the Berga labor camp. A special area of the Berga cemetery was set aside for the bodies of twenty-two Americans, some of whom were buried in the same grave without coffins. The helmet displays the insignia of the 28th Division. Source: National Archives.

Exterior view of the seventeen tunnels where the POWs from Berga worked. Prisoners worked six to twelve hours, seven days a week in freezing temperatures for nearly two months in the damp, dusty shafts. The Germans would blast the slate loose with dynamite, and the Americans would break up the rock so it could be shoveled into mining cars. Civilian overseers beat prisoners who worked too slowly. Source: National Archives.

Maj. Fulton Vowell (left) and Capt. Herschel Auerbach (right) apprehend an SS guard, assistant warden at the Berga labor camp. When American troops entered the camp, the guard fled to an old woman's home but was betrayed by German civilians and taken into custody. Source: National Archives.

Photo from the German identity card issued to First Lt. James D. Hastin, one of the eighty-two Americans sent to the Buchenwald concentration camp in August 1944. For two months they learned what life was like for European Jews. The POWs were later transferred to Stalag Luft III. Years later Hastin and the others discovered they were supposed to be executed at Buchenwald. Photo used by permission of James D. Hastin, Lt/Col USAF (Ret).

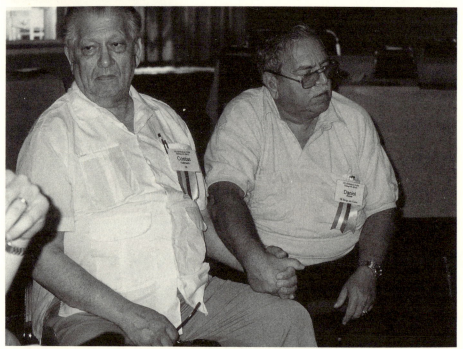

Costa Katimaris (left) and Daniel Steckler (right) talk about their experience at the Berga labor camp during a reunion of Stalags IX-A, IX-B, and IX-C in Jacksonville, FL, April 18–21, 1991. Photo by Mitchell G. Bard.

9

The Death March and Liberation

THE POLITICAL PRISONERS left Berga in early April. "Day and night the SS marched us farther away from the ever-increasing thunder of the guns," Eugene Heimler recalled.[1] The Commandant, a man named Schwarzbach, ordered anyone who fell to be shot dead. The road behind them was splattered with blood and strewn with corpses. The American POWs followed this trail of carnage.

Three hundred fifty healthy, young GIs had left Stalag IX-B two months earlier. According to the camp log, 24 died in Berga, 26 went to hospitals (at least one other POW died on route) and 10–20 escaped. Now, fewer than 300 walking skeletons—actually a number could not even stand and rode in a cart—began to march away from the rapidly approaching Allied forces. Some men had no shoes or overcoats. If the Americans were quick enough, they could sometimes get extra clothes from dead men. But this was only if the Germans did not get them first.

At first, the POWs had blankets they had taken from the camp. When they reached their first stop, Greiz, their blankets were taken away. Metz said it was because they belonged to Schwalbe 5. At his war crimes trial he testified that he protested but went on to say the POWs all had either field jackets or overcoats and still had plenty of blankets. Metz went so far as to claim the prisoners had better clothes than the Germans. These were men who were wearing the same uniforms they had been captured in nearly five months earlier.

The POWs marched from daylight to ten P.M. or midnight, 9–16 miles, with a break every hour and a half. Once a day, they were given one loaf of bread per 10 men and potato soup with rotten potatoes. They received no water unless they passed a stream. Meanwhile, the Germans had plenty of canned meat and bread.

The men who could not walk when they left Berga were put on a "sick wagon." Metz decided who could ride in the wagon. A POW "had to be practically dead," Milton Shippee said, to be allowed to ride.[2] The cart was packed so tightly at least one American was said to have suffocated. Israel Cohen had been recaptured after trying to escape from Berga and was badly beaten and forced to work in the latrine. According to Norman Martin, he was the first man put on the sick wagon. Other men were subsequently thrown on top of him and Martin believes he suffocated "because his face was a picture of agony and from the position of his body he looked as if he had been struggling to get air."[3]

According to Metz, about 35 men were sick each day, but there was plenty of room on the three sick wagons he said were available. Contradicting POWs who said he determined who would ride, Metz claimed the medics made these decisions.[4] Regardless, according to Shippee, the Germans made no effort to get another cart, though they never hesitated to commandeer food when they wanted to.

The POWs usually slept in barns and open fields. Whenever the POWs asked where they were going, the guards would say: "Next town, next town."

The German civilians they passed on the journey treated the Americans well and gave them food. This was in contrast to the treatment they got from the civilians at Berga, who Samuel Fahrer said had ridiculed them at every opportunity. "The Hitler Youth members threw stones at us many times," he said.[5]

Whenever they could, the Americans would steal food. "One night, I stole some potatoes from a barn," Winfield Rosenberg recalls. "A guard caught me and hit me in the back with his rifle. But," Rosenberg says with a smile, "I got to keep the potatoes."[6]

"Most men barely had the strength to stand let alone march 12–14 hours," Fahrer recalled. "The Germans were irritable and merciless in driving us onward. When prisoners lagged, the guards would prod them with rifles. Men began falling to the rear of the column and some attempted to escape." Fahrer said he had many opportunities to flee but decided to help the men who were sick. "At night, I would travel around the countryside seeking information of our troops, which I would take back to the rest of the men. The guards never bothered me because I'd tell them I'd been on the road bringing in men who had collapsed during the day."[7]

The medics were also in better physical condition than the other POWs because they had not been forced to work in the mines. "Some days they'd help those who could barely walk by holding them under the arms," Shippee recalled. Fahrer and the other medic had practically no supplies. Steckler recalled Fahrer wrapping his injured hand with toilet paper.

The second stop, 16 miles away, was Muehltroff, where the POWs were housed in an old castle used as a home for juveniles. Four Americans died there.[8]

After traveling another 9 miles, they stopped in Dobareuth for the night. It had been raining and the ground was wet, but the Germans said they would have to sleep in the field. Norman Martin spoke German, so he protested to Metz. "If men were forced to sleep on wet ground in their weak condition," he said, "at least 15 would die during the night." Metz answered by slugging Martin, knocking out three of his teeth.[9] Four men died that evening.

Nighttime was when most of the prisoners died. "They'd stick out the day's march, then fall asleep and never wake up," Shippee said. At his trial, Metz portrayed himself as sympathetic in treating American dead because he granted medics' requests to immediately bury them rather than wait until they reached a town.[10] The former POWs had different memories.

The Americans, who had suffered dehumanization in the camp, were not even allowed to die with dignity. Winfield Rosenberg recalled waking up one morning and finding six men dead. "They left the bodies outside a farm house, next to a manure pile. I can still remember how they looked lying there."[11] Steckler said the POWs could tell what stage of death a man was in by looking at him.[12]

For some Americans, the sight of the political prisoners was the worst part of the march. "Dead Jews were everywhere with bullet holes in the head. You could see pieces of skull," Leo Zaccaria recalled. "We didn't stop once, walking through thousands—every five feet for six or seven hours, sometimes on both sides of the road."[13]

Unlike the civilian prisoners who were shot when they fell out of line, the Germans did not kill Americans who could not keep up. "If you weren't walking fast enough, they would hit you with a rifle, kick you and punch you," Shippee told investigators after his liberation. After one American was beaten in the back with a bayonet because he had collapsed from exhaustion, Metz said: "Beat them if they don't walk."[14]

"One night we were standing in line for soup and made too much noise or something that upset the Kommandofuehrer," Shippee recalled. "So he took the bucket of soup and threw it on the ground and then grabbed a guard's rifle and charged our line swinging it. He hit Norman Martin in the shoulder blades with the rifle butt and knocked another man unconscious."[15]

One survivor testified that in at least one instance a POW was killed from such a beating. Marcel Ouimet said Pvt. Donald Rowe collapsed and could not get up. A guard then struck him in the forehead with the butt of his rifle and killed him.[16]

The POWs also remained uncertain about their fate. They could never be sure if the Germans would decide to kill them. Lawrence Gillette climbed up on some hay one night. "An officer got mad at me and pointed his gun at my head, and I crawled off. I don't know whether he'd have shot or not, probably would have if I hadn't got off."[17] It did not take much to end the life of a man who had barely survived the weeks in the mines and the beatings from the guards in the camp. Many of those who died on the march were really killed in Berga but did not expire until later.

By the time the column reached Hof, the third stop, some men could no longer eat. Two prisoners died during the night and two others were semiconscious and expected to die. "The Germans put the bodies of the two dead men outdoors in the snow and then ordered us to put the two men who were not yet dead outdoors and strip them of their clothes," recalled Roy Moser. "They were left in the snow to die. The men were still conscious and knew what we were doing but were too weak to take any action."[18] Moser said they protested putting the men outside, but the Germans shoved a bayonet in their backs.

After having marched more than 50 miles since leaving Berga four days earlier, the column stopped to rest for a few days. The Americans stayed in a barn. "We thought the Kommandofuehrer wanted to get rid of us," Shippee said. "We were afraid that he might set fire to the barn and burn us all to death."[19]

Altogether, 10 POWs died during this "rest" stop. Their bodies were found after the war in Topen, buried without grave markers or coffins.[20] This was about the time President Roosevelt died. The Germans were dancing, but the POWs were somber. "We felt as though he went in our place and we had to carry on his work," Daniel Steckler said.[21] The POWs held a service led by Leon Trachtman, a Rabbi's assistant from Cleveland. They read the 23rd Psalm.

On April 14, the POWs marched 15 miles to Rehau. Eight men died. Their bodies were buried in a single grave with eight small iron crosses in a field near Durenich.[22] Another prisoner died after they left the town. He was buried on the road. The corpse was found with a Bible in the pocket with the name Pvt. Lawrence Leighton Osborn.

Four more Americans died the next day. Actually, one man who was supposed to have died was still alive when he reached the cemetery at Thierstein.[23] The bodies were buried in a single grave without coffins but with a wooden cross that said in German: "Here Lay 4 American Prisoners of War 15 April 1945."[24]

Over the next three days, another three men died. Metz told Fahrer to take the most seriously ill prisoners to a hospital in Fuchsmuehl "over his protest." Thirty-one American POWs were admitted to the Fuchsmuehl hospital, but they received no medical treatment and slept on straw until being liberated. One of the men died. Approximately 14 prisoners escaped from the hospital.[25]

After nearly two weeks of marching, the column consisted of gaunt figures stumbling and groping along, many too weak to walk unassisted. "Some men were delirious, crying aloud with pain, with tears streaming from their eyes," said Roy Moser. "Some of the men knew they were dying and were crying out that they were afraid and did not want to die."[26]

Metz testified he tried to find doctors on the march but did not succeed. According to Moser, about 25 men had pneumonia or strep throat before leaving the camp. He suffered from the former. A doctor examined them before they left and advised that three or four of the men be sent to a hospital. The commandant said there was no transport to take them.[27]

Moser said the sick cart could only hold one or two men along with German baggage and that days sometimes passed without any place for the sick. Moser was too weak to walk because of the aftereffects of pneumonia and spent much of the time on the cart. At the end, he spent a week straight on it before being taken to a hospital near the Czech border.

Those prisoners who still were strong enough took advantage of the opportunity to escape from the march. The column had few guards and, for the first time, the prisoners had some hope of being sheltered by German civilians who now were more interested in currying favor with the Americans than with the Nazis. The healthier Americans did not want to risk being killed after having survived the hell of the camp.

Milton Shippee, for example, escaped near Hof and hid in the town of Weiden until he was liberated on April 20.[28] Robert Widdicombe buried himself in a haystack. Earlier, he had been asleep, curled up in a blanket with his best friend, George Burdeski. When the sun came up, Burdeski was dead. "That's when I realized it could happen to me," he said. "If I had stayed with the column, I believe now I would have died, too."[29]

The POWs were marching through some woods one night. Laurence Gillette and Jack Kemper hung back. "There was a little light outside, but under the trees it was black as black. We saw a place under the trees and just both fell down. They just walked on and left us." After the column passed, they hid in a cow barn. "Jack had never been around a cow," but Gillette milked it and filled their canteen cups. In the course of moving from house to house, they came upon a Polish slave laborer who said the SS were around and hid them in a hayloft. "He'd get us a boiled egg or two. . . . he did cut our hair, and we just threw away those old clothes. There were some clothes that got dumped from the troops, kind of pajamas and we crawled into those clothes."

A couple of days later the American troops arrived. "We tried to run to them, but all we could do was walk; we couldn't run. We had no strength left. I don't know how they even knew we were Americans, except that we could speak English. That's the only time in my life I ever saw Superman was when I saw those American troops."[30]

Those Americans who were too weak to escape were usually found by the liberating forces at the verge of death.

One night, the prisoners sharing a barn sensed something different was happening as they awoke for another day on the road. They heard no German voices, only shooting outside. One POW climbed a ladder and looked out from a window to investigate. "I see a big white star! It looks like a Sherman tank!" he hollered down to his companions. The men cheered. The vehicle was indeed American. "Before we knew it, the barn door flew open and it wasn't a Kraut standing there," Bernie Melnick recalled. "I ran over to some tank and the commander picked me up and lifted me inside. I was hysterical." Melnick weighed 90 pounds and was suffering from dysentery, jaundice, infected wounds and shell shock.

By the time the Americans arrived, the German guards had apparently fled. "Who are you guys?" the liberators asked. "They didn't believe us," Joe Guigno said. "The GIs were crying when they saw us. We were all stretcher cases. We couldn't go to the bathroom. We just went where we were."[31]

Steckler was in a beer hall at the end of the march. Two men were dead, laying naked in a corner. In another corner, the very sick were bleeding. Only four men could stand, but they were incoherent. An American infantryman broke down the door of the house and held a gun on Steckler. "I was so scared I got up and stumbled on top of him and kissed his rifle. He was disgusted and knocked me off." Steckler told him not to shoot because they were Americans. Everyone started screaming and babbling. The soldier was about to shoot when another officer arrived and stopped him. Steckler was asked his name, rank and serial number. Then he asked him where he was from, which baseball team played in Brooklyn, who played center field for the Dodgers and how many home runs their first baseman hit. In a daze, Steckler blathered the answers. An officer came in and screamed: "Look what they've done to our guys!"

George Tabele was a "walking zombie" weighing less than 90 pounds when Patton's 1st Armored Division liberated him April 28. He told his local newspaper nearly 40 years later how a "big, heavy-bearded (tank driver) picked me up like a 10-pound baby, put me inside the tank and started to feed me food he got from home—canned peaches, cake and cookies. But the order came over his radio not to feed the POWs. A little real food might kill them." He was picked up by an ambulance, which took him to a hospital run by Catholic nuns in Cham, Germany.

Louis Crain escaped from the column and was trying to make his way to the American lines. Weakened by exposure and the lack of food, he developed pneumonia and collapsed. A German priest found him along the side of the road and took him to his home. Two weeks later, American troops found him in a bedroom in the priest's home.

The Associated Press's Edward Ball described the men he found when the 90th Division arrived at a German hospital April 21, 1945:

> Freedom arrived just ahead of death from starvation for a number of American soldiers in a German hospital overrun by the 90th Division.
>
> 47 American Doughboys, captured in the Belgian breakthrough last December, were liberated yesterday by the 90th. All of them were suffering from acute malnutrition, overwork and frequent beatings administered by the Germans, who had worked them in a rock quarry.
>
> 15 of the 47 were wasted away to little more than living skeletons. All of the men were crawling with lice; some still bore welts and infected sores from the beatings by German civilian and military guards.
>
> Medicos said some were in so advanced a stage of starvation that they could not have survived much longer. One man died at Fuchsmuehl where the Americans stayed for five days after they were abandoned by the Germans. . . . A number of litter cases were too weak from hunger and excitement to talk. Others were only half-conscious. "I see only rainbows in those lights," one delirious 19-year-old said as he was brought into the clearing room.[32]

Most men were liberated between April 20–24, 1945, approximately four months after being captured. The ordeal had finally ended.

Of the 350 Americans who were originally sent to Berga, no more than 280 returned to the United States. At least 36 men died on the march to nowhere. The fatality rate in Berga, including the march, was nearly 20 percent, and the 70–73 men who were killed represented approximately six percent of *all* Americans who perished as POWs during World War II.

10

The Meaning of Survival: Life After the Camps

WHEN THE FORMER POWs returned to the United States, they found neither their government nor their friends believed their stories of imprisonment in concentration camps. One Berga survivor, for example, said in an interview he was sent to a psychiatrist because the army thought he was fabricating the whole story. Most former POWs were reluctant to talk about their experiences.

Initially, the only concern of the men who survived their ordeals was to recuperate. Dan Steckler's condition at liberation was typical:

> When we got to the hospital in Paris, I weighed less than 85 pounds. We were lice-ridden, millions of lice in my hair, all over my body. I was shaved from head to foot, except for my moustache, my eyebrows, my eyelids. I was shaved completely. We looked so bad that the nurses, the French nurses' aides used to cry when they came to our bedside. Ran from the bed sometimes. We were in such bad shape that they fed us vitamins intravenously, and then finally within a few days were told we were gonna be shipped back to the States by airplanes because there wasn't much more they could do for us and they were afraid that they weren't doing enough and it might not be possible to save us. If we were to die, we were going to die home.[1]

"I was quite well, just suffering from malnutrition," Lawrence Gillette recalled. "So I just ate. For breakfast I'd have six big hotcakes, a bowl of cereal and half a dozen eggs. Then I'd take a bunch of food home with me, back to my barracks there. Then I'd wake up in the middle of the night and eat. The hunger just wouldn't go away." When Gillette got back to the States, he went to a dentist and had most of his teeth pulled because they had rotted from malnutrition. "I was still hungry, so I kept eating. I put on 60 pounds in 60 days I ate so much."[2]

The impact of having been starved had longer lasting effects as well. Daniel Steckler virtually surrounds his food with his body when he eats. "God forbid anyone should reach for something on my plate. I don't know what I'd do," he says now. Steckler's experience also affected his family. His wife believes their children are more high-strung because Dan was so obsessed. Steckler's daughter said she thought it would have been better if her father had forgotten Berga. "It changed our lives," she said. "We knew we were different. From the time I was three, instead of hearing Dr. Seuss I heard about delousing and other stories about Berga."[3]

Gillette also found that he was more than just malnourished. When he was still recovering, he went out to play baseball one day. "I'd throw the ball to second base, and the damned ball would go to first base. I had no coordination."[4]

When he reflected on why he survived, Gillette said he had more of a reason than some other guys. "My family, my [Mormon] church and my religion. I had more to live for; I still have more to live for," he said.

Sam Lubinsky told the VA about his experiences at Berga. "They sent me to see a psychiatrist. They said no such thing happened." When he first got back to New York, Lubinsky became paralyzed from heart blockage. He got better and became a master plumber in his hometown of Lima, Ohio. He could not stand the cold, however, and moved to Florida. Like most of the other POWs, he had difficulty talking about his experience and often had nightmares. He only began to speak about Berga in 1991, and that was because he had suffered a worse trauma, his wife's death.[5]

Many former POWs complain about the treatment they received from the VA. Most did not think they were given the compensation they deserved for their injuries. Irving Pastor, for example, had problems with his stomach after he returned and got 100% disability. After a year, it was dropped to 10%.

Winfield Rosenberg was only 24 when he was liberated from Berga and returned home. "I had nightmares and would jump up in the middle of the night," he said. But the nightmares did not end even after years and decades passed. "I still dream about it," he said. It's no wonder the memory never leaves him. This is the condition he was in when he was liberated:

> I had urethritis blockage. I had pneumonia, malnutrition, yellow jaundice, dysentery, full of lice, frozen feet. I weighed less than 90 pounds and my hair started to fall out. They did not touch my feet for over a month because they were so sore. The clothes I wore when I went overseas were the same clothes I had on when I was liberated, so you can imagine how we smelled. I was given plasma and fed very little, because if I ate anything too heavy it came back up. I was isolated in a private room on account of pneumonia.[6]

Rosenberg could not work for a year after the war and had to live with his family. He could not wear shoes because his feet would swell up. Eventually, Rosenberg worked for the Post Office, then as a salesman for a furniture company and finally as a salesman for Gulf Oil. He had to stop working in 1971, however, because he was not physically able to continue even though he was only fifty. Despite the mental and physical anguish, Rosenberg never talked about Berga. The people in his hometown—even his wife of 37 years—did not know what happened to him until 1985, when he told his story to the local paper. Today,

Rosenberg has many ailments typical of the elderly. He wears glasses and a hearing aid. He has had stomach hernias, his gall bladder removed, a hiatal hernia operation, kidney stone operations, a prostate operation, a cartilage removed from his left knee and spurs in his lower back removed. At least some of these problems can be attributed to his days in Berga. He still has trouble with his stomach, for example, and problems with his feet. "My feet burn all of the time while I'm up," he says. "When I go to bed my feet go numb; when I get up in the morning my feet are ice cold. It's an effort for me to walk."

Others underwent similar experiences. When Joe Guigno was liberated from Berga he weighed 85 pounds and his feet were frozen up to his ankles. He was lucky to lose only two toes. He had dysentery and his clothes had rotted so that he was only wearing shoes. When he returned home, he learned the government claimed Berga did not exist.

George Tabele lived with a "rotten" stomach, was frightened by thunderstorms and was prone to nightmares after the war. He was a "walking zombie" weighing less than 90 pounds when Patton's 1st Armored Division liberated him April 28. Tabele had been captured in the Huertgen Forest near St. Vith, Belgium, December 17, 1944. He had been wounded, shrapnel in the hand and a tracer bullet in the shoulder. The shrapnel was not removed until he returned to the States. He was in an infantry company that he said was nearly two-thirds Jewish. "Those Jewish boys were good soldiers," he told his local newspaper 40 years later. "They had a lot more to fight for than we did."[7]

When Leo Zaccaria was flown from Germany to Riems, he carried a gun and a knife. "I was a mean bastard at liberation," he said. "We were a bunch of animals. I may have been one of the worst." The hospital staff wanted to delouse him, but he threatened to shoot them. He could not sleep in the bed and stayed on the floor. Once he saw some German prisoners in the mess hall and went over to their table and tipped over all the food. "They had to wait for their supper."

Another time a nurse came in to give him a pill. "When she woke me up, I grabbed her and had her on the ground. I almost killed her before I realized where I was." Zaccaria was out of control and beginning to drink heavily. He said a Catholic priest settled him down by telling him he was behaving as badly as the Germans. Zaccaria said he got over his hate in three months. Still, the adjustment to civilian life was difficult. "Through life you are taught right from wrong," he said. "Then you are put in a situation where there's only wrong. And the people doing wrong are succeeding over you." Zaccaria wanted to forget his experience so he did not tell his family what happened. "I avoided the VA like the plague because it was a reminder." He could not escape the memories, however, and suffered from nightmares. Even low-flying airplanes scared him.[8]

"When we got back, we were ashamed, and the government was ashamed of us being captured," Gerald Zimand said. He had spent four months in a hospital in Europe because of a frozen foot. The other survivors of Berga did not even know he was alive. After he returned home, his wife says, he would celebrate his rebirth every April 23—the anniversary of his liberation—and get drunk. Once under the influence, he would talk a little about his experience "but never enough," she said.

Zimand has only recently told his son and daughter what happened to him, but they did not believe it. Had they known earlier, they might have better understood some of their father's behavior. For example, when his son bought his first car, a Volkswagen, Zimand would not let him put it in the garage.

"The government tried to cover up Berga," Myron Swack related in an interview. "Even when I joined an ex-POW group, they called it 9C. It was like it never existed. They tried to suggest I was at a resort," he recalled bitterly.

Unlike many other survivors, Swack says he could put the experience behind him. "I was back at Ohio State in September 1945. I never looked back. I was able to divorce myself from the experience."

Bob Widdicombe also tried to block out the experience. "When I look back now, it seems like something that could have happened on TV," he told his local paper.[9]

The impact of the POW experience on Gerald Daub was to make him more aware of life and death and to have a greater appreciation for the former. He was determined not to drift through the rest of his life. Ultimately, he became an architect.[10]

The survivors have differing opinions as to why they were singled out to be mistreated. Some said that Hitler had ordered that Jewish POW's be removed from all camps but that the commandant at Bad Orb was the only one who carried out the order. Others said the commandant was anti-Semitic and made the decision independently.[11] No records were produced at the war crimes trials or elsewhere to provide a definitive answer.

The families of the POWs who died never were told by the government exactly what had happened to their loved ones. Those who found out were told by the Berga survivors. "I wrote letters to Rodgers' wife and to the wife of this other fellow who died on the march," Gillette said. "My letters were their first notifications of their husbands' deaths."[12] Bernard Vogel's mother received a cryptic note about her son's death. It was only after his uncle investigated the matter, and located Vogel's comrades, that she learned the truth. Six months later, Vogel's body was disinterred from the German cemetery and buried in the United States.

The POWs from Stalag IX-B never knew what happened to the Jews and others taken from the camp that cold day in February. "I have asked for years if anyone knew what happened," Pete House said. "It was in 1989 at our 106th Division Association reunion that someone told me what happened."[13]

The former POWs who express anger at the government's failure to acknowledge what happened at Berga, and at its subsequent treatment of them, remain patriotic. Dan Steckler, now 67, said: "I'm as much American as anyone. I'm as dedicated as any American who ever lived. I carry on the torch of Americanism that is reminiscent of Abraham, Isaac and Jacob. We are in the forefront of the fight for liberty."

Lawrence Gillette said his experience in Berga had a significant impact on his life. "I appreciate America and I appreciate democracy. I never miss a chance to vote. I appreciate that privilege we have in America. I appreciate what I have more and love my country that much more."[14]

Similarly, Roy Moser considers himself lucky despite his experience. "No one could ever imagine what we suffered," he wrote to Winfield Rosenberg. "The memories will be with us until we die. The way I look at it, we have 42 years on the comrades we left over there so that every morning I wake up I say 'thank you' for another day.'" Moser had triple-bypass surgery in 1972 and an operation for colon cancer in 1986. "The radiation therapy and chemo were tough," he told Rosenberg, "but I just keep fighting, like we did at Berga."

Costa "the Greek" Katimaris has a similar attitude. He breaks down when he tries to talk about Berga. "We should thank God we're still here."[15]

One man who was in IX-B but was never sent to Berga, is no less thankful. He carries reports in his briefcase on how many people died in the camp. "When I have a bad day," Pete House says, "I take them out and I don't feel bad anymore."[16]

The experience of being sent to a concentration camp created special bonds among the men sent to Buchenwald. Those men formed the K.L.B. Club while they were in Hut 58 of the Little Lager at Buchenwald. K.L.B. stands for Konzentrationslager Buchenwald. After the war, the club did not meet, however, until 1979. Of the 82 USAF survivors of the camp, 22 had died by 1991, 45 had been located by club members and 15 were unaccounted for. It was not until their 1983 reunion that they decided to go public. "The shock of what happened still lingered and many did not want to dig into the hidden recesses of their minds and find facts that they did not want to believe happened," club president Arthur Kinnis wrote.[17]

Kinnis himself kept a diary but did not take it out of his drawer. He never discussed his experience with his kids. He had nightmares and talked in his sleep. Most of the survivors found it too discouraging to mention because most people did not believe their story. Kinnis, a Canadian, was an interior decorator. He had to give up his profession after the war. "I couldn't stand being confined. I had headaches until I quit." He ultimately became the sales manager for a building construction firm. He built his own home in British Columbia as therapy.

"If you weren't there, you can't believe a person could go through it," Bill Gibson said. "You can't believe that one person could do such things to another human being."[18]

Today, most of the survivors bear physical as well as psychological scars. Many still have holes in their legs from the fleas and lice.

A British veteran wrote to Park Chapman about his feelings, sentiments shared by all the men who had been in Buchenwald:

I was most interested to hear of your personal emotional reactions to the recalling of those awesome events of the past—to anyone who has never experienced fear, and such traumas as we in our early youths, experienced in those few dramatic months—the shock of being shot down and losing one's close flying friends, the drama of the weeks of "freedom," the shock of capture, in civilian clothes, and the shame and mishandling of the evil and ruthless Gestapo. The privations and confinement of the dreadful old Fresnes prison in Paris, the nightmare of the five days shut up in the boxcars in the heat and overcrowding, and the unbelievable world that we found ourselves at the end of the journey when we found ourselves in the Camp—lost to the world. The narrow escapes of the bombing, a few yards from us, and the extra privations that followed with the loss of the water supply to add to our torments. . . . And the cruel thing is that nobody has ever wanted to know, nor even really believed our story when we have attempted to retell some of the more dramatic events. Such indifference I am certain has only made us all the more bitter and frustrated, and somewhat bitter of authority who should have taken our welfare to heart and monitored our health over the years.[19]

The former POW added that he had suffered from bad dreams over the years and had kept his bitterness and resentment bottled up. It was only after he returned to Buchenwald that he could discuss his experience. Now, he says, he seems to talk about it constantly. "I am a little worried that it might all come back again to trouble me, there is hardly a day that the subject of Buchenwald doesn't come up in conversation in one way or another, and I'm sure my dear lady wife, as patient and understanding as she is, must be a little anxious the way the situation is developing."[20]

The U.S. government did nothing to recognize the ordeal these men survived. Moreover, it has hidden the facts and refused to compensate the men. By contrast, the Australian and New Zealand governments paid their servicemen $10,000 and $13,000, respectively, for their suffering. The British government got some money from the Germans for people who were illegally detained. According to Jim Hastin, RAF officers got about 300 pounds out of the millions the government got from Germany. Hastin says he never got any compensation because the State Department does not want to open the floodgates for reparations claims, but Park Chapman said he got about three dollars for each day of imprisonment.[21]

One of John Chalot's friends asked him why he did not apply for a Florida POW license plate. He wrote to the Air Force Records Center and was told they had no record of his being a POW. They could only provide him with a copy of his mission orders. Chalot's only proof that he had been a POW were the letters and telegrams his mother had received and saved. When Chalot wrote to other agencies in Washington, he was always told: "There were no Allied airmen in Buchenwald." It was not until he received a reply from the International Tracing Service in 1989 that Chalot received documentary evidence showing he was in Buchenwald.

Bill Powell applied for assistance at a VA hospital and told his story to the examining physician. At the end, the doctor wrote in his record: "*Claims* he was in Buchenwald" (emphasis added).[22]

One K.L.B. member believed the form ex-POWs had to fill out about their medical history for the VA typified the government's attitude. One question reads: "Despite the many negative aspects of your POW status, were there any positive aspects to your experience?"

During his imprisonment, Hastin was optimistic. "I never thought anything would happen to me," he said. "It was like the poem, 'I am a mother's son.' I was young—22—we all accepted the situation because we couldn't do anything about it." But the experience scarred him. "I could never get close to someone after Buchenwald," Hastin admitted. "Mentally, I had to block out emotions. I still do." Hastin had nightmares and found it difficult to talk about his experience. "It was so inconceivable, people did not believe it. They said, 'Oh yeah, it must have been kind of rough,' and talk about something else." It has only been in the last few years that Hastin began to talk about what happened. In fact, until recently he had not even told his kids; they knew only that he had been in a POW camp.

In 1988, Hastin and his wife went to Buchenwald. "That helped quite a bit. Like taking a load off," he said. "Now it's gone, but just enough remains to remind you it was there. I wanted to go back a free man, knowing that I could go and leave it." Although a non-Jew, Hastin considers himself a survivor. "We were so close. The orders were in camp for our execution when we left. We heard the SOE names called over the loudspeaker before they were executed." Hastin does not blame the U.S. government for what happened to him, but he is angry it did not compensate the POWs or acknowledge they were treated as political prisoners. He did get a POW medal but wants the recognition that they were in Buchenwald. "I go to the VA and show them the spots on my leg, but the doctors just think I'm another ex-POW."[23]

None of the former POWs received any decorations after the war for their incarceration. In the 1980s, some finally received the POW medal created originally to honor men held captive in Vietnam. The citation says nothing about Berga. The attitudes of the veterans toward the decoration were mixed. Some believed it was belated recognition by the government of their treatment and more importantly an acknowledgment that what they said did happen. Others had no interest in medals that would remind them of their experience. And a few felt like William Rudnick. Although he received a medal, he said he did not think "being a prisoner was something to be proud of."[24]

Most of the former POWs never gave any thought to the question of whether they were Holocaust survivors. When asked, the opinions were again mixed. "I was never in fear of going to the gas chamber," Milton Filler said in denying he was a survivor. Similarly, Ernest Kinoy said they were victims of "one nut who acted on his own authority." He said what happened to the men in Berga could not be compared with what Jews went through in the concentration camps. Dan

Steckler disagrees: "Of course we were in the Holocaust. We were Holocaust victims." Perhaps Costa Katimaris put it best: "I think I became a Jew since I was in Berga."[25]

The American civilians who were victims of the Holocaust were, with only a couple of exceptions, impossible to locate. New Jersey–born Margaret Pogany was raised in Hungary and imprisoned in Bergen-Belsen, Raguhn and Theresienstadt. She applied to the German government for war reparations. Her claim was rejected. She then appealed to the U.S. government for help but was told by the State Department that American citizens living in Europe at the beginning of hostilities had the opportunity to return home. Mrs. Pogany said she did not have the necessary papers to prove her citizenship and, even if she had, it would not have helped her because, according to Hungarian laws, she was not an American but a Czech like her deceased father.[26]

11

The War Crimes Trials: Justice Half-Served

DURING THE WAR, a decision was made not to pursue war criminals until after an Allied victory for fear of provoking reprisals against POWs. Instead, officials were secretly to gather evidence of war crimes for use after the war.[1] But most Nazis who might have been tried for war crimes against Americans either evaded capture, were purposely allowed to come to the United States (and other countries) or were simply not prosecuted.

Evidence of the mistreatment of American soldiers was introduced at two concentration camp trials but did not play a major part in the prosecution of the Nazis in either one. In the trial of Germans responsible for the Flossenbürg camp, for example, evidence was presented that English and American POWs were placed in dark, isolated cells. Some remained in these cells for 11 months. An American Second Lieutenant who was confined in this prison was hanged in April 1945.[2]

The Buchenwald concentration camp case, *U.S. vs. Josias Prince Zu Waldeck, et al.*, was tried from April 11 to August 14, 1947. The prosecution established that Buchenwald and its 100 subcamps, with a population of 80,000 men and 23,000 women, was operated by the accused who participated in the general mission of torture and abuse of the inmates by starvation, beatings and systematic mistreatment and killing. The death rate reached a high of 5,000 a month toward the end of the war. The defense denied the charges and attempted to justify and explain the large number of deaths by attributing them to natural causes, legal executions and superior orders.

In the Buchenwald trial, mention was made that approximately 178 (the actual number was 168) Allied airmen were held, but their imprisonment was minimized. "A transport of American and Canadian prisoners of war was sent to Buchenwald by mistake," the trial record says. "Due to overcrowding of the camp, they had to sleep under the open sky. Within a week they were placed in buildings and, after an investigation, sent to a prisoner of war camp at Oberursel." One

Buchenwald official, Stabsscharführer Friedrich Wilhelm, told interrogators he saw an American in the dispensary.[3]

No mention was made of the horrors witnessed and experienced by Americans like Jim Hastin, Park Chapman or the other 166 Allied airmen who spent *two months* in Buchenwald. None of the Germans were held accountable for the deaths of Philip Hemmens or Levitt Beck.

Obviously, Americans were not the principal victims at Buchenwald. The evidence of atrocities was sufficient for the court to convict all 31 of the accused for violations of the laws and usages of war. The judges imposed 22 death sentences, five life terms, one 10-year term, two of 15 years and one of 20. But six death sentences were commuted to life, one to 20 years. Two life terms were reduced to 20 years, one to 15, and another to 4 years. One 15-year sentence was reduced to 5 years. One 10-year sentence was reduced to 3 years.

The man who commanded the camp until early 1942, Col. Karl Koch, was executed by the Nazis for the embezzlement of SS funds and for the murder of someone with whom he had personal difficulties.[4] His wife was sentenced at Nuremberg to life imprisonment, though this was subsequently reduced to four years because reviewers said there was no convincing evidence that she selected inmates for extermination to secure tattooed skin or that she possessed any articles made of human skin.[5] When Americans learned the "Bitch of Buchenwald" had been let off the hook, it caused a major furor in the United States that ultimately led to a Congressional investigation.[6]

Col. Koch's successor was Herman Pister. At the trial, it was said that he visited the Allied airmen several times and called them "terror fliers." Pister told interrogators that 80 American flyers had come on a transport from France. He said he notified the Main Reichs Security Office at once and then a commission came and they were taken away. Later, he said they stayed three weeks.[7] Pister was sentenced to hang but died in prison.[8]

After the review of the Buchenwald convictions, Solomon Surowitz, one of three prosecutors in the Buchenwald case, wrote to the Secretary of the Army to protest the sentence reductions. "Based on the most stringent principles of Anglo-Saxon jurisprudence, the original sentences imposed on Ilse Koch, Prince (SS Lt. Gen.) Waldeck, Katzen-Ellenbogen and all the other Buchenwald accused were fair to the verge of leniency." He said the charges against Koch went beyond those rejected in the review, that is, her involvement in beatings and deaths and "her proven participation in the common plan or design to abuse, starve, torture and kill."[9]

Surowitz also said "there were at least 300 Americans at Buchenwald: medics from infantry, airmen from Bomber and Fighter commands, those who fell into the Nazi dragnet when France was occupied and others. By heart, I can mention the names of many Americans who died there as a direct result of maltreatment and willful refusal of medical care. It's all in the Record."

A check of the trial record does not indicate this information was introduced by the prosecution. Surowitz's letter proves, however, the U.S. government knew Americans were in concentration camps. In fact, as early as July 1945, Canadian and American war crimes investigators were working together to identify nationals who were victims at Buchenwald.[10] Furthermore, testimony from at least 15 former POWs was in government hands.[11] Introduction of that evidence could have been used to obtain justice for American victims like Lt. Levitt Beck and might have prevented subsequent reviewers from reducing the sentences of at least some convicted war criminals.

It is peculiar that information about the mistreatment of Americans would have been excluded. Public knowledge of atrocities against Americans surely would have helped generate more support for the trials and verdicts.

In February 1945, acting Secretary of State Joseph Grew said it was clear the American people want the guilty punished and that the State Department shared that "inexorable determination."[12]

In the Mauthausen trial, one of the star witnesses was an OSS officer, the only concentration camp trial where an American citizen testified. Lt. Jack Taylor described his six weeks in Mauthausen. He was a valuable eyewitness who testified that 250–300 people died each day of starvation when he first arrived. By the end of April, the figure was 400–500. As someone forced to construct a crematorium, he also gave first-hand accounts of the gassing and burning of prisoners. Taylor also testified that other Americans were in Mauthausen. Another former prisoner, Wilhelm Ornstein, said 14 English and American officers were killed on January 26, 1945. One American he specifically named was Nelson Paris, the OSS photographer.[13]

In his dying confession, Mauthausen commandant Frank Ziereis admitted an Anglo-American mission from Croatia had been brought into the camp and was interrogated. He denied being present and claimed the mission was sent to Dachau. Evidence was presented, however, that Ziereis executed two American airmen—Leroy Teschendorf and Halsey Nisula—at the beginning of February. The executioner of most of the OSS officers, Georg Bachmayer, committed suicide before he could be interrogated. The camp adjutant, Viktor Zoller, testified that he was called in to take part in the execution of three parachute agents whom he believed to be British or American. Ziereis said he had been looking forward to killing them for a long time and wanted to give them the "honor" of being shot by SS leaders. The prisoners were brought in and told to face the wall. Ziereis, Zoller and a third man then shot each in the back of the head.[14]

"The purpose of the camp was to kill as many prisoners as possible," Oberscharführer Andreas Trum testified. Another SS officer said "Ziereis repeatedly reminded us to treat the prisoners as severely and inhumanely as possible."[15] Most guards needed little encouragement as they were all members of the Totenkopf, the Death-head unit of the SS.

In his closing argument, prosecutor William Denson observed: "There was no other camp under the German Reich where the conditions were as terrible, where beatings were more severe, where the prisoners received less food, than at Maut-hausen." He said the 61 men being tried were charged with "participating in a common design to beat, kill, to torture, to starve, and to subject these prisoners to the indignities that has been established here."

Denson said, "Virtually every known form of killing was used at Mauthausen. To list some, inmates were killed by gassing, hanging, clubbing, heart injections, driving inmates into the electric fence, kicking in genitals, being buried alive and by putting a red-hot poker down the throat."

The court found "it was impossible for a governmental, military or civil offi-cial, a guard or a civilian employee, of the concentration camp Mauthausen . . . [not to have] acquired a definite knowledge of the criminal practices and activi-ties therein existing."[16]

Most of the Mauthausen defendants were hung. It is difficult to know how much weight the evidence regarding the mistreatment of Americans carried, but the defendants in this case did not receive the same leniency that most convicted war criminals ultimately obtained. As in the Buchenwald trial, evidence of crimes against Americans was not needed to convict the perpetrators of the Mauthausen atrocities. Nevertheless, those crimes should have been part of the record.

After learning the "Dawes" team was executed at Mauthausen, OSS General Counsel Commander James G. Donovan (no relation to OSS chief Major Gen-eral William Donovan) had said his organization had "a very deep interest in bringing the perpetrators of this crime to justice."[17] The OSS also wanted Ernst Kaltenbrunner to be interrogated regarding his order to execute the agents.[18] This apparently was not done. Moreover, the government failed to introduce evidence it possessed about the Dawes agents, and the Associated Press reporter who accompanied them, who were executed at Mauthausen. The incident involving Taylor and the other OSS agents was not included in the testimony during the Nuremberg trial, but there was a reference to the case of the 47 Allied prisoners who were killed in the quarry.[19]

William Denson, chief prosecutor of the major concentration camp trials—Buchenwald, Flossenbürg, Mauthausen and Dachau—tried 177 criminals in the four cases. He said little was known about Americans in the camps, but one of the first things investigators did was to try to find Americans. The prosecutors had to rely on information provided by the war crimes teams that went into the camps. For some reason, they did not seem to have access to, or were not given, other information in the government's possession indicating Americans had been mistreated. "If we had an inkling of Americans, we'd have put them on," he said in an interview. As an example, he recalled having problems in getting the money to bring Lt. Jack Taylor to testify: "We busted our ass to get Taylor for the Mauthausen trial." He did not remember, however, knowing of any Americans in Buchenwald. "If I'd known, I'd have gotten them." On the other hand, Denson also argued that the trials only had jurisdiction for crimes committed against for-eign nationals.[20] In the Nuremberg trial of the heads of the Nazi regime, prosecutor Telford Taylor says the mistreatment of Americans was supposed to have been handled in the Dachau trials.[21]

Twelve other trials were held in Nuremberg to prosecute groups of Nazis who had the chief responsibility for a variety of crimes. These included the "Medical Case," the "I.G. Farben Case" and the *"Einsatzgruppen* Case." The trial dealing with the mistreatment of POWs was the twelfth, *U.S. vs. Wilhelm von Leeb, et al.,* the "High Command Case."

The head of the POW department of the High Command, Herman Reinecke, and 13 others were charged with "murder and ill-treatment, denial of rights and status, and employment under inhumane conditions and prohibited circumstances" of enemy belligerents and POWs. Reinecke was found to have been responsible for the segregation and liquidation of POWs and was sentenced to life imprisonment. The evidence, however, was almost entirely focused on the mistreatment of Soviet POWs. Despite the wealth of information about abuse of Americans, the only reference to U.S. POWs concerned the murder of 15 uniformed soldiers near La Spezia and the execution of 12 to 15 American POWs in Mauthausen in January 1945.[22]

The most dramatic example of American Jews being singled out for mistreatment, the segregation at Bad Orb and deportation to the slave labor camp at Berga, ultimately did result in a trial. Initially, however, it did not look as though any of the guards would be prosecuted. Dr. Jacob Cantor, whose son died in Berga, sent many letters to war crimes investigators urging them to bring the murderers to justice. In December 1945, he was assured by Maj. Clarence Yancey, Executive, War Crimes Office, that this is what the government planned. A few months later, however, he received a response that seven volumes of evidence had been compiled on Stalag IX-B and Berga but "inadequacy in naming and describing the perpetrators has made apprehension difficult." In fact, the government *was* able to find those responsible. One of the men (Merz) who ultimately was tried had been taken into custody on April 23, nearly eight months before Yancey's letter.

As was generally the case, a decision was made to prosecute only the higher ranking officers who ran the camp. This was particularly appropriate in the case of Berga since most of the guards were elderly men who were not guilty of mistreating the Americans. The Germans who were tried were the commandant of the camp, Erwin Metz, and his superior, Ludwig Merz.[23]

The United States government knew exactly what happened at Berga, but it is impossible not to conclude that its prosecution of the case lacked the vigor associated with the Nuremberg trials. In April 1946, the War Department sent a letter to Charles Vogel, the uncle of a GI killed in the camp, acknowledging his offer to provide information about Berga.[24] Internal correspondence suggested, however, that the Department did not take Vogel seriously and viewed him as a nuisance. It was therefore not surprising that investigators seemed to pay little or no attention to the more than 70 eyewitness accounts he provided them. Still, the War Crimes

Branch of the War Department had in its possession debriefings of at least 38 Berga survivors, conducted as early as May 23, 1945, by its own investigators. Accounts about individuals also appeared in several local newspapers; nevertheless, no witnesses were brought to testify at the trial and only seven former POWs provided written testimony.[25] To this day, few survivors are aware a trial took place.

Three charges were brought against Metz: that he shot and killed an unarmed POW, that he assaulted POWs "by beating them about the body and face" and that he failed to provide adequate food, medical care and clothing to POWs, which resulted in the death of several unknown members of the U.S. Army. Metz pleaded not guilty to each charge. Merz was tried only on the third charge to which he also pled not guilty.

The trial was conducted at Dachau during the first two weeks of September 1946, a year and a half after the survivors of Berga were liberated. Both defendants were present for the trial, but not one former POW attended.

Ludwig Merz, a 59-year-old elementary school teacher from Haardt, was the company commander for Home Guard Battalion 621 based in Greiz. The battalion belonged to Stalag IXC in Bad Sulza. Merz was in charge of POW work details, of which he supervised 60–70 with a total of 2,500 men. One of those he oversaw was the American detail at Berga. According to his testimony, Merz did not spend much time in Berga, visiting the camp only 18–20 times.

Erwin Metz, 53, was a manager in the food industry in Erkmannsdorf in Thuringia. He denied even being a member of the Nazi Party: "I am an anti-fascist and belong to the politically persecuted," he said, claiming the Gestapo, the Party and the state police hounded him. Metz had been in charge of the Slovak detail before being sent to oversee the Americans on March 15, 1945.[26]

The defense stated, with regard to the charge of failing to provide adequate food, medical care and clothing, that the general conditions in Germany precluded Metz and Merz from furnishing everything the POWs required. The commandant from the Moosburg POW camp and the medic at Stalag 18C testified to the general conditions at German POW camps, but neither had any knowledge whatsoever of Berga. Two other defense witnesses maintained the Germans had difficulty getting food and medicine in the region where the camp was located but again knew nothing about Berga.[27]

The image the defense tried to create was of two dedicated German officers who did everything in their power under adverse circumstances to improve the conditions of the POWs. Captain Friedrich Bauch, an inspector in the company commanded by Merz, said the Sergeant had given better food to the POWs than to the guards. Bauch admitted the work details were severe—he mentioned the dust and lack of visibility in the tunnels—but said Merz complained to the SS and had the POWs taken out of the mines. Although Bauch was on the march after Berga was evacuated, he claimed he did not see any POWs die.[28]

One of the Berga guards, Paul Hockart, an older man who suffered from asthma, a spine out of place and an injured hand, also testified for the defense. Hockart said he put kitchen utensils in the barracks and three blankets for each of the 350 men. He also suggested medical attention was adequate. A doctor came from the town, he said, four to five times a week. Hockart said many men got sick because the latrine at the new camp was not ready when the POWs moved in so they had to leave the "warm" barracks to use a bucket in the cold outside.

Hockart admitted some Americans died—he said 15–20. They were not buried for 2–3 days, he said, because it took that long to get a casket. He suggested this was not unusual in Germany. Later, Hockart testified that approximately 30 men died on the march. The guards talked among themselves about the number of deaths of prisoners in Berga, Hockart admitted, "but everybody minded his own business and there was only some interest in the cause." Hockart did notice the POWs lost weight, but he attributed this to arriving at Berga sick. He also claimed he never was in the barracks or saw what the prisoners ate. He did see the men come out of the tunnels covered with dust and coughing.[29]

In his testimony, Merz maintained that he did everything in his power to make the POWs' imprisonment pleasant but was thwarted by the SS. He complained to the man in charge of Schwalbe 5, First Lt. Hack of the SS, for example, that the windows of the barracks had bars on them so it was impossible to open them. Hack told him this was an emergency and the camp would eventually be enlarged. Merz said he refused to take responsibility for the camp.

Merz also testified that one American told him Berga was better than Bad Orb. Merz insisted the POWs arrived pale and fatigued and without any health certificates or army papers. He sent a report saying the prisoners were unfit for hard work and needed doctors. Two doctors were brought in to attend to the prisoners. Later, Merz said Rudolf Miethe was the only doctor for the town but still managed to visit the Americans every day. Merz also said sick POWs were sent to hospitals—10 to Schleiz, 6 to Eisensch, 6 or 7 to Schleiz again and 10 were supposed to go to Muehlhausen but were sent back from the station because there was no train.

Dr. Miethe told Merz the POWs got diarrhea from drinking water from the Elster River, but Merz did not believe him. Merz testified that the river was beyond the camp fence and thus out of the POWs' reach. Moreover, Merz did not consider diarrhea an illness; it certainly did not warrant a reprieve from work or a trip to the hospital. Dr. Miethe testified that he took care of the Americans from February 16 until March 22.[30] When he first saw them, they had lost weight and appeared malnourished. During the nearly five weeks he went to the camp, Miethe said he saw approximately 12 cases of pneumonia, enteritis of a nonspecific type that lasted 3–14 days and three cases of diphtheria. He thought there were also 10 Americans who suffered from pulmonary tuberculosis, but he could not confirm the diagnosis. He believed that 17–18 prisoners died; two or three he said had been shot dead. One of those, Goldstein, was shot in the back of the head and the lower back.

The doctor also testified that both prisoners and guards told him they did not have enough to eat. The prisoners were badly malnourished, he said, and should not have had to do the work they were made to do, but the SS at the camp forced them.

Part of Merz's defense was that he would have done more if he had known problems existed. He said the Americans did not complain about their treatment. When Merz came on his visits, he always talked to the prisoners. "They had plenty of chances to report mistreatment by Metz," he said. "They didn't."

Norman Martin had a different story. In his written testimony, he said the POWs protested to Metz that conditions violated the Geneva Convention. Metz said "he was the only Geneva Conference available."

According to Merz, the prisoners' clothes were in good condition. In fact, throughout his testimony, he said the POWs were better off than the guards. The Americans had shoes, overcoats and jackets whereas the Germans did not. The prisoners had more meat in their soup. And the camp latrines were the same as the German Army used.

Investigators found several empty Red Cross cartons in an orderly room. The former prisoners had said they only received a total of three parcels, and that was toward the end of their incarceration. Merz said a shipment of Red Cross parcels arrived containing only boxing gloves and shoes. He said he gave the shoes to the Americans. None of the former prisoners recalled ever getting shoes from the Germans.

The POWs were given as much food as possible, Merz said, but he later recognized they were not getting enough rations to do the work, so he complained to Schwalbe 5 to no effect. Merz also told First Lt. Hack "this was no kind of work" for U.S. prisoners. Slovaks were working outside the mountain at Berga drilling a tunnel through which the railroad was supposed to be laid. They were more accustomed to this type of work, he said. He also suggested that Russians be brought in to replace the Americans. About three weeks later, 500 Russians were put in the tunnels and the Americans were taken out, Merz testified. Another action he took to ease the POWs' burden, he said, was to move them to a new camp that was much closer to where they worked. In his testimony, Metz took credit for these same changes. When asked why, as the commander, he did not just give the order to take the men out of the tunnels, Merz replied that only the employer could do that.

Even on the march, Merz claimed he was looking out for the POWs' welfare. He said he arranged horse carts to transport the sick and protested when the Americans were forced to give up their blankets at the first stop in Greiz. He defended the blankets being taken, however, saying they belonged to the employer Schwalbe 5 and had to be returned. Besides, he maintained, the Americans still had plenty of blankets.

At one point, Merz said he was prepared to defy his orders and take infirm prisoners to a hospital, but he never did. He was ordered to be sure to have all the

POWs when it came time for peace negotiations. "Every American soldier is something precious in the hands of the führer when it comes to peace negotiations with America," a Nazi officer told Merz. Altogether, Merz testified he knew of only about 19 Americans who died. He subsequently said 15–17 died on the march.

Erwin Metz could not claim ignorance since he was in command of the camp. He testified that when he took over at Berga, he immediately found that more than 50 POWs were ill. He met with Dr. Miethe and told him he wanted to transfer ailing men to the hospital. He said 26 were sent to two different hospitals. Dr. Miethe himself got sick and visited for the last time in late March. Another doctor then took over. The number of POWs reporting each morning at sick call grew from 50 to as many as 70 a day. Metz said the American medics determined if someone was feigning illness. If they were, Metz warned them of possible punishment but testified no one ever was disciplined. The prisoners were just forced to work in the barracks the rest of that day. The doctor decided if men were well enough to work.

This was not how Pfc. Leon Trachtman remembered the process. He testified that Metz "fancied himself sort of a doctor. When the fellows went on sick call, he would examine them by asking them to stick out their tongues. He would say, 'Healthy tongue. Go to work.'" Metz later argued the American medics "bore the sole and complete responsibility for the medical care" of their fellow POWs.[31]

In his statement, Metz said bodies were kept in front of the barracks until the doctor came. If anything unusual was wrong with a prisoner he sent them to the doctor in town. This, he said, happened about once a week.

Like Merz, Metz also maintained that he had no power to assign workers and that he told First Lt. Hack the Americans were unfit. He did take measures, however, to protect the POWs. Metz said four guards from the camp went to the mines to make sure the foremen did not abuse the POWs. The first week, the guards reported that the foremen did mistreat them. Metz investigated the incident and said he reported it to his superiors.

Around March 22 (later he said the 26th), Metz testified that 400 Red Cross parcels, 50 with special diets for the sick, arrived, along with 25 pairs of shoes. These were given to the Americans. Then, the Sunday before Easter, Red Cross parcels were distributed for every two men. At the time of the evacuation, he gave out parcels for every four men. Special parcels, he said, were given out "at once depending on need."

His version of meals at the camp was also quite different from that of the former prisoners. Metz said the men got sausage five days a week and twice a week either cheese or marmalade. For lunch, they received a liter of stew with vegetables, potatoes and meat. Dinner consisted of a half liter of soup. In the morning they were given coffee.

Metz also said the Americans were better dressed than the Germans. He testified the POWs had overcoats, field jackets and caps, some even had helmets and fur coats. They never asked for any additional clothes, he stated. Meanwhile, the former POWs all said they were still wearing the clothes they'd been captured in two months earlier.

Metz made Berga sound more like a recreational camp than a prison. He said prisoners "sunbathed" outside the barracks—this in the midst of the German winter. He talked about prisoners who escaped or faked illness being "rewarded" with lighter work. Also, he maintained that the POWs complained to him that the American medics kept food and diet packages for themselves.

Stanley B. Cohen, Leon Trachtman and Norman Martin provided statements to the prosecution asserting that Metz's actions had resulted in the death of David Young. According to Martin, Young was ill and was given two days of bed rest. He was still sick at the end of the two days, but Metz dragged him out of bed. Young lost consciousness and Metz threw water on him. A half hour later he was dead.

According to one guard, a member of the *Volksturm,* this was standard proce-dure for Metz. Americans had to be carried from the tunnels almost every day because of exhaustion, Kurt Seifert testified. "When one fell down coming to or from work, Metz ordered a helmetful of water, cold water, thrown on the man to see if he was really out or only feigning."[32] Metz offered several excuses and said Cohen's testimony was an effort to get revenge because he probably thought Metz was responsible for his demotion from being the Man of Confidence. He denied ever killing or slapping a prisoner.

One former guard, Otto Ritterman, testified against Metz. Again, Metz claimed his accuser was trying to take revenge for something he had done to the man earlier. According to Metz, he had punished Ritterman for trading a knife for some cigarettes. He did not explain why a guard would ever be willing to give a prisoner a knife. In his statement, Metz said he never traded with the POWs, but they would give him cigarettes "out of appreciation for his kindness."

Metz claimed only 10–12 men died after he took over the camp; 8–9 died be-fore. All the prisoners were buried in coffins by an American detail that took them to a cemetery. The Americans had an American and a German dog tag. When a man died, the lower half of the tag was taken away and sent to the com-pany with a report; the other half was buried with the corpse.

The sick men who had been turned back on the way to Muehlhausen were put in the dispensary. They were taken on the march and then put in a hospital at Wiesau. Metz said he had tried to get them into a hospital earlier, but they had been overcrowded.

Norman Martin said that POWs who tried to escape and were recaptured were forced to stand outside near the fence all night and then go to work in the morn-ing without having any food or sleep. Metz denied this. He said POWs who were recaptured after escaping were turned over to the American camp leader and put to work within the camp.

One crime for which Metz was being tried was the murder of Morton Goldstein, who had escaped and been recaptured before being shot. Concern over escapes was evident by the fact that the original commandant at Berga was relieved in early March because too many escapes had occurred.

Merz testified that punishment for POWs who were captured after trying to escape varied depending on how long they were away and how much work they missed. He said the men were supposed to be confined, but instead they were assigned two hours of "light labor" for every day they were supposed to be confined. Thus, the most severe penalty would have been about 10 hours of work.

Metz's version of Morton Goldstein's death was quite different from that of his accusers. Metz said he had been told by Hockart that two prisoners escaped on the way to pick up coffee one morning. About two days later, the rural police station called and said one had been picked up. Metz went to the mayor's house where Goldstein was having breakfast with the mayor's family. According to the mayor, Walter Zschaeck, the police brought Goldstein to his home because the town had no jail. The mayor testified that Metz told the prisoner he was going to beat him up and shoot him while the other American prisoners watched.

Metz told the mayor there had been 20 escapes and that "if one takes off he walks the way of death." Metz said this was just a figure of speech and he did not mean it literally. In a sworn statement on June 19, 1945, Metz said he had told the Burgermeister that "prisoners who ran away should be shot on sight and that there was [an] order to that effect." His attorneys claimed many things Metz told the Americans earlier had been taken the wrong way.

Metz told Goldstein he was disappointed because he had given him lots of liberty, including the opportunity to go out of the camp now and then. Goldstein agreed and said his comrades had led him astray. On the way back to the camp with Goldstein, Metz said he ran into a member of the construction firm and began talking to him. Goldstein kept walking. Metz shouted: "Take it a little slower, because I want to come along too." Goldstein then jumped an embankment and ran into the woods. Metz yelled "Halt!" three times, then shot and killed him. Metz said he brought the American medics to see Goldstein. The POWs said it was careless of him to try to escape during the day. The following day, Merz investigated the incident.

Goldstein had a bullet in the head and back, but Metz said he'd shot him only once. The prosecution argued that Metz had shot Goldstein in the head when he was lying on the ground, but the ballistics test indicated both bullets had been fired from more than 50 feet away. Metz claimed he had never fired a pistol before, yet he managed to hit a running man about 90 feet away.

Four medics brought Goldstein's body back on a stretcher and left it between the two barracks. The prosecution said Metz called two details in the barracks out to view the body. Metz denied this but admitted everyone could see the corpse, which stayed outside for three days.

Several weeks after Goldstein's shooting, Hans Grieshammer shot a POW in the back. Metz said the man had run away three times before. I could find no record of Grieshammer being tried.

The defense admitted that 59 Americans died (the number was actually 70–73). But the defense attorneys said only about 12 men "were sufficiently disturbed by the experience to dictate to anyone their recollections." He said this "made the vote 279–12 against the thought that what happened at Berga was a crime or even worthy of complaint."

The defense further tried to suggest that those prisoners who did testify confused Sgt. Kunz (who was apparently never brought to trial) with Sgt. Metz. Others who testified against the defendants did so because they had ulterior motives, he argued. The Burgermeister, Walter Zschaeck, whose testimony suggested Metz intended to kill Goldstein, for example, was accused of doing so to ingratiate himself with the Americans.

Metz also said that "not a single guard beat the prisoners during the march." But Martin said in his statement that during the march, in the town of Hof, Metz took a rifle and used the butt to beat some of the men. Martin also charged that Metz was responsible for the death of Pvt. Israel Cohen, the POW who suffocated underneath a pile of prisoners on the "sick wagon." Metz denied throwing unhealthy prisoners on top of others on the cart during the march.

A German guard testified he saw Hans Grieshammer beat a man with a bayonet because he had fallen from exhaustion. Metz watched this and told Kurt Seifert and his companions: "Beat them if they don't walk." Seifert said Metz's assistant, Gefreiter Andreas Pickart, another *Landeschutz* man, beat prisoners indiscriminately. Metz denied anyone was beaten, starved or worked to death.

Major Herman Bolker, a pathologist for the War Crimes Investigating Team, examined 22 bodies buried at Berga.[33] The cemetery had three rows of graves of unequal sizes. Most of the graves had one body, one contained four, another three. Six had marker crosses with names of Americans, German POW numbers and the date of death. Several crosses had helmets hanging on them. The majority of bodies were buried in coffins, but several were not. One marker, "David Young—PW26133—died 19 March 1945," had no corresponding body. Bolker could identify 19 of the 22 corpses. All the bodies, he said, indicated malnutrition. He also found evidence of pneumonia and diarrhea. Bolker followed the march route in search of other bodies and discovered those described in Chapter 9.

The court found Ludwig Merz and Erwin Metz guilty on all charges. Metz issued a plea to the court that he had cared for the prisoners "in a fatherly manner and did everything in my power to lighten the work and living conditions of the prisoners."[34] Merz said he "felt sorry for every sick and deceased American prisoner of war" but blamed his superiors for tying his hands. The court sentenced both men to hang. On October 15, 1945, the trial was adjourned.

A year later, the two men petitioned for clemency and pardons. The petition for clemency said Metz and Merz "did everything possible for the interests of their PWs. They were not in a position to do more." A certificate of good character signed by 48 people was enclosed to show that Merz was a man "of irreproachable character" who could not possibly have consciously committed offenses against humanity.[35]

Ironically, two American officers also petitioned on their behalf and argued that "the confused conditions which prevailed inside Germany" limited the ability of Metz and Merz to alleviate the hardships of the American POWs. Moreover, they said "the absence of the American witnesses during the trial made it difficult, if not impossible for the Court to accord the proper weight to their different testimonies, to test their credibilities," and so on.

Thus, U.S. officials were using their colleagues' failure to bring witnesses to the trial as justification for clemency. Further, they said other German witnesses who ended up in the Russian Zone were not available to testify so the Court could not obtain a "clear picture of the true conditions" at Berga.[36]

The petitioners had a point when they said that the defense had no opportunity to cross-examine the Americans, that their testimonies contained contradictions and that they were taken at different places and times. Apparently, a policy had been established not to bring witnesses from the United States. The petition asserts many other errors in the conduct of the trial. Reviewers ultimately agreed.

On January 29, 1948, the War Crimes Review Board recommended commuting Merz's death sentence to five years. It said that Merz was named only in the third charge and that the evidence was sufficient to sustain the guilty verdict but that unspecified "extenuating factors should be given considerable weight."[37] Another review approved this recommendation on February 13, 1948, with imprisonment to start October 15, 1946.

The January review also concluded that a reasonable doubt existed regarding the charge that Metz killed Goldstein. The evidence was sufficient to sustain the guilty verdicts on the other charges, which led the board to recommend a 20-year sentence.

On February 20, 1948, the War Crimes Board of Review rejected Metz's petition, concluding it lacked merit.[38] Strangely, however, a week earlier, on February 13, 1948, Gen. Lucius Clay commuted the sentence of Erwin Metz to life imprisonment at War Criminal Prison #1 at Landsberg, Germany. He reduced Merz's sentence to five years in the same prison. Three years later, on May 21, 1951, almost exactly six years after his conviction, Metz's sentence was reduced again, this time to 15 years. The Chief of the War Crimes Branch, Col. W.H. Peters, Jr., said, however, the sentence should be commuted to the time served from June 19, 1945. He said that ballistics evidence and insufficiency of proof made it impossible to sustain the charge against Metz for murdering Goldstein. Peters also dismissed the third charge, that Metz had not provided adequate medical care, after a member of the U.S. Army Medical Corps said he was satisfied the POWs were given adequate treatment given the available supplies.

This finding was bolstered by a posttrial statement June 30, 1947, by former POW Milton Stolon that said he served as an official interpreter in Berga and that he did not fault Metz because of the lack of food in the camp. The petitioners' attorney colored the statement considerably because Stolon went on to say he did blame Metz for their treatment during the march. "The German civilians were pretty good to us," he said, "and they wanted to feed us, but Metz prohibited it." Stolon also said, for example, that he was told by a guard (who did not witness the act) that Metz had shot Goldstein. He testified that "we had no deaths until Metz took over. He seemed to disregard the pleas the men made to him." Furthermore, Stolon said, "Metz was so brutal in his attitude that when one of them got a little sick, Metz made sure that he would stay that way, and he took away their hope."

During the march, Stolon said Metz beat him. He also saw Metz beat another prisoner. He then volunteered that while Metz may claim to have had orders to treat the men as he did, "he added to them, and carried them out severely." Stolon claimed Merz gave orders to Metz to distribute Red Cross parcels, clean up the camp and not be too harsh on the prisoners. Stolon said Israel Cohen suffocated on the sick wagon but *not* because the Germans threw sick men on top of him.

The defense partly relied on Stolon's statement that he did not believe Metz's actions warranted the death penalty and that he did not know much about Merz but thought 5–10 years would be sufficient punishment for him. The defense ignored his final statement about what he thought would be appropriate punishment: "What I really think they both ought to get is six months in that digging of the underground factory; give them the same conditions, food and treatment and see how long they last that out."[39]

Another posttrial statement, this one by Paul Arthur Van Horne, said he never heard of POWs being beaten on the march and that Metz did everything in his power to help prisoners. Van Horne blamed the dysentery on his fellow prisoners' failure to take adequate precautions.

In fact, Van Horne's testimony was confused. He was not sure if he recognized the photo he was shown of Metz. At first he said he looked like the man who had beaten and mistreated prisoners at Berga; later he said the opposite. When Van Horne started to say that Metz had beaten Charles Clark, the attorneys cut him off. Later, he repeated that Metz did beat Clark, which caused his death.[40]

Peters did find sufficient proof to sustain the second charge, that Metz had been guilty of assault and battery. A civilian attorney who reviewed the case also recommended that Metz be released after the six years he had served, concluding that "the only thing we have in this case to justify the holding of this accused is some testimony in the form of pre-trial statements to the effect that he committed *a few assaults*" (emphasis added).[41]

Stanley Cohen told prosecution attorney Richard Ruppert on June 30, 1947, that Metz "heightened rather than diminished the rigors of the system" in the camp. According to the transcript of the deposition, Ruppert only asked Cohen two substantive questions.[42]

Ironically, one justification for the appeal of Merz and Metz was the denial of their right to cross-examine witnesses, yet prosecutors failed to question the survivors the defense used as posttrial witnesses.

The reduction of the sentences of Merz and Metz might be attributable to both political and emotional factors, which also influenced the outcome of other cases. Michael Berenbaum, project director of the United States Holocaust Memorial Museum, explained:

> While the trials were in progress public attention shifted to the unfolding of the Cold War, the struggle between the United States and the Soviet Union that seemed to embody a worldwide battle between capitalism and Marxism. The 1948 Berlin Blockade made the future of Germany central to American geopolitical interests. The American government did not want to provoke the German people, especially when their support was vital to the future. The Korean War only intensified the desire to get on to other things. Interest in the trials faded. No sooner had they ended than clemency boards were established. In the next few years, sentences were reduced, pardons were granted, and time off was given for good behavior.[43]

Former war crimes trial prosecutor Denson had another explanation for why so many convicted war criminals had their sentences reduced. He said it was hard for anyone who had not been in the camps to believe what had taken place. "It was so horrible, it was incredible," he said. "The hardest thing for me was presenting evidence the court would believe." Denson admitted he had omitted some evidence because it was just too unbelievable. Nevertheless, he was confident he had done a good enough job to prove the guilt of those he tried. When he found out that Ilse Koch's sentence had been reduced to four years for insufficient evidence, he took that to be a statement that he did not know how to try a case. Gen. Clay had said that *he* (that is, the people reviewing the case for him) did not believe the witnesses. But this was not up to them. "If they'd been in the court, they'd have believed them," Denson asserted.

John J. McCloy, the United States High Commissioner for Germany, came under tremendous pressure from the Pope, the German government and others to grant clemency to convicted war criminals. Subsequently, he commuted the sentence of Ernst von Weizsacker, a Nazi foreign office official convicted of complicity in the deaths of 6,000 Jews transferred from France to Poland; and commuted or reduced the sentences of all convicted concentration camp doctors, 20 of the 25 SS officers convicted of serving in the *Einsatzgruppen* (mobile killing units) as well as Nazi industrialist Alfred Krupp.[44] In 1951, McCloy issued a general amnesty, which apparently applied to Metz and Merz.

One Berga survivor who was not asked to testify, though he had told officials about his experience, protested the reduction of Metz's sentence. Marvin Gritz said Metz "was overzealous in his cruel punishment of our group. Metz not only carried out orders of his superiors, but also took it upon himself to see to it that these orders were unduly severe and unbearable."[45]

The War Department told Charles Vogel the sentences of Metz and Merz were reduced because they were underlings and "the defendant Metz, though guilty of a generally cruel course of conduct toward prisoners, was not directly responsible for the death of any prisoners except one who was killed during the course of an attempt to escape."[46]

Vogel said he knew nothing about Merz but had provided a 10-page verbatim account to the War Crimes Branch on April 27, 1946, relating the experiences of Stephen Schweitzer, Robert Lamb, Costa Katimaris and Samuel Fahrer. At other times he had sent communications from survivors he had contacted. This information, Vogel maintained, should have enabled the court to determine that Metz was guilty of murder.

Moreover, he noted, the conditions in Berga did not differ markedly from those in concentration camps like Flossenbürg. At Nuremberg, he said, the report on Flossenbürg sounded much like Berga:

> The work at these camps mainly consisted of underground labor, the purpose being the construction of large underground factories, storage rooms, etc. This labor was performed completely underground and as a result of the brutal treatment, working and living conditions, a daily average of 100 prisoners died.[47]

Thus, for reasons that are unfathomable, the United States failed to use all of the evidence and witnesses at its disposal to ensure the perpetrators of atrocities against American soldiers would be punished. A group of Berga survivors formed a group to protest the sentences Metz and Merz received. They obtained 5,000 signatures on a petition to President Truman, but nothing was ever done to reopen the case.

12

Recognition of the Victims

ALFRED FELDMAN, a survivor of Berga, said he gave a deposition about his ordeal to military war crimes investigators after the war. But what happened to this information is a mystery to Feldman. "It makes me bitter. Our government buried the whole thing. Our depositions were never used against our captors. Why, I don't know. I guess we were just a very small group of men, a few hundred fellas who got lost in the shuffle and confusion," Feldman said. "No one cared what happened to us. It was the end of the war."[1]

Why has Alfred Feldman's story and that of other American victims of the Holocaust gone untold?

Part of the reason has to do with the government's desire to prevent this story from being disclosed. It would have been embarrassing to admit that American Jews were victims of the Nazis, that their government would not or could not protect them. Furthermore, by avoiding the subject, the government saved the American people from a painful reexamination of the nation's commitment to people in need, its obligations to its citizens and its treatment of minorities. Although the war ended more than 45 years ago, it is not too late to scrutinize the government's behavior because lessons can still be learned that are of relevance today.

With only a handful of little-known exceptions, such as Mary Berg's diary and Barry Spanjaard's memoir, American civilians did not relate their stories. Many did not know the full extent of their abandonment; those who did had no one to tell.

Still, the government knew civilians were held by the Nazis and withheld the information. The State Department did not release a list of 27 Americans deported to Germany from occupied territories in Europe until the end of March 1945.[2] As Chapter 2 documented, officials knew about Americans being arrested by the Nazis as early as 1942.

Meanwhile, many returning POWs were forced to sign secrecy pledges that precluded them from discussing activities in the camps related to intelligence and escapes.[3] This might have intimidated some people from speaking about their general experience, but, as we saw in Chapter 10, most former POWs often felt too ashamed at having been captured or simply preferred to put the episode behind them. Most of the surviving Jewish POWs say their comrades still know nothing of their ordeal. Those who heard something about Berga, for example, joke as though it were a resort.

Ample evidence exists to demonstrate that the government and the press knew what happened at Berga, and yet it received virtually no attention. One reason may be that it was overshadowed by other stories, such as the mistreatment of Americans in the Pacific theater.

Another explanation, however, is the government's policy of denial. As the survivors testified in Chapter 10, U.S. officials rejected their claims of mistreatment. Sam Lubinsky being sent to a psychiatrist was probably the most dramatic indication of the government's approach.

Most former POWs absolve the U.S. government of responsibility for their plight in the camps. They do not believe the government knew where they were or what was happening to them. What they find unforgivable, however, is the government's treatment of them after officials learned of their fates. The government denied many of the atrocities took place, resisted compensating them for their injuries and failed to bring the perpetrators to justice.

The United States never publicly acknowledged that American Jewish POWs were mistreated. It is true that Merz and Metz were tried for war crimes, but this was an unpublicized case and the charges against them were narrow. Moreover, the trial did not specify that many prisoners had been placed in Berga because they were Jews.

The information made public attracted little attention. On April 21, 1945, for example, Associated Press correspondent Edward Ball wrote his account of the liberation of the Berga survivors. The men he spoke to estimated that only 142 of 308 men survived. A reported (though exaggerated) mortality rate of well over 50 percent for a single POW camp—by far the highest of any prison camp—should have raised eyebrows and at least provoked an investigation by the press or the Pentagon. The story itself did not.

The uncle of Bernard Vogel, one of the men who was killed at Berga, also provided the government with extensive evidence of what happened at the slave labor camp. Nevertheless, months after receiving testimony about the events at Berga, a report by the Military Intelligence Service of the War Department said Jews were segregated at Bad Orb but "no other discrimination was made against them."[4] Ultimately, as Chapter 11 explained, the Berga trial was one of hundreds held at Dachau that went completely unnoticed by the public and the press.

The *New York Times* also had a couple of tiny stories about the mistreatment of American Jews. On April 2, it was reported that Americans were in Bad Orb, that privates worked in slate mines and that "all Jews were segregated and shackled and made to do whatever the Germans desired."[5] On April 20, mention was made of two American Jewish soldiers who "were singled out for kickings and cuffings and blows by rifle butts" in Stalag XI-B. The following month, the *Times* reported that "for reasons of military security imposed by American authorities," it was impossible to provide individual accounts of the experiences of POWs freed by the Russians.[6]

The *New York Times* reported part of the story of Berga on June 13, 1945. It said Daniel Steckler, 20, of Brooklyn told authorities that U.S. POWs were beaten with picks, shovels and rubber hose at Berga Elster. Steckler told the paper that 70 out of 350 POWs died. He related the story of how he was beaten and his thumb mangled when an overseer stomped on it with his boot. The report also talked about the segregation of the Jews at IX-B. Accounts of individuals who had been in Berga also appeared in local newspapers as early as July 20, 1945.[7]

A report that AP war correspondent Joseph Morton was captured by the Germans first appeared in the *New York Times* on March 7, 1945. On May 11, the military newspaper, *Stars and Stripes,* published a report about an American citizen who had been a prisoner at Mauthausen since 1939 and an American officer who said a U.S. Air Force navigator and an American naval officer were executed in April at Mauthausen.

The government had reports as early as November 1944 about the Allied POWs who had been in Buchenwald, yet it declined to make the information public. Officials subsequently denied knowing anything about the incident despite having debriefings from at least 15 POWs who had been in Buchenwald dating back to July 18, 1945.[8] An August 1946 document is attached to a list of American POWs and the amounts of money they were forced to surrender upon entering Buchenwald.[9] The National Archives has a reference paper written by an archivist in 1989 listing the POWs who were in Buchenwald.[10]

Even after American forces began to liberate POW camps, the government was censoring information about the treatment of prisoners until late April. "Third Army troops are becoming increasingly bitter over German treatment of American prisoners of war," the *New York Times* reported April 21. "Army censors have been wary of passing stories about conditions in these camps [liberated by Patton's troops]. Everything indicating severe cruelty had been stopped until recently. The policy has now been relaxed. Correspondents may report what they see."

Actually, the shift in policy had taken place a week earlier when the Secretaries of State and War issued a joint statement denouncing the Germans' "deliberate neglect and shocking treatment" of American POWs. They accused the Nazis of imposing "deplorable" conditions on the prisoners and failing to abide by the Geneva Convention. The "atrocities," the statement said, "are documented by the pitiable conditions of liberated American soldiers. The American nation will not forget them." The secretaries vowed the "perpetrators" of these "heinous crimes will be brought to justice."

According to the *Times,* the statement "was viewed in official quarters here [Washington] as an indication the State and War Departments, perhaps despairing of inducing Germany by normal methods to live up to her obligations to prisoners, had taken off the kid gloves in dealing with a topic heretofore handled with extreme delicacy."

The government's attitude was also evident after the liberation of Stalag IX-B. Spokesmen for the Red Cross, the State Department and the Army admitted the conditions in that camp were deplorable and might be found in other camps, but, they said, "such suffering is one of the prices the Allies must pay for the success of their drive on Berlin."[11]

Whereas the U.S. government usually maintained it did not know what was happening, the Red Cross position was that it could not do anything, even about incidents of which it was aware. In what became the standard response to criticism of the International Committee of the Red Cross's (ICRC) behavior during the war, Roger Du Pasquier, head of the Information Department, explained:

> No relief action of any sort by the Red Cross in Germany or the occupied territories could have been undertaken without the approval of the authorities. . . . Conforming to the letter, if not to the spirit of the Geneva Conventions . . . the Nazi government permitted the ICRC and its delegates to act on behalf of the several millions of prisoners held in the Stalags and Oflags. It refused, however, to allow any intervention on the part of the Red Cross in the concentration camps. . . .
>
> In the face of such an obstinate refusal which covered up the horrifying reality, about which one was then ill-informed, the ICRC certainly could have made itself heard; it could have protested publicly and called on the conscience of the world. By doing so it would, however, have deprived itself of any possibility of acting in Hitler's Empire; it would have deliberately given up what chances there still remained to it to help, even in a restricted manner, the victims of the concentration camp regime. But, above all, it would have made it impossible for it to continue its activity on behalf of millions of military captives. For the Nazi leaders viewed this activity with suspicion which they would have ruthlessly suppressed on the slightest pretext.[12]

The Red Cross did much good work, but it is clear from many of the examples in the preceding chapters that it often failed POWs as miserably as it did the inmates of concentration camps. The organization's options were limited by the Nazis, but the idea that the Red Cross therefore had no moral responsibility to speak out on behalf of concentration camp inmates because it threatened the good work it was able to do for POWs is, in retrospect, obscene.

Morality aside, it is simply false to say the ICRC was "ill-informed" about the "horrifying reality" of the camps. The American Red Cross files contain a collection of newspaper clippings that indicate it was well aware of events in Europe. Here are a few of the headlines of those stories:

25,000 JEWS SEIZED IN SOUTHERN FRANCE
(*New York Times*, August 28, 1942)

JEWISH CHILDREN INTERNED BY VICHY
(*Chicago Sun*, August 31, 1942)

35,000 JEWS EXECUTED IN FIVE POLISH TOWNS
(*New York Herald Tribune,* March 21, 1943)

50,000 JEWS PUT IN NAZI PRISON 'DIE LIKE FLIES'
(*Washington Times Herald,* September 3, 1943)

50,000 JEWS DYING IN NAZI FORTRESS
(*New York Times,* September 3, 1943)

NAZI SLAYINGS NEAR 250,000
(*Baltimore Sun,* September 22, 1943)

POLES REPORT NAZIS SLAY 10,000 DAILY
(*Washington Post,* March 22, 1944)

1,000,000 HUNGARIAN JEWS FACE MASSACRE, HULL SAYS
(*Chicago Sun,* July 15, 1944)[13]

It is clear from these clips the Red Cross knew about the Nazi atrocities as early as August 1942. In February 1945, the President of the Red Cross wrote to a U.S. official: "Concerning the Jewish problem in Germany we are in close and continual contact with the German authorities."[14] The fact that the head of the Red Cross would use the Nazi phraseology—"the Jewish problem"—may also be an indication of the organization's attitude that Jews were more of a problem than a people who were being annihilated.

The Red Cross also knew about crimes against POWs but did little to publicize them. One might have thought the U.S. government would have an interest in fomenting anger toward the Germans and would have broadcast stories of mistreatment of soldiers, but officials took the opposite tack. Virtually all the information made public about POWs emphasized their welfare. For example, a December 17, 1944, *Washington Post* headline was reassuring: "Nazis Play Fair in Prison Camps, Families Told." This news came from the director of POW relief of the ICRC. He told the *Post* the Germans "have endeavored to accord the same standards of treatment to American and British prisoners that were set up in the Geneva Convention."

The ICRC maintained that there was no inequality of treatment of Jewish prisoners, for example, though the organization did acknowledge that Jewish POWs were sometimes segregated. The Red Cross accepted the Nazi contention that such actions were permissible under Article 9 of the Geneva Convention, which provides that belligerents shall not house prisoners of different races or nationalities together.

Perhaps this is why no notice seems to have been taken of a story that appeared under the March 8, 1945, headline in *PM:* "Nazis Accused of Plan to Murder Jewish Captives." The report cited concerns expressed by the Emergency Committee to Save the Jewish People of Europe that the Nazis were segregating Polish Jewish POWs with the intention of exterminating them. No mention of American

POWs is made, but the Committee hinted they could be next if no action was taken. In a telegram to Eisenhower, cited in the article, the Committee said:

> The high command of the triumphant Allied armies is powerful enough to per-
> suade the Germans to abandon this fiendish scheme. ... We are confident that
> whatever you proclaim, whether warning of stern retaliation against German pris-
> oners held by the Allies, or ... any other convincing means will have an impressive
> effect. Positive action is urgent, not alone to save the remnants of Polish Jews, but
> to save the lives of other Allied soldiers, for you know it was always the practice of
> the Nazis to massacre Polish Jews first and then, if done with impunity, to proceed
> to Jews of other nationalities.

The U.S. government knew American Jews were being segregated even before this report. The ICRC visited Stalag VII-A on January 27, 1945, for example, and reported that 110 American Jewish POWs had been segregated but said they were not otherwise mistreated.[15]

The American Red Cross, meanwhile, adopted the attitude that it should not do anything to upset families; therefore, its *Prisoner of War Bulletin* was filled with glowing reports of POW camps, letters from cheerful prisoners and photos of happy Americans. But those who returned home came back with a different account of life in a POW camp.

The Red Cross never visited Berga, but it did go to Stalags IX-B and IX-C, Berga being a subcamp of the latter. A Swiss representative visited IX-B on March 23, 1945, and reported that the camp commander and his staff had "no interest whatsoever in the welfare of the prisoners of war." A representative of the International Red Cross who visited Stalags IX-A, IX-B and IX-C on March 13 said the situation was "very serious." He described prisoners as "nothing but skin and bones" and said many were suffering from acute diarrhea and pneumonia. A thousand men lacked eating utensils and ate with their hands out of helmets, old tin cans or pails, the report said. The POWs received only one shipment of Red Cross parcels. The minimum ration an inactive man needs to survive is 1,700 calories; the POWs in Bad Orb received about 1,400. In just over one month, between February 8 and April 1, 32 Americans died of malnutrition and pneumonia.

The report briefly mentions that the Man of Confidence refused to single out Jews for segregation. The Germans then selected those they thought were Jews and put them in a separate barracks. The report said "no other discrimination was made against them."[16]

In June 1945, the head of the ICRC repeated that its officials had regularly vis-ited POW camps and that Allied prisoners enjoyed the protection of the Geneva Convention.[17] After reading this, Herman Vogel wrote to the chairman of the American Red Cross and asked how the ICRC had failed to know about IX-B and Berga. He received an unsigned reply that falsely asserted IX-B had never been visited and minimized the brutality suffered by the POWs: "Some of the prisoner of war camps, later liberated, were never reported to the International Red Cross and their existence was not known until the men were freed. Bad Orb was one of those camps. Abuses were made by individual camp commandants, and no effort was made to gloss over such abuses. They are deeply regretted by all concerned."[18]

As the war was ending, the Red Cross reported that 99 percent of American POWs survived.[19] This figure probably underestimated the fatalities. For example, given that the organization knew nothing about Berga, the deaths there undoubtedly were excluded. Regardless, the emphasis on the survivors minimized the deaths of more than 1,100 POWs.

Besides the documentary evidence available earlier, war crimes investigators received testimony from survivors of Berga as early as May 23, 1945, that Jews were segregated at IX-B and sent to work in mines. An investigation was recommended. They continued to receive reports and testimony as ex-POWs were interrogated.[20]

Reports of Nazi mistreatment of Americans did filter out and provoke anger, especially when compared with stories that Nazi POWs in the States were being "coddled." For example, *Newsweek* reported (May 7, 1945): "About the same time GIs released from Berga told of being forced to dig tunnels under the eyes of SS guards who beat them with rubber hose, 300 Nazi POWs sullenly refused to work in Southern Idaho pea fields. (Punishment: bread-and-water and sleeping outdoors.)"[21] Note, too, the fact that reference is made here to Berga, showing the press had the story by May 1945.

"Pictures and descriptions of the conditions at this camp cannot adequately portray what we saw there," a Congressional investigative commission said of Buchenwald. "And it is only when the stench of the camps is smelled that anyone can have complete appreciation of the depths of degradation to which the German Nazi government and those responsible for it and its agencies, organizations, and practices had dropped in their treatment of those who had failed to embrace the doctrines of the 'master race.'"[22] If members of Congress had learned of the Americans who were held in Buchenwald just six months earlier—and, as noted above, this information was available as early as November 1944—it is hard to imagine they would have failed to react. But the commission found no evidence Americans had been in Buchenwald and no further inquiry was pursued.

The U.S. government learned details about Jews being gassed at Auschwitz in June 1944. In May, telegrams sent from the Orthodox community in Bratislava, Czechoslovakia, to the representative in Switzerland of the Union of Orthodox Rabbis called for the bombing of the railway lines to Auschwitz. These were forwarded to the War Refugee Board. John Pehle took the proposal to Assistant Secretary of War John McCloy, the man who would later decide to commute the sentences of many convicted Nazi war criminals. McCloy said he would look into the matter. Two days later, the Operations Division of the War Department

General Staff said the suggested air operation was "impracticable" because "it could be executed only by diversion of considerable air support essential to the success of our forces now engaged in decisive operations." The Operations Division concluded, as most government officials would later maintain, that "the most effective relief to victims of enemy persecution is the early defeat of the Axis, an undertaking to which we must devote every resource at our disposal."[23]

The same argument could not be made concerning other camps. We have seen, for example, that the Allies did attack Buchenwald, though they did not do so with the intent of eliminating its extermination capability. If in August 1944 the Allies were targeting factories at Buchenwald, they could have easily bombed the crematoria and the rail lines without diverting any resources from "decisive operations."

One question that arises is the failure of the press to devote more attention to Nazi atrocities in general and those directed at Americans specifically. Deborah Lipstadt investigated the former and gave her 1986 book a title that fit her conclusions: *Beyond Belief.* Atrocity stories had little credibility because of the phony reports circulated during World War I. In addition, editors were skeptical of accounts they received from their correspondents. Consequently, when they did print horror stories, they were usually buried in the back of the paper. The fact that the Nazis' campaign of annihilation was directed at Jews was obscured by government officials' general references to victims: Whatever happened to the Jews was likely to happen to others. Finally, the magnitude of what was taking place strained credulity. As Lipstadt wrote:

> The extreme nature of the news fostered doubts in the minds of victim and bystander. The systematic annihilation of an entire people seemed beyond the realm of the possible. It certainly was beyond the realm of the believable. Both the means of murder—gas—and the size of the victim population—many millions— reinforced the natural barriers of incredulity. In a certain respect these were healthy doubts—the mind's rebellion against believing that human beings were capable of sinking to such levels of depravity—but they made it easier for the perpetrators to camouflage their plans.[24]

Lipstadt believes the *New York Times* was one of the worst offenders in terms of failing to report atrocities committed on a grand scale against Jews with the same fervor it devoted to the deaths of small numbers of non-Jews. "Had the *Times* reacted with less equanimity, it is possible that other American papers would have followed suit," she observes.[25]

The press usually relegated "horror stories" to the back pages where they got the attention reports with little credibility deserved. But the information was published and therefore known almost from the beginning of the "Final Solution." Occasionally, a dramatic incident did make the front page. For example, on April 22, 1943, a small article appeared in the *New York Times* reporting that a secret Polish radio broadcast a frantic message before going off the air: "The last

35,000 Jews in the ghetto at Warsaw have been condemned to execution. Warsaw again is echoing to musketry volleys. The people were murdered and children defend themselves with their naked arms. Save us." Almost immediately, the *Times* lost interest in the uprising and relegated it to inside pages. Ironically, a year later (April 21, 1944), the paper editorialized that the ghetto fighters "set for the rest of us an example of courage that history can scarcely match."[26]

Lipstadt labels the evolution in press coverage of the Holocaust "Yes, but." She explains:

> At first it argued, *Yes*, bad things may be happening *but* not as bad as reported. Subsequently it was willing to acknowledge that *Yes*, many Jews may be victims *but* not as many as claimed. *Yes* many may have died, *but* most probably died as a result of war-related privations and not as a result of having been murdered. *Yes*, many have been killed *but* not in gas chambers. *Yes*, some Jews may have died in death camps, *but* so did many other people.[27]

The information about the systematic extermination of the Jews did not move Roosevelt or provoke concern for American Jews largely because, throughout the war, the President and his advisers minimized the Jewish aspect of the Nazi policy.

But what could have been done?

A precedent was set as early as May 1897 when the U.S. Ambassador to Persia interceded on behalf of the Jews in Teheran who were being subjected to mob violence by Muslims. "His course was approved with the statement that his 'good offices in this somewhat delicate question seem to have been discreetly used in the interest of common humanity and in accordance with the precepts of civilization.'"[28] Ironically, this reference was found in a State Department file on the protection of persons during the war.

How simple it would have been for American ambassadors to act "in the interest of common humanity before their embassies were closed." They could have done what the Swedish diplomat Raoul Wallenberg did, provide visas or passports to as many Jews as possible, regardless of whether they were American citizens. In those cases where citizenship was claimed, applicants could have been given the benefit of the doubt, especially after the fate of those denied passports became known. This would have been the least U.S. officials could do. They could have been less reluctant to exchange Germans interned in the States for Americans. The Germans were willing to exchange several U.S. POWs for one German. At least one life, that of Barry Spanjaard's father, likely would have been saved by such a policy.

U.S. officials could have also warned the Nazis earlier and more frequently about the consequences of harming Americans and then taken action after learning of German crimes. For example, steps toward prosecuting war criminals might have begun long before the end of the war to send the message that Germans who were caught faced serious consequences. The Germans were concerned that the Allies would take punitive action against their prisoners if they mistreated Allied captives. Had the United States been willing to treat the Germans it held more harshly, Hitler might have been persuaded to adhere to the POW conventions. On March 25, 1945—already long after most of the atrocities had occurred—Eisenhower did warn the Germans not to execute Allied prisoners on pain of "severe punishment" for any person taking part in such executions.[29] By this time, the Germans knew that no punitive measures would be taken and were therefore less restrained in the way they treated their prisoners.

The military should have known from the beginning that American Jewish GIs would be in greater danger after capture than other soldiers and taken precautions, in particular, deleting the "H" from their dog tags. This certainly should have been done after reports of mistreatment of American Jewish soldiers reached Washington.

Army regulations specifically state that the religious identification "may *at the request of the wearer* be stamped on the ID Tag" (emphasis added).[30] Thus, wearing an "H" was (and still is) supposed to be voluntary, but it appears no one informed the Jewish GIs.

The Red Cross could have given greater publicity to the Nazi genocide, used its influence to obtain access to more camps and mobilized world opinion to crusade for an end to the atrocities. The Red Cross could have also told the truth to the public about the mistreatment of POWs, especially American Jewish soldiers, so the people would have known that it was not just foreigners who were being abused. Hitler may not have been moved by an outcry, but the absence of one allowed him to conclude that his annihilation of the Jews was of little concern, even to his enemies.

Secretary of State Cordell Hull had said in 1944 that his department was "exercising special vigilance to prevent discrimination by German authorities against American prisoners of war upon racial or religious basis."[31] At the time of his statement, Hull claimed no evidence of discrimination, but by April of that year the State Department learned Jewish soldiers faced persecution by their captors. Hull received a report that an American POW named Levanthal had been paraded through the streets of Frankfurt with a sign reading: "I am a member of the race which started the war." A few months later, Hull also received a report that Americans had been sent to Dachau. Even after the government received this information, no action was taken.

Eisenhower acknowledged publicizing atrocities would increase support for the war effort when he was asked if the wide publication of such information was going to be useful:

> When I found the first camp like that I think I was never so angry in my life. The bestiality displayed there was not merely piled up bodies of people that had starved to death, but to follow out the road, and see where they tried to evacuate them so they could still work, you could see where they sprawled on the road. You could go

to their burial pits and see horrors that really I wouldn't even want to begin to describe. I think people ought to know about such things. It explains something of my attitude toward the German war criminal. I believe he must be punished, and I will hold out for that forever. I think it did good. I think the people at home ought to know what they are fighting for and the kind of person they are fighting. Yes, it did good.[32]

Unfortunately, Eisenhower did not speak until June 1945, after the liberation of the camps. Imagine the outrage that might have been provoked had the American people known U.S. soldiers were in the same camp less than a year earlier? Isn't it conceivable that such knowledge would have convinced officials to attack the concentration camps or to ease the restrictions impeding people from escaping to the United States?

As we saw in Chapter 11, the criminals could have also been brought to trial and given sentences that fit their crimes. Evidence of abuses against Americans could have been introduced into the record and witnesses been brought to testify who could have insured that sufficient proof existed to prevent verdicts from being reversed and sentences from being reduced.

In 1948, Bernard Vogel's uncle circulated petitions protesting the sentence reductions given to Metz and Merz, but they generated no attention. And why should they? After all, most of the survivors of the camp were not aware they had been tried. Had their mistreatment of Americans become widely known, the clemency shown to them might have provoked the kind of widespread outrage and Congressional investigation that followed the reduction of Ilse Koch's sentence.

In addition, trials might have been held in the United States for crimes committed against Americans. These would have brought the guilty to justice, let the public know how their fellow citizens were brutalized and educated Americans about the Holocaust.

Is there anything that can still be done to make amends for the failure to save American lives during the war or to compensate the survivors?

Several things can and should be done.

First, American victims of the Holocaust received no reparations from the German government. Hugo Princz, an American who claimed he had been in the Warsaw Ghetto, Dachau and Auschwitz, applied for reparations in the mid-1950s. The party handling his case said he was the first American to apply and that he would be the first one to receive reparations from Germany. In 1956, however, he received a letter of rejection because he did not reside in Germany in 1947 and was an American citizen.[33] In fact, the German compensation law did not permit American victims to receive reparations. That law required applicants to prove they had been subject to persecution *and* were stateless after the war. The second test would not have been met by American citizens. Many people fell through this loophole in the law. In some European countries, bilateral agreements were reached with Germany to compensate their citizens.[34]

The filing deadline for compensation under the German law was 1965; however, new arrangements are being made to give people in Eastern Europe who were denied the opportunity to apply for reparations another chance. The U.S. government should negotiate a similar agreement with the German authorities to allow Americans to apply as well. The German government should provide compensation to any American citizens who can prove that they were persecuted under the Nazis, even if they did not subsequently become classified as "stateless." In late 1993, Rep. Charles Schumer introduced an amendment to the Foreign Sovereign Immunities Act that would allow U.S. citizens victimized by the Nazis to sue the German government for reparations.

Second, all Americans who were held as POWs in Berga and Buchenwald should receive the POW medal with a citation acknowledging their special treatment.

Third, a Congressional hearing should be held to investigate the treatment of American citizens and soldiers during the war. The government should release all documents that it has related to this subject and publicly acknowledge that Americans were held in concentration camps, that American Jews were harmed and that government inaction was responsible for some of their deaths and mistreatment.

Fourth, the Office of Special Investigations, the Justice Department agency responsible for gathering information on suspected Nazi war criminals, should review all cases where crimes were committed against Americans and investigate whether the perpetrators are still living. If so, they should be brought to justice.

Fifth, researchers should examine concentration camp and deportation records for evidence of American citizens. In particular, new information available from the International Tracing Service of the Red Cross, the archives of the former Soviet Union and the French government should be checked.

Sixth, Holocaust museums, memorials and scholars should provide accounts of the American victims.[35]

What lessons can we learn from the events of nearly a half century ago?

One lesson is that American citizens cannot always count on their government to protect them. As we have seen more recently with Americans taken hostage in Lebanon, officials may consider foreign policy interests more important than individual citizens. The government may be limited in what it can do, but it may also be unwilling to take action for reasons of state that are never explained.

The U.S. government did take extraordinary action after Iraq's invasion of Kuwait in 1990. The State Department allowed entire families to come to the United States if one person, usually a child, was an American citizen. The director of the Citizens Emergency Center at the State Department said the U.S. Embassy in Kuwait was cut off and there was no way to determine eligibility for immigration. "So we made a decision," he said. "If there was one American in the family, the entire family would be evacuated. We did that to save lives."[36]

At the same time, however, American Jewish soldiers were again sent into battle during Operation Desert Storm wearing dog tags identifying them. The history of Arab treatment of Jewish POWs from Israel is horrifying and familiar to the Pentagon. Saddam Hussein's hatred for Jews and Israel was also well known (and demonstrated by Iraq's Scud missile attacks on civilian population centers in Israel); therefore, the possibility existed that Jewish military personnel could have been captured and mistreated. Apparently, no Jewish soldiers were captured. A Jewish journalist covering the war, CBS correspondent Bob Simon, was taken by the Iraqis, however, and abused.[37] It is time for the Pentagon to reevaluate whether it is necessary to identify the religion of GIs on their dog tags.

After reading the evidence presented here, Jews should see that the phrase "Never Again!" has even greater meaning. Not even America could or would protect them. Sadly, the story of the American victims of the Holocaust was never deemed important enough to investigate or report.

American Jewry has long maintained that what happened in Germany could never happen here. But the insensitivity to American Jewish citizens is cause for reappraisal.

Notes

Chapter 1

1. David Wyman, *The Abandonment of the Jews,* (NY: Pantheon, 1984), pp. 339–340.

2. See for example the *Washington Post* (June 25, 1992) on Vietnam POWs and the *Washington Times* (June 12, 1992) on the treatment of POWs during the Gulf War.

Chapter 2

1. "Policy of the United States Government in Regard to Repatriation of United States Nationals," March 1944, Record Group 59 [henceforth RG], Special War Problems Division, Policy Books, 1939–45, Vol. 22, Folder 1, Box 8, National Archives and Records Administration [henceforth NARA].

2. Letter from G.S. Messersmith to Leland Harrison, November 25, 1939, Breckinridge Long Papers, Special Division General, 1940–42, Container 205, Manuscript Division, Library of Congress [henceforth LC].

3. "Summary of Present Facilities For the Extension of Assistance to: (A) American nationals under enemy jurisdiction and (B) enemy nationals under American jurisdiction," April 15, 1942, RG200, 619.2/01, General Plans and Policies, Box 990, NARA.

4. Letter from G.S. Messersmith to Leland Harrison, November 25, 1939, Breckinridge Long Papers, Special Division General, 1940–42, Container 205, LC.

5. William Leahy to the Secretary of State, March 10, 1941, *Foreign Relations of the United States,* 1941, Vol. II (DC: Government Printing Office), p. 505 [henceforth *FRUS*].

6. Hull to Chargé in Germany (Morris), January 11, 1941; William D. Leahy, Ambassador to France to Hull, March 10, 1941; Hull to Morris, May 29, 1941, *FRUS*, 1941, Vol. II, pp. 503–5, 507.

7. Leahy to Hull, June 19, 1941, *FRUS*, 1941, Vol. II, p. 509.

8. Welles to Leahy, June 27, 1941; Leahy to Hull, July 26, 1941, *FRUS*, 1941, Vol. II, p. 509–511.

9. Hull to Pell, May 1, 1941; Pell to Hull, June 17, 1941, *FRUS*, 1941, Vol. 1, pp. 403–406.

10. Morris to Hull, August 12, 1941, *FRUS*, 1941, Vol. II, pp. 632–33.

11. Memo of conversation by Welles, June 16, 1941; Morris to Hull, June 19, 1941, *FRUS*, 1941, Vol. II, pp. 629–31.

12. Hull telegram, February 6, 1942, RG84, 703, Box 20, A1, U.S.-Rumania, NARA.

13. Memo, April 21, 1943, RG84, 350, General Jewish, Box 17, NARA.

14. Minister in Rumania (Franklin Mott Gunther) to Hull, January 30, 1941, *FRUS*, 1941, Vol. II, p. 860.

15. Gunther to Hull, April 2, July 1, and August 19, 1941, *FRUS*, 1941, Vol. II, pp. 863–868.

16. Gunther to Hull, October 3, 1941, *FRUS*, 1941, Vol. II, pp. 868–869.

17. Gunther to Hull, November 4, 1941, *FRUS,* 1941, Vol. II, pp. 871–874.

18. Gunther to Hull, November 14, 1941, *FRUS,* 1941, Vol. II, pp. 876–77.

19. Hull to Gunther, December 1, 1941, *FRUS,* 1941, Vol. II, pp. 878–879.

20. Wyman, p. 99.

21. Robert Alexander of the State Department Visa Division to Long, May 7, 1943, BLP, B 203, Ref Mvt & Natl Groups, quoted in Wyman, p. 99.

22. Long to Roosevelt, January 6, 1941 and an undated letter to Roosevelt. Several other letters and memos in the file express concern about enemy agents infiltrating the United States. Breckinridge Long Papers, General Correspondence, Container 139, LC.

23. Henry Feingold, *The Politics of Rescue,* (NJ: Rutgers University Press, 1970), p. 138.

24. James Keeley, Jr. to Mr. Travers, December 15, 1942, RG59, Vol. 22, Folder 2, Box 8, NARA.

25. Wyman, p. 131–32.

26. James Keeley, Jr. to Mr. Travers, December 15, 1942, RG59, Vol. 22, Folder 2, Box 8, NARA.

27. Long to Rep. Emanuel Celler, September 20, 1943, Breckinridge Long Papers, General Correspondence, 1943, Container 145, LC.

28. James Keeley, Jr. to Mr. Travers, December 15, 1942, RG59, Vol. 22, Folder 2, Box 8, NARA.

29. Letter from A.M. Warren to Ludwig Pollock, August 19, 1941, Breckinridge Long, General Correspondence, Container 138, LC.

30. Letter from Long to Ruth Kelm, December 19, 1941, Breckinridge Long, General Correspondence, Container 138, LC.

31. Wyman, pp. 125–26.

32. George Kennan, *Memoirs: 1925–1950,* (MA: Little Brown, 1967), pp. 136–141.

33. Memo from Joseph Green to Brandt, May 4, 1942, Breckinridge Long Papers, Special Division, General Cases, 1942, Box 206, LC.

34. Memo from Joseph Green to Brandt, May 4, 1942, Breckinridge Long Papers, Special Division, General Correspondence, 1942, Box 206, LC.

35. Breckinridge Long to George Brandt, May 6, 1942, Breckinridge Long Papers, Special Division, General Correspondence, 1942, Box 206, LC.

36. Green to Brandt, May 4, 1942, Long Papers, Special Division, General Correspondence, 1942, Box 206, LC.

37. George Brandt memo, June 5, 1942, Special Division, General Correspondence, 1942, Box 206, Breckinridge Long Papers, LC.

38. David Wyman, *The Abandonment of the Jews,* (NY: Pantheon, 1984), pp. 5–15.

39. Morris to Hull, May 10, 1941, *FRUS,* 1941, Vol. II, pp. 505–6.

40. January 26, 1942 letter from Swiss Consulate, Amsterdam; November 17, 1942 telegram from Hull to American Interests Norway; December 14, 1942 letter from Francis James, Special Representative of American Red Cross to George Tait; RG84, 711.5, Individuals, Box 42, NARA.

41. Green memo, March 17, 1942, Breckinridge Long Papers, Special Division, General Correspondence, 1942, Box 206, LC.

42. Green memo, March 17, 1942, Breckinridge Long Papers, Special Division, General Correspondence, 1942, Box 206, LC.

43. Telegram from Huddle to State Department, March 6, 1942, and cable from Harrison to State Department, July 4, 1942, Harrison telegram September 22, 1942; Hull response September 26, 1942; RG84, 711.5, American Civil Prisoners, Box 38, NARA.

44. Huddle to State Department, February 12, 1942; RG84, 703, U.S. Slovakia, Box 20, NARA.

45. Memo from Joseph Green to Atherton and Shipley, June 9, 1942, attached to memo of same date from Harrison to Hull, RG59, 703.5462/32, General Records of Department of State, Decimal File, 1940–44, Box 1952, NARA.

46. Hull to American Legation Bern, January 20, 1943, RG59, General Records of Department of State, Special War Problems Division, Policy Books, 1939–45, Box 6, NARA.

47. Tait message to Hull, April 3, 1943, reporting message from Swiss in Vichy, RG84, 350, General Jewish, Box 17, NARA.

48. American Legation letter to Federal Political Department, September 17, 1943, RG84, 350, Individuals, Box 18, NARA.

49. Bern Legation report, June 8, 1943, RG84, 711.5, Civil Prisoners in France, Box 38, NARA.

50. Memos from Harrison to the State Department dated July 11 and August 7, 1944. Message from Secretary of State Hull dated August 22, 1944, RG84, 711.5, Countries G-Z, Box 69, NARA.

51. Harrison telegram to State Department, July 4, 1944; translation of *Hungarian Reports* newspaper, July 4, 1944; Harrison report to State Department, July 10, 1944; *Pester Lloyd,* July 6, 1944; Report from Hungarian Legation, July 4, 1944; *Pesti Hirlap,* July 13, 1944. Estimates of the number of people killed in air raid ranged from 89 to 111. The Swiss confirmed in Harrison's July 10 memo at least 96 dead and the Hungarian Legation report on July 4 said only 37 of 144 people in the camp remained, RG84, 711.5, Countries G-Z, Box 69, NARA.

52. Hull message to McClelland, September 20, 1944, RG84, 840.1, Jews-Europe, Box 41, NARA.

53. Note concerning assistance which might be given to the Jews in Europe, July 7, 1943, 619.2, Jewish Internees and POWS Europe, Box 1016, NARA.

54. Hull message to Bern, October 7, 1944, RG84, 840.1, Jews-Europe, Box 41, NARA.

55. Harrison message to State Department, October 24, 1944, RG84, 840.1, Box 41, NARA.

56. "Approximate Whereabouts of American Nationals in Continental Europe," September 12, 1944, RG59, Vol. 22, Folder 2, Box 8, NARA.

57. *FRUS,* 1944, Vol. 1, p. 1205; "Approximate Whereabouts of American Nationals in Continental Europe," RG59, Vol. 22, Box 8, Folder 2, NARA.

58. Camp reports, RG84, 711.5, Box 38; Long to Welles, May 12, 1943, *FRUS,* 1943, Vol. 1, pp. 93–94; Airgram from American Legation, Lisbon, July 12, 1943, RG84, 711.5, State Department, Box 34; Monthly Report, March 8, 1944, RG84, 711.4, Box 63, NARA.

59. Testimony of Henry Kloczynski to War Crimes Office, April 23, 1945, RG153, 12-618, Box 312, NARA.

60. Russell Singleton, "Civilian Internment Camps in Germany," *Prisoners of War Bulletin,* (January 1941), pp. 2–3.

61. Memos, October 14 and November 3, 1944; State Department report January 5, 1945, RG338, T2, 11-416, Box 74, NARA.

62. Roswell McClelland message, February 10, 1945, RG84, 711.5, American Civilian Prisoners—France, Box 89, NARA.

63. Memorandum for files, January 12, 1943 and April 5, 1943, RG84, 701.1, Box 19, NARA.

64. Report of February 9, 1945, visit to Ilag Biberach, RG84, 711.5, American Civilian Prisoners—France, Box 89, NARA.

65. For example, an April 25, 1945 cable from Harrison to State said no Americans were found at Ravensbrück, RG84, 711.5, General, Box 89, 1942–47, NARA.

66. September 21, 1944, Hull to McClelland; September 29, 1944, Harrison to State; October 9, 1944, Bonn report; November 8, 1944, Stettinius message to State; December 14, 1944, McClelland to Tait, RG84, 840.1, Box 41, NARA.

67. Dec. 23, 1944 message from Huddle to State, RG84, 840.1, Box 42, NARA. An October 12, 1944, message regards a woman in Bergen-Belsen who says her husband is a naturalized American. The Swiss Legation asked if she could be included in a list of unaccompanied alien close relatives of American citizens desiring to be repatriated. No answer is in the files, RG84, 711.5, Box 70, NARA.

68. Barry Spanjaard, *Don't Fence Me In!*, (CA: B&B Publishing, 1981). Another case for which no details were available involved a woman named Margaret Pogany. Born in Newark, her mother took her back to her native Hungary. She ended up not only in Bergen-Belsen, but also Raguhn and Theresienstadt.

69. Spanjaard, pp. 110–111.

70. Alfred Spanjaard is buried in Muensterlingen, Switzerland. The tombstone reads: "Victim of camp Bergen-Belsen. Your strength lasted until entering free ground. You witnessed the premature end of six million Jews in the years 1933–1945."

71. *PM*, (April 23, 1945).

72. July 19, 1945, testimony of Emil Weiss, RG153, 12-180, Box 176, War Crimes Branch Case Files, p. 10; May 29, 1945, testimony of Isidore Weiss, RG153, 19-110, Box 571, NARA.

73. *New York Times*, (April 26, 1945).

74. May 22, 1944 and December 26, 1944, RG84, Box 70, 711.5, Individuals, NARA.

75. Martin Gilbert, *Atlas Of The Holocaust*, (Oxford: Pergamon Press, 1988), pp. 134–35.

76. From "Nazi Death Camps" document collection provided to the author by The Jewish Historical Institute in Poland, July 11, 1991.

77. Letter from Jerzy Wroblewski, Director of the State Museum of Auschwitz, to the author, November 22, 1991. Wroblewski also said that all the papers of American citizens in Auschwitz were destroyed by the SS in January 1945 during the liquidation of the camp. He notes also that Serge Klarsfeld wrote that 10 Americans were deported to Auschwitz in *Le memorial de la deportation des Juifs de France*. Wenger's testimony is also mentioned in Olga Lengyel, *Five Chimneys*, (NY: Howard Fertig, 1983), pp. 168–170.

78. Letter to the author, July 7, 1991, from Vaclava Sucha, Department of Collections, Memorial Gedenkstätte Monument-Památník Terezín.

79. Paul Berben, *Dachau*, (London: The Norfolk Press, 1975); *Dachau*, OSS Section, Seventh Army (NY: Benchmark Publishing Co., 1945), p. 65; Document supplied by the Dachau Museum in letter to the author from Barbara Distel, KZ-Gedenkstatte Dachau, June 3, 1991.

80. *Stars and Stripes*, dispatch dated May 11, 1945.

81. Evelyn Le Chene, *Mauthausen*, (London: Methuen and Co., Ltd., 1971), p. 168.

82. November 10, 1942 memo, RG84, 711.5, Individuals, Box 42, NARA.

83. Memo from War Problems Division to Le [probably Swiss Legation], November 3, 1944, RG59, Vol. 13, Folder 2, Box 6, NARA.

84. Tait to Hull, October 15, 1943, RG84, 320, A-Z, Box 15, NARA.

85. Series of memos regarding Mrs. Rosa Lewy-Busch and a cable from Stettinius, October 31, 1944, RG84, 711.5, Box 70, NARA.

86. Hull message to Bern, May 5, 1944; Harrison message to State Department, June 9, 1944; Hull message to American Interests, France, June 22, 1944; German Minister of Interior letter, June 5, 1944; Berlin Foreign Office letter to Swiss Legation, July 31, 1944; Hull message, August 17, 1944, RG84, 711.5, Box 70, NARA.

87. Telegram from Cordell Hull, September 9, 1944, RG84, 711.5, Box 70, NARA.

88. Translation of message from German Foreign Office, November 24, 1944, RG84, 711.5, Box 70, NARA.

89. Memorandum of Conversation with M. Pilet-Golaz written by J.K.H., December 7, 1944, RG84, 711.5, Box 70, NARA.

90. *New York Times*, (March 27, 1945).

91. Harrison telegram to State Department, February 20, 1943; and Harrison telegram April 1, 1943; RG84, 711.5, American Prisoners in Germany, Box 38, NARA.

92. Secretary of State Hull to Attorney General Biddle, May 10, 1943, *FRUS,* 1943, Vol. 1, pp. 90–93.

93. Breckinridge Long memo to Adm. Land, February 13, 1942, Breckinridge Long Papers, Special Division, 1939–44, Container 205, LC. A December 15, 1942, memo from Keeley in the Special Division to Travers in the Visa Division revealed the rationalization for failing to exchange Germans interned in the U.S. for Jews in Europe. Keeley said less than 2,000 Germans were interned in the U.S. and that the number of Jews in concentration camps was undoubtedly much larger; therefore, "it is unlikely that it would be possible to reach with the German Government an agreement which would provide for more than an exchange of a person for a person rather than for the exchange of the entire group of German internees for all the Jews held by the Nazis." Keeley went on to warn about the danger of Jews who were brought to the U.S. becoming spies. Though Jews were anti-Nazi, he said, they would be susceptible to intimidation because of relatives they left behind. Finally, he opposed exchanging Germans for Jews because other people would be upset that they were not being rescued. "While the plight of the Jews in Germany and German-occupied territory is pitiful, it is no less precarious than the plight of the Poles and Czechs," Keeley wrote, RG59, Vol. 22, Box 8, Folder 2, NARA.

94. RG84, 711.4, Repatriation 1/15/45, Box 86, NARA.

95. Letter dated July 7, 1943, RG59, Vol. 26, Protection, Folder 1, Box 8, NARA.

96. Letter from Ruth Shipley, chief of the Passport Division, to Mr. Keeley, February 19, 1944, essentially told him to stay off her turf and that PD would handle all citizenship questions, RG59, Vol 26, Protection, Folder 1, Box 8, NARA.

97. September 5, 1944, Tait to Paul Squire, American Consul Geneva concerning information that Jacob Silverman is at Birkenau and requesting an effort to get documents from him regarding his citizenship, RG84, 840.1, Jews-Europe, Box 41, NARA.

98. Letter from Ruth Shipley, chief of the Passport Division, to Mr. Keeley, February 19, 1944, RG59, Vol 26, Protection, Folder 1, Box 8, NARA.

99. Letter from Secretary of War Henry Stimson, April 7, 1944. A memo from the Secretary of State to American Diplomatic and Consular officers, July 21, 1944, informed them they would be given military rank, RG84, 711.4, Box 60, NARA.

Chapter 3

1. This chapter is based on *Warsaw Ghetto: A Diary by Mary Berg*, (NY: L.B. Fischer, 1945).

2. *New York Times*, (March 20, 1945).

3. Raul Hilberg, et. al., *The Warsaw Diary of Adam Czerniakow*, (NY: Stein & Day, 1979), pp. 362 and 380. Czerniakow also mentions an American Jew named Fanny Rapaport whose property was returned because she was an alien. No further mention is made of what happened to her (pp. 319–20).

4. Memo of conversation, September 4, 1942, State Department 1939–44, Container 205, Breckinridge Long Papers, LC.

Chapter 4

1. Stan Sommers, *The European Story*, (WI: American Ex-Prisoners of War, Inc., July 1980), p. 1.

2. Sommers, p. 1.

3. Sommers, p. 4.

4. I. Kaufman, *American Jews in World War II*, (NY: Dial Press, 1947), pp. 349–50; "American Jews in World War II," in Isaac Kowalski, ed., *Anthology on Armed Jewish Resistance, 1939–1945*, (NY: Jewish Combatants Publishers House, 1984), vol. 1, pp. 38–39.

5. The treatment of black GIs was of particular interest, but it was almost impossible to find any information in the archives. Relatively few blacks were allowed to serve in frontline positions during the war and I could find no evidence of systematic mistreatment. In fact, I found only one reference to an unprovoked attack on a black soldier (RG153, 100-425, Box 35, Folder 1, Book 6, NARA). According to a story by Curtis Whiteway, SS divisions bayoneted and beat black soldiers to death after overrunning their units. They also mutilated their bodies ("POW/Battle of the Bulge," *The Checkerboard*, (September 1990), p. 5). Foy reported "scattered instances of mistreatment" of black soldiers (p. 129). In an interview, Pete House recalled two black artillerymen being in his section at Stalag IX-B, but said they were not segregated or mistreated.

6. International Military Tribunal, *Trial of the Major War Criminals*, Vol. 22, (Nuremberg, 1947), pp. 257–58 [henceforth IMT].

7. Szymon Datner, *Crimes Against POWs*, (Poland: Zachodnia Agencja Prasowa, 1964), pp. 98–99.

8. Kurt Lindow, a Gestapo official, testified that Himmler gave orders in 1941–42 to execute captured Soviet political commissars and Jewish soldiers, IMT, Vol. 4, p. 260; IMT, Vol. VII, p. 380; Vol. XI, p. 415.

9. In the Spring of 1945, Lt. Gen. Gottlob Berger, the SS general in charge of POW affairs, told Hitler that the West had approximately 12 million Germans in custody, Arthur Durand, *Stalag Luft III*, (LA: Louisiana State University Press, 1988), p. 131.

10. Undated letter to the author.

11. Walter Gray, *Beverage News*, no date.

12. Undated letter to the author.

13. Durand, pp. 65–66.

14. Testimony of Second Lt. Edgar Denton, Sept. 24, 1945; Testimony of T/Sgt. John Ray, August 14, 1945; and Testimony of S/Sgt. Billy Walker, RG153, 12-839, Box 324, p. 7, NARA.

15. Leonard Winograd, "Double Jeopardy: What an American Army Officer, A Jew, Remembers of Prison Life in Germany," *American Jewish Archives*, (April 1976), p. 7.

16. Winograd, p. 11.

17. Sam Kalman, letter to editor of the *Jewish Week*, October 5, 1990; also letter to the author, November 14, 1987.

18. Letter to the author from Hubert Zemke, November 7, 1990.

19. Interview with Ed Neft.

20. Letter to the author from Eugene Hayes, October 22, 1990.

21. Irving Lifson, "Loneliest and Happiest Point in One's Life," in William Richarz et al., eds., *The 390th Bomb Group Anthology*, Vol. 1, (AZ: 390th Memorial Museum Foundation, Inc.), pp. 194–195.

22. Sam Kalman "An Ex-POW Remembers," *The Jewish Veteran*, (July-August 1986).

23. John Vietor, *Time Out*, (NY: Richard R. Smith, Inc., 1951), p. 156.

24. Letter to the author from Maurice Fridrich, January 2, 1991.

25. Kalman letter, October 5, 1990; David Foy, *For You The War Is Over*, (NY: Stein and Day, 1984), p. 101.

26. Irving Lifson, "Loneliest and Happiest Point in One's Life," in William Richarz et al., eds., *The 390th Bomb Group Anthology*, Vol. 1, (AZ: 390th Memorial Museum Foundation, Inc.), pp. 194–195.

27. Sam Kalman "An Ex-POW Remembers," *The Jewish Veteran*, (July-August 1986).

28. Foy, pp. 129–131.

29. *New York Times*, (February 20, 1945).

30. Testimony of Joseph Boros, February 23, 1945, RG338, Box 372, 40-L4, Vol. XLIII and Testimony of Raymond Allaby, RG338, Box 369, 40-L4, Vol. 28, NARA.

31. Letter to the author from Stanley Wojtusik.

32. Report on International Red Cross visit to Stalag VII-A, January 27, 1945, RG59, Special War Problems Division, Subject Files 39-54, Box 128, NARA; "American Prisoners of War In Germany," Military Intelligence Service, War Department, November 1, 1945.

33. Curtis Whiteway, "POW/Battle of the Bulge," *The Checkerboard*, (September 1990), p. 5; *The Checkerboard*, (March 1989), pp. 8–9.

34. Durand, pp. 209, 306–307.

35. Letter to the author, November 30, 1990.

36. IMT, Vol. 37, p. 610.

37. *New York Times*, (May 1, 1945).

38. Datner, pp. 317–318.

39. Investigation of killing and mistreatment of Allied POWs in Flossenbürg Concentration Camp, Headquarters, Third U.S. Army Judge Advocate Section, War Crimes Branch, June 21, 1945, in *Nazi Conspiracy and Aggression*, Vol. IV. (DC: Government Printing Office, 1946), pp. 1001–2.

40. *New York Times*, (April 25 and December 14, 1945); Datner, p. 300; *Times-Herald*, (April 25, 1945).

41. *U.S. vs. Friedrich Becker, et al.*, May 21, 1947, RG153, 12-583, Vol. 1, Trial Record, Part 1, Folder 2, Box 293, NARA.

Chapter 5

1. Eugen Kogon, *The Theory and Practice of Hell,* (NY: Berkley Books, 1980).

2. Quotes from a tape given to me by one of the survivors, Park Chapman, which contains the stories of several of the POWs from Buchenwald. Since the speakers are not identifiable, their quotes are henceforth cited as "Chapman tape."

3. Chapman tape.

4. Chapman tape.

5. Special Treatment of Allied Aircrew. Hitler's Directive—Archive RW 4/v.700 [archive kept at Wehrmacht High Command/Liaison Staff]—May 20, 1944—found in Bundesarchiv-Koblenz.

6. Robert Conot, *Justice at Nuremberg,* (NY: Carroll & Graf, 1983), pp. 314–316.

7. Testimony of S/Sgt. Thomas Richey, June 20, 1945, RG153, 12-811, Book 1, Box 322, NARA.

8. Albert Kadler, "Special Report of Conditions On Transfer Of Allied Prisoners of War from Fresnes Prison, Paris to Concentration Camp at Buchenwald, Germany and of Conditions at Concentration Camp At Buchenwald Near Weimar, Germany," Berlin, November 24, 1944, File MD/JAG/FS/21/54 from JAG Office, Spring Gardens, London, July 13, 1945.

9. Testimony of William Powell, August 3, 1945, RG153, 12-390, Book 2, Folder 2, Box 245, p. 104; Testimony of William Edge, August 1, 1945, RG153, 11-581, Box 146, NARA; interview with Jim Hastin; also Kadler report, November 24, 1944.

10. Interview with Park Chapman.

11. Letter to author from Wolfgang Roll, head of the Historical Department at the National Memorial of Buchenwald, July 2, 1990.

12. Hastin interview.

13. Chapman tape.

14. Letter to the author from Jim Hastin, May 8, 1991.

15. Chapman tape; Kadler report, November 24, 1944.

16. Kinnis interview.

17. Carr testimony.

18. Chapman interview.

19. Kadler report, November 24, 1944; United States, 79th Congress, first session, May 15, 1945, Senate Document No. 47: Report of the Committee requested by Gen. Dwight D. Eisenhower through the Chief of Staff, Gen. George C. Marshall to the Congress of the United States Relative to Atrocities and Other Conditions in Concentration Camps in Germany, pp. 6–8.

20. Chapman tape.

21. Chapman tape.

22. Hastin interview.

23. Testimony of Second Lt. Stratton Appleman, August 8, 1945, RG153, 12-811, Book 1, Box 322, NARA.

24. Testimony of Frederick Carr, July 25, 1944, RG153, 12-390, Box 244, NARA.

25. Chapman interview.

26. Kinnis interview.

27. Testimony of William Edge, August 1, 1945, RG153, 12-390, Book 2, Folder 2, Box 245, NARA.

28. A Sgt. Ritter, quoted in "Ex-Report No. 621 (Stalag 7A)," Prepared by MIS-X Section, CPM Branch, June 23, 1945, RG153, 12-390, Folder 1, Box 244, NARA.

29. Chapman interview.

30. Chapman tape.

31. Chapman interview.

32. Testimony of William Powell, August 3, 1945, RG153, 12-390, Book 2, Folder 2, Box 245, NARA.

33. Carr testimony.

34. Kogon, pp. 166–167.

35. Chapman tape.

36. Chapman tape.

37. Correspondence supplied to the author by John Chalot.

38. Testimony of Second Lt. William Granberry, III, RG153, 12-811, Book 2, Box 322, NARA.

39. Hastin interview.

40. Chapman tape.

41. Testimony of First Lt. Harold Brown, August 10, 1945, RG153, 12-811, Book 2, Box 322, NARA.

42. "Operations against Weimar (Buchenwald)," report from the USAF Historical Research Center at Maxwell AFB, quoted in a letter from Stan Bauer to Park Chapman, April 18, 1988.

43. "Ex-Report No. 621 (Stalag 7A)," Prepared by MIS-X Section, CPM Branch, June 23, 1945, RG153, 12-390, Folder 1, Box 244, p. 62, NARA; Report by the SS Garrison Medical Officer, SS Captain Gerhard Schiedlausky, to the Head of Section D.III at the WVHA (Wirtsch-Verw-HA) Berlin, on August 27, 1944. Document provided to the author by Park Chapman.

44. Chapman interview; Chapman tape; Hastin interview.

45. Testimony of Second Lt. Joseph Pedersen, July 28, 1921, RG153, 12-811, Book 2, Box 322, NARA; Chapman tape.

46. Kinnis interview.

47. Chapman tape.

48. Kinnis interview; Chapman tape.

49. Testimony of Second Lt. William Powell, RG311, 12-811, book 1, Box 322, NARA.

50. Chapman tape; Hastin interview.

51. Chapman interview.

52. Chapman tape.

53. Testimony of Second Lt. William Granberry, III, RG153, 12-811, Book 2, Box 322, NARA.

54. Eugene Weinstock, *Beyond the Last Path,* (NY: Boni And Gaer, 1947), p. 248.

55. Interview with Jim Hastin.

56. Chapman interview.

57. Chapman interview.

58. Chapman tape.

59. Arthur Durand, *Stalag Luft III,* (LA: Louisiana State University Press, 1988), pp. 269–270.

60. Testimony of Sgt. William Lee, RG153, 12-811, Book 2, Box 322, NARA.

61. *U.S. vs. Josias Prince zu Waldeck et al.,* November 15, 1947, RG153, 12-390, Box 243;

Vol. 1, Trial Record Exhibits, Part 3, Folder 2, Box 252; interrogation of Herman Helbig, Vol. 1, Trial Record Exhibits, Part 2, Folder 2, Box 252, NARA.

62. Letter from Solomon Surowitz to Secretary of the Army Kenneth Royall, September 27, 1948, RG153, 12-390, Book 5, Box 245, NARA.

63. Kogon, pp. 281–282.

64. Edward R. Murrow, "They Died 900 a Day in 'the Best' Nazi Death Camp," *PM,* (April 16, 1945).

65. Chapman tape.

Chapter 6

1. War Crimes Information, June 26, 1945, RG153, 5-88, Box 59, NARA.

2. Testimony of Dr. Karl Helfrich, May 15, 1945, RG226, Entry 110, Folder 86, Box 4, OSS Files, NARA.

3. Evelyn Le Chene, *Mauthausen,* (London: Methuen and Co., Ltd., 1971), p. 127.

4. "Day" to Jake, October 23, 1944, RG226, Entry 139, Box 29, "Day," Folder 200, OSS Files, NARA.

5. Chapin to Dawes, September 27, 1944, RG226, Entry 136, Box 26, Folder 264, OSS Files, NARA.

6. "War's End Brings Story of Morton's Death," *AP World,* no date, pp. 10–12.

7. Messages from Dawes, October 25–28, 1944, RG226, Entry 136, Box 26, Folder 264, OSS Files, NARA.

8. Messages to Dawes, October 25 and November 7, 1944, RG226, Entry 136, Box 26, Folder 264, OSS Files, NARA.

9. Cables dated March 4 and 14, 1945, RG226, Entry 154, Box 42, Folder 642, OSS Files, NARA.

10. Chief SICE to Chief X-2, OSS, Operational History, Dawes and Associated Teams—Slovakia, January 27, 1945, RG226, Entry 190, Box 22, Folder 1, NARA.

11. Cables dated March 4 and 14, 1945, RG226, Entry 154, Box 42, Folder 642, OSS Files, NARA.

12. Cables dated February 1 and 14, 1945, RG226, Entry 190, Box 22, Folder 1, OSS Files, NARA.

13. Lt. Kelly O'Neall, Jr., War Crimes Investigation Committee, HQ, 2677th Regiment, OSS, July 19, 1945, RG153, 8-9, Box 116; report on Interview of Anton Novak, RG226, Entry 190, Folder 1, Box 22, OSS Files, NARA.

14. Report on Green Mission, OSS, no date, RG153, 8-9, Box 116, NARA.

15. Lt. Col. H.M. Chapin, Chief SICE to Chief X-2, "Operational History, Dawes and Associated Teams—Slovakia," January 27, 1945, OSS Files, RG226, Entry 190, Folder 1, Box 22, NARA.

16. Testimony of interpreter from Mauthausen, undated and untitled, RG153, 8-9, Box 116, NARA.

17. Testimony of Dr. Hans Wilhelm Thost attached to memo from Capt. Wallace Wharton, Office of the Chief of Naval Operations to Capt. J.J. Robinson, Navy Division (JAG) War Crimes Office, Sept. 22, 1946, RG153, 8-9, Box 116, NARA.

18. UN War Crimes Commission, Mauthausen Trial, RG153, 5-31, Volume 1, Trial Record, Book 1, Folder 1-2, Boxes 9-10; First Lt. W.A. Underwood, War Crimes Section,

U.S. Forces in Austria, War Crimes Section progress report for the month of August 1945, August 31, 1945, RG153, 8-9, Box 116, NARA.

19. Appendix III, OSS Slovakia Mission, no date, RG153, 8-9, Box 116, NARA.

20. Lt. Kelly O'Neall, Jr., War Crimes Investigation Committee, HQ, 2677th Regiment, OSS, July 19, 1945, RG153, 8-9, Box 116, NARA.

21. Bennett to Billman, et al., January 26, 1945, RG226, Entry 154, Box 42, Folder 642; OSS Casualty Report, January 29, 1945, RG226, Entry 190, Box 22, Folder 1, OSS Files, NARA.

22. Col. C.W. Christenberry, Allied Force Headquarters, "Capture of Anglo-American Group of agents," February 13, 1945, RG153, 8-9, Box 116, NARA.

23. Memo from Saint Caserta to Saint Bari, February 9, 1945, RG226, Entry 190, Box 22, Folder 1, OSS Files, NARA.

24. Lt. Howard Chapin, Chief, SICE, to Whitney Shepardson, June 25, 1945, RG226, Entry 124, Box 26, Folder 195, OSS Files, NARA.

25. Debrief of "Dupont," June 13, 1945, RG226, Entry 154, Box 42, Folder 657, "Dupont," OSS Files, NARA.

26. Letter from Lou Biagioni to Curtis Whiteway, December 6, 1991.

27. "Dupont Mission" and report by Lt. Jack Taylor, RG226, Entry 110, Folder 86, Box 4, OSS Files, NARA.

28. Lt. Howard Chapin, Chief, SICE to adjutant HQ, 2677th Regiment, OSS, May 13, 1945, RG226, Entry 124, Box 26, Folder 195, OSS Files, NARA.

Chapter 7

1. Interview with Pete House.

2. Curtis Whiteway, "POW/Battle of the Bulge," *The Checkerboard,* (September 1990), p. 5.

3. "*P.O.W.—Americans In Enemy Hands,*" (CA: Arnold Shapiro Productions, 1987).

4. Letter from Edwin Cornell to *The Jewish Veteran.*

5. Testimony of Gaetano D'Angelo, July 28, 1945, RG153, 100-425, Box 35, Book 6, Folder 1, NARA.

6. "American Prisoners of War in Germany," report prepared by Military Intelligence Service War Department, November 1, 1945.

7. Testimony of Charles Green, June 18, 1945, RG153, 100-425, Book 6, Box 35, Folder 1, NARA.

8. Testimony of Pfc. Arthur Homer, September 7, 1945, RG153, 100-425, Book 4, Box 35, NARA.

9. Testimony of Sgt. Howard Gosett, July 25, 1945, RG153, 100-425, Book 7, Box 36, NARA.

10. Testimony of Cpl. Richard Ramsey, September 27, 1945, RG153, 100-425, Book 6, Box 35, Folder 1; Testimony of Pfc. Smith Bee, July 13, 1945, RG153, 100-425, Book 7, Box 36, Folder 2, NARA.

11. "A POW's Diary of Survival On Faded Photographs," *Detroit Free Press,* December 8, 1985.

12. Willis and Roberta Carpenter, *I was the Enemy,* (IN: Willis and Roberta Carpenter, 1990), pp. 55–56.

13. Testimony of Cpl. Joseph Aborn, August 20, 1945, RG153, 12-1668, Box 372, NARA.
14. Interview with Gerald Zimand.
15. Deposition of Stanley B. Cohen, June 19, 1947, RG153, 100-486, Box 49, NARA.
16. Interview with Reme Bottcher.
17. Letter to the author from Pete House, March 1, 1991.
18. Testimony of Leroy Erlandson, RG153, 100-486, Box 49, Book 3, Folder 2, NARA.
19. Letter from Edwin Cornell to *The Jewish Veteran*.
20. Testimony of Marcel Ouimet, August 8, 1945, RG153, 12-1618-19, Box 368, NARA.
21. Testimony of Sgt. Jack Sulser, July 23, 1945, RG153, 100-425, Book 1, Box 34, NARA.
22. Testimony of Samuel Fahrer, May 23, 1946, RG153, 100-486, Folder 1, Box 48, NARA.

Chapter 8

1. Interview with Myron Swack.
2. Statement of Pfc. Norman Martin, May 24, 1945, RG153, 12-745, Box 319, NARA.
3. Otto Ritterman statement, Record Group 153, Records of the Office of the Judge Advocate General, War Crimes Branch, Section 100-486, Trial Record, Prosecution Appendix, Vol. 1, Exhibits, Folder 2, Box 51, NARA.
4. Testimony of Stephen Schweitzer, May 28, 1946, RG153, Folder 1, 100-486, NARA.
5. Interview with Joseph Guigno.
6. Interview with Winfield Rosenberg.
7. Interview with Daniel Steckler.
8. Metz testimony, RG153, Vol. 1, Trial Record, Part 4, Box 51, NARA.
9. Ray Weiss, "Soldiers Of Berga," *Fort Myers News-Press,* (May 1, 1983).
10. Interview with Winfield Rosenberg.
11. Interview with Bernie Melnick.
12. Interview with Daniel Steckler.
13. Interview with Daniel Steckler.
14. Testimony of Milton Shippee, RG153, 100-425, Book 6, Folder 2, Box 35, NARA.
15. Interview with Leo Zaccaria.
16. Interview with Costa Katimaris.
17. Interview with Winfield Rosenberg.
18. Interview of Joseph Guigno.
19. Interview with Daniel Steckler.
20. Interview with Daniel Steckler.
21. "Death March Survivors Relive Ordeal At Reunion," *Florida Today,* (April 21, 1986).
22. Testimony of William Minto, RG153, 12-1668, Box 372, NARA.
23. Interview with Tony Drago.
24. Interview with Milton Filler.
25. Interview with Leo Zaccaria.
26. Interview with Milton Filler.
27. Interview with Sam Lubinsky.
28. Interview with Gerald Zimand.
29. Letter from Vogel, based on survivor responses to his questionnaire, sent to the War Department Special Staff, War Crimes Branch, Civil Affairs Division, June 18, 1948. Copy given to the author by Winfield Rosenberg.

30. Interview with Daniel Steckler.

31. *West Warwick Journal-Bulletin,* (November 11, 1983).

32. Interview with Daniel Steckler.

33. *Delmarva Crossroads* (Delaware), (September 18, 1985).

34. Interview with Robert Rudnick.

35. Testimony of Pfc. Edward Petty, Oct. 1, 1945, RG153, 100-486, Folder 1, Box 48, NARA.

36. Paul Arthur Van Horne, statement in Prosecution Appendix, RG153, Vol. 1, Exhibit, Folder 2, Box 51, NARA.

37. Marvin Gritz, testimony August 1, 1945, RG153, 100-486, Book 3, Folder 2, Box 49, NARA.

38. Milton Stolon response to Vogel questionnaire, RG153, 100-486, Book 3, Folder 2, Box 49, NARA.

39. Donald Hildenbrand report on treatment as POW, RG153, 100-486, Book 3, Folder 2, Box 49, NARA.

40. Shippee ibid.

41. Merz testimony, RG153, Trial Record Part 3, Folder 2, Box 50, NARA.

42. Marvin Gritz testimony June 1, 1945, RG153, 100-486, Book 3, Folder 2, p. 105, Box 49, NARA.

43. Leon E. Trachtman testimony, Prosecution Appendix, RG153, Vol. 1, Exhibits, Folder 2, Box 51, NARA.

44. Testimony of Pvt. Stanley B. Cohen; also that of Pvt. Norman Martin, Prosecution Appendix, RG153, Vol. 1, Exhibits, Folder 2, Box 51, NARA.

45. Metz testimony, RG153, Vol. 1, Trial Record, Part 4, Box 51; Ellis Geyer told investigators October 30, 1945, that Ray Gornic died in a boxcar on the way to the hospital for treatment of a throat infection, Memo for the officer in charge from Eugene Burris, first lt., Chief Intelligence Branch, RG153, 100-425, Box 35, Book 6, Folder 1, NARA.

46. Interview with Myron Swack.

47. Hospital Log in RG153, Vol. 1, Exhibit, Box 51, NARA.

48. Summary of facts about Berga compiled by Dr. Jacob Cantor in Vogel file.

49. Interview with Winfield Rosenberg.

50. Interview with Leo Zaccaria.

51. Interview with Tony Drago.

52. Interview with Myron Swack.

53. Interview with Winfield Rosenberg.

54. Norman Martin testimony, Prosecution Appendix 1, RG153, Vol. 1 Exhibits, Folder 2, Box 51, NARA.

55. Metz testimony in War Crimes Trial, Vol. 1, Trial Record, Part 4, Box 51; testimony of Hockart, RG153, Trial Record, part 2, folder 2; Metz, Vol. 1, Trial Record, Part 4, Box 51; and Walter Zschaeck, Prosecution Appendix, Vol. 1, Exhibits, Folder 2, Box 51; Shippee ibid., NARA.

56. Metz statement, RG153, Vol. 1, Exhibits, Folder 1, 100-486, Box 51, NARA.

57. Alan Reyner response to Vogel questionnaire, RG153, 100-486, Book 3, Folder 2, Box 49, NARA.

58. Interview with Daniel Steckler.

59. Interview with Winfield Rosenberg.

60. Testimony of Merz and Metz, RG153, Trial Record Part 3, Folder 1, NARA.

61. Interview with Ernest Kinoy.
62. Interview with John Marek.
63. Eugene Heimler, *Night of the Mist*, (Bodley Head, 1959), p. 178.

Chapter 9

1. Eugene Heimler, *Night of the Mist*, (Bodley Head, 1959), p. 182.
2. Testimony of Milton Shippee, October 8, 1945, RG153, 100-425, Box 35, Book 6, Folder 2, NARA.
3. Norman Martin, Trial Record, Vol 1., Exhibits, Folder 2, Box 51, NARA.
4. Testimony of Erwin Metz, Vol. 1, Trial Record, Part 4, Box 51, NARA.
5. Testimony of Samuel Fahrer, May 23, 1946, RG153, 100-486, Folder 1, Box 48, NARA.
6. Interview with Winfield Rosenberg.
7. Fahrer testimony.
8. The war crimes examiner found a record of three who were buried in the cemetery on April 6: Ernest Strada, Frank Fladzinski and Joseph Rhlagar, testimony of Major Herman Bolker, RG153, 100-486, Vol. 1, Exhibits, Folder 2, Box 51, NARA.
9. Testimony of Norman Martin, November 13, 1945, RG153, 100-486, Book 1, Folder 2, Box 48, NARA.
10. Testimony of Erwin Metz, Vol. 1, Trial Record, Part 4, Box 51, NARA.
11. *Delmarva Crossroads* (Delaware), (September 18, 1985).
12. Interview with Daniel Steckler.
13. Interview with Leo Zaccaria.
14. Testimony of Seifert, Vol. 1, Exhibits, Folder 2, Box 51, NARA.
15. Statement by Norman Martin, RG153, 100-486, Vol. 1, Exhibit Folder 2, Trial Record, Box 51, NARA.
16. Testimony of Marcel Ouimet, Vol. 1, Exhibits, Folder 2, Box 51, NARA.
17. "Dad's Prisoner of War Experiences," written by Lawrence Gillette's daughter.
18. Testimony of Roy Moser, RG153, 12-2163, Box 412, NARA.
19. Testimony of Milton Shippee, RG153, 100-425, Book 6, Folder 2, Box 35, NARA.
20. Six of the bodies had dog tags: Bernard Vogel, Leonard Domb, Merle Smith, Robert Kessler, Joseph Land, Jr., and Russell Johnson. William Maxwell was also identified among the dead, but three other bodies were not.
21. Interview with Daniel Steckler.
22. Leo Wildman and Milton Kornetz were identified, the rest could not be; however, Norman Martin lists as dying that day: Parkins, Deaver, Martin, Ed Cooper, Bruin, and Milsap.
23. Merz statement to war crimes investigators, June 19, 1945, Trial Record of Erwin Metz and Ludwig Merz, RG153, 100-486, Vol. 1, Exhibits, Folder 1, Part 4, Box 51, NARA.
24. The four were identified as James Cullina, John Weller, Arnold Ascher [perhaps Asher], and Hardy Millserg [perhaps Millerg].
25. Moser testimony, RG153, 12-2163, Box 412, NARA; Trial Record of Ludwig Merz and Erwin Metz, RG153, 100-486, Vol. 1, Trial Record, Parts 2-4; Exhibits, Folders 1-2, Boxes 50-51, NARA.
26. Moser testimony, RG153, 12-2163, Box 412, NARA.
27. Moser testimony, RG153, 12-2163, Box 412, NARA.

28. Testimony of Milton Shippee, October 8, 1945, RG153, 100-425, Book 6, Folder 2, Box 35, NARA.

29. Letter from Robert Widdicombe to Winfield Rosenberg, July 22, 1988; *Naples Daily News,* (April 10, 1988).

30. "Dad's Prisoner of War Experiences," written by Lawrence Gillette's daughter.

31. Interview with Joseph Guigno.

32. AP, (April 21, 1945).

Chapter 10

1. *"P.O.W.—Americans In Enemy Hands,"* (CA: Arnold Shapiro Productions, 1987).

2. "Dad's Prisoner of War Experiences," written by Lawrence Gillette's daughter, unpublished.

3. Interview with Stecklers.

4. Gillette's story.

5. Interview with Sam Lubinsky.

6. Interview with Winfield Rosenberg.

7. *Warwick Journal-Bulletin,* (November 11, 1983).

8. Interview with Leo Zaccaria.

9. *Naples Daily News,* (April 10, 1988).

10. Interview with Gerald Daub.

11. Ray Weiss, "Soldiers of Berga," *Fort Myers News-Press,* (May 1, 1983).

12. Gillette story.

13. Letter to the author from Pete House, March 27, 1992.

14. Gillette story.

15. Interview with Costa Katimaris.

16. Interview with Pete House.

17. Letter from Arthur Kinnis to the author, January 7, 1991.

18. Quotes from a tape given to me by one of the survivors, Park Chapman, which contains the stories of several of the POWs from Buchenwald. Since the speakers are not identifiable, their quotes are henceforth cited as "Chapman tape."

19. Letter to Park Chapman dated April 18, 1988, supplied to the author.

20. Ibid.

21. Chapman tape.

22. Arthur Durand, *Stalag Luft III,* (LA: Louisiana State University Press, 1988), p. 270n.

23. Interview with Jim Hastin.

24. Interview with Robert Rudnick.

25. Interviews with Milton Filler, Daniel Steckler and Costa Katimaris.

26. Letter to the author, November 13, 1990.

Chapter 11

1. Secretary of State Cordell Hull to Representative on Politico-Military Commission at Algiers, November. 26, 1943, *FRUS,* 1943, Vol. 1, pp. 427–8.

2. *U.S. vs. Friedrich Becker, et al.,* May 21, 1947, RG153, 12-583, Vol. 1, Trial Record, Part 1 and 6, Folder 2, Boxes 293–4, NARA.

3. Interrogation of Stabsscharfuhrer Friedrich Wilhelm, March 4, 1947, RG153, 12-390, Vol. 1, Buchenwald Trial Record, Exhibits, Part 3, Folder 1, Box 252, NARA.

4. Ann Tusa and John Tusa, *The Nuremberg Trial,* (NY: Atheneum, 1986), p. 168n.

5. Press release from the National Military Establishment, Department of the Army, September 23, 1948, RG153, 12-390, Book 5, Box 245, NARA.

6. See for example, United States, 80th Congress, second session, Senate Report No. 1775, Part 3: Conduct of Ilse Koch War Crimes Trial, Interim Report of the Investigations Subcommittee of the Committee on Expenditures in the Executive Departments.

7. Interrogation of Herman Pister, March 4, 1947, RG153, 12-390, Vol. 1, Buchenwald Trial Record, Exhibits, Part 2, Folder 1, Box 252, NARA.

8. *U.S. vs. Josias Prince zu Waldeck, et al.,* November 15, 1947, RG153, 12-390, Box 243, NARA.

9. Letter from Attorney Solomon Surowitz to Secretary of the Army Kenneth Royall, Sept. 27, 1948, RG153, 12-390, Book 5, Box 245, NARA.

10. Memo from J.W. Blaine, Canadian War Crimes Investigation Unit, July 24, 1945, provided to the author by a former POW in Buchenwald.

11. Besides the testimony of individual POWs, the War Crimes Branch had a copy of a list of POWs and the amount of money surrendered by them upon entering Buchenwald, memo from C.E. Straight, JAGD, to War Crimes Branch, August 22, 1946. Investigators also had a copy of the Kadler report on conditions at Buchenwald that discussed the Americans' imprisonment. Documents provided to the author by a former POW.

12. *New York Times,* (February 2, 1945).

13. Testimony of Ornstein, Mauthausen Trial Record, Box 9, NARA.

14. Mauthausen Trial Record, Part 5, Box 10, p. 1498-99, Exhibit 137A, NARA.

15. Mauthausen Trial Record, pp. 1379 and 1408, Exhibit 101A and 113A, Box 10, NARA.

16. RG153, 5-31, Vol. 1-2, Mauthausen Trial Record, Book 1, Parts 1, 5, 8, Folders 1–3, Boxes 9–10, 11; Exhibits, Box 12, NARA.

17. Commander James Donovan to Brigadier Gen. John Weir, Asst. JAG, March 26, 1945, RG153, 8-9, Box 116, NARA.

18. Kelly O' Neall, Jr., War Crimes Investigation Committee memo, July 19, 1945, RG153, 8-9, Box 115, NARA.

19. International Military Tribunal, *Trial of the Major War Criminals,* (Nuremberg, 1947), Vol. 6, p. 186.

20. Interview with William Denson.

21. Interview with Telford Taylor.

22. *U.S. vs. Wilhelm von Leeb, et al.,* in *Trials of War Criminals,* (DC: Government Printing Office, 1950), Vol. X, p. 32; Vol. XI, pp. 463, 495, 654–661, 696.

23. Record of testimony in trial of *U.S. vs. Erwin Metz, et al.,* tried at Dachau, September 3–16, 1946, RG153, 100-486, Trial Record, Boxes 50–51, NARA.

24. Maj. Gen. O.P. Echols, Director, Civil Affairs Division, War Department to Charles Vogel, April 4, 1946, provided to the author by a former POW.

25. The number of accounts given to investigators may have been greater, but I could find only 38 in the National Archives. Charles Vogel said he had obtained more than 70 statements and forwarded them to investigators. The seven ex-POWs who provided state-

ments were Leon Trachtman, Stanley B. Cohen, Marcel Ouimet, Stephen Schweitzer, Arthur Van Horne, Meyer Lemberg and Norman Martin.

26. Trial Record, pp. 830–1088, 1096–1109, NARA.

27. Trial Record, pp. 109–118, 123–173, 291–310, 415–445, NARA.

28. Trial Record, pp. 179–209, NARA.

29. Trial Record, pp. 311–414, 449–479, NARA.

30. Testimony of Dr. Rudolf Miethe, June 7, 1945, RG153, 100-486, Exhibits, Vol 1, folder 1, Box 51, NARA.

31. Letter from Erwin Metz to the Reviewing Authority, Munich, February 8, 1948, RG153, 100-480, Vol. 1, Clemency, Part 1, Folder 1, Box 49, NARA.

32. Kurt Seifert testimony, RG153, 100-483, Vol. 1, Exhibits, Folder 2, Box 51, NARA.

33. Testimony of Major Herman Bolker, RG153, 100-486, Vol. 1, Exhibits, Folder 2, Box 51, NARA.

34. Trial Record, p. 1167, NARA.

35. Petitions of October 17, 1946, and December 12, 1946, RG153, 100-486, Vol. 1, Clemency, Part 1, Folder 1, Box 49, NARA.

36. Plea for Clemency, November 18, 1946, RG153, 100-486, Vol. 1, Clemency, Part 1, Folder 2, Box 49, NARA.

37. Report of War Crimes Board of Review No. 1, January 29, 1948, RG153, 100-486, Vol. 1, Review, Box 50, NARA.

38. Report of War Crimes Board of Review No. 1, RG153, 100-486, Vol. 1, Clemency, Part 1, Box 49, NARA.

39. Statement by Milton Stolon, June 30, 1947, RG153, 100-486, Vol. 1, Clemency, Part 1, Folder 2, Box 49, NARA.

40. Deposition of Arthur Van Horne, June 19, 1947, RG153, 100-486, Box 49, NARA.

41. Military Government Court Order On Review and Action of the Modification Board, RG153, 100-486, Vol. 1, Action of the Modification Board, Box 49, NARA.

42. Deposition of Stanley B. Cohen, June 30, 1947, RG153, 100-486, Box 49, NARA.

43. Michael Berenbaum, *The World Must Know: The History of the Holocaust as Told in the United States Holocaust Memorial Museum,* (MA: Little, Brown and Co., 1993), pp. 200–202.

44. Jacob Heilbrunn, "The Real McCloy," *New Republic,* (May 11, 1992), p. 44.

45. Letter from Marvin Gritz to Edward Young, Chief, War Crimes Branch, August 3, 1948, RG153, 100-486, Book 4, Box 49, NARA.

46. Col. Edward Young, Chief, War Crimes Branch, Civil Affairs Division, to Charles Vogel, June 11, 1948, provided to the author by Vogel's nephew [henceforth Vogel file].

47. Vogel to War Department Special Staff, June 18, 1948, Vogel file.

Chapter 12

1. Ray Weiss, "Soldiers of Berga," *Fort Myers News-Press,* (May 1, 1983).

2. *New York Times,* (March 27, 1945).

3. The Security Certificate for Ex-Prisoners of War signed by Joseph Guigno on April 24, 1945, said that "some activities of American prisoners of war within German prison camps must remain secret not only for the duration of the war against the present enemies of the United States but in peace-time as well. . . . I may not reveal, discuss, publish or

otherwise disclose to unauthorized persons information on escape from enemy prison camps or evasion in enemy occupied territory, clandestine organizations among prisoners of war, any means of outwitting captors or of promoting intelligence activities within prison camps."

4. Report by Military Intelligence Service of War Department, November 1, 1945, RG200, 619.2/08, "American POWs' in Germany," NARA.

5. The State Department had received reports in January and February 1944—a full year before American Jews were sent to Berga—that Americans were working in slate mines at Stalag IX-C, RG59, Special War Problems Division, Box 128, NARA.

6. *New York Times,* (March 20, 1945).

7. LaGrange, Illinois, (July 20, 1945).

8. In an interview, Bill Powell said he worked for a company that sponsored the documentary on POWs that featured Daniel Steckler. He wrote to the producer about what happened to him and the other Allied POWs in Buchenwald. The producer contacted the U.S. government and the International Red Cross and was told no Americans had been in Buchenwald.

9. Memo from C.E. Straight, Deputy Theater Judge Advocate for War Crimes to War Crimes Branch, "Money Surrendered at Buchenwald Concentration Camp," August 22, 1946, provided to the author by a former POW.

10. Reference Paper, C.C. Buchenwald 77001-80000 Zugangsbuch, 71, RG238, NARA.

11. Story datelined, Washington, April 4.

12. Roger Du Pasquier, "The Red Cross Speaks Only Through Its Actions," undated, RG200, 619.2, American and Allied Internees and POWs, Box 990, NARA.

13. RG200, 619.2, Box 990, Hospitalized Soldiers, NARA.

14. Letter from International Committee of the Red Cross President Carl Burckhardt to George Tait, First Secretary of the U.S. Legation at Berne, February 6, 1945, RG84, 711.5, Individuals, Box 89, NARA.

15. Report on ICRC visit to Stalag VII-A, January 27, 1945, RG59, Special War Problems Division, Subject Files, 39-54, Box 128, NARA.

16. "American Prisoners of War in Germany," report prepared by Military Intelligence Service War Department, Nov. 1, 1945; Report of Werner Buchmuller, representative of Swiss Legation, regarding conditions in Stalag IX-B on his visit February 15, 1945, RG153, 100-425, Book 1, Box 34, NARA; Report of Albert Kadler, representative of Swiss Legation, regarding conditions in Stalag IX-B on his visit March 23, 1945, RG153, 100-425, Book 1, Box 34, NARA.

17. *New York Times,* (June 2, 1945).

18. Letter from Herman Vogel to Basil O' Conner, June 13, 1945; Unsigned reply, June 21, 1945, RG200, 619.2/91, Criticisms and Controversial Subjects, Box 1014, NARA.

19. *New York Times,* (June 2, 1945); a study by Charles Stenger of the Veterans Administration, dated April 6, 1977, arrived at a similar figure, citing 1,121 POWs as the number who died in captivity, out of a total of 93,941 captured and interned in the European and Mediterranean theaters, in "German Treatment of American Prisoners of War in World War II," by Ben Goldman, Chief, Office of TAC History, U.S. Air Force, excerpted in Stan Sommers, *The European Story,* (WI: American Ex-Prisoners of War, Inc., July 1980), p. 4.

20. No less than 38 Berga survivors provided information between May 23, 1945 and July 16, 1948. For example, see the testimony of Melvin Eder, June 21, 1945, RG153, 100-425, Book 1, Box 34; Col. Mastin White, deputy director War Crimes Office to Commanding

General, Second Service Command, Governors Island, July 28, 1945; similar memo to Commanding General 9th Service Command, July 27, 1945, RG153, 100-425, Book 1, Box 34; memo from Russel Sweet to War Crimes Office, August 17, 1945, RG153, 100-425, Book 2, Box 34, NARA.

21. "Anger at Nazi Atrocities Is Rising but U.S. Treats Prisoners Fairly," *Newsweek,* (May 7, 1945), p. 21.

22. United States, 79th Congress, first session, May 15, 1945, Senate Document No. 47: Report of the Committee requested by Gen. Dwight D. Eisenhower through the Chief of Staff, Gen. George C. Marshall to the Congress of the United States Relative to Atrocities and Other Conditions in Concentration Camps in Germany, p. 10.

23. Martin Gilbert, *Auschwitz and the Allies,* (NY: Holt, Rinehart and Winston, 1981), pp. 231–239; Wyman, 288–307.

24. Deborah Lipstadt, *Beyond Belief,* (NY: Free Press, 1986), pp. 136–142.

25. Lipstadt, p. 171.

26. Lipstadt, p. 217.

27. Lipstadt, p. 270.

28. Excerpts from Moore's International Law Digest, Vol. IV, Section 653, p. 592, copy in Protection of Persons file, RG59, Box 6, Vol. 13, Folder 1, NARA.

29. *New York Times,* (March 25, 1945).

30. "Personal Identification System, United States Army," August 1971, p. 2, citing GO 122-111, HQ, A.E.F., France, July 26, 1918, provided by U.S. Army Center of Military History.

31. "The Special Treatment of Jewish POWs," *Wiener Library Bulletin,* (April 1964), p. 23.

32. Press conference of General Dwight Eisenhower at the Pentagon, June 18, 1945.

33. Letter from Hugo Princz to Sen. Bill Bradley, June 4, 1984.

34. Interview with Saul Kagan, Executive Director of the Jewish Restitution Successor Organization.

35. I have been working with the U.S. Holocaust Memorial Council during the course of my research and have been told elements of this story will be a part of the U.S. Holocaust Memorial Museum when it opens in April 1993.

36. *Washington Post,* (Oct. 10, 1991).

37. Bob Simon, *Forty Days,* (NY: G.P. Putnam's Sons, 1992).

Bibliography

Abzug, Robert, *Inside the Vicious Heart* (NY: Oxford University Press, 1985).

Adler, Stanislav, *In the Warsaw Ghetto* (Jerusalem, Yad Vashem, 1982).

Barker, A.J., *Behind Barbed Wire* (London: B.T. Batsford Ltd., 1974).

Berenbaum, Michael, *The World Must Know: The History of the Holocaust as Told in the United States Holocaust Memorial Museum* (MA: Little, Brown and Co., 1993).

Burton, Gerry, "POWs of Germans Get Together," *Avalanche-Journal* (Lubbock, TX), around 1987.

Carpenter, Willis and Roberta, *I Was the Enemy* (IN: Willis and Roberta Carpenter, 1990).

Carter, Kit and Robert Mueller, eds., *The Army Air Forces in World War II* (Office of Air Force History, 1973).

Central Commission for Investigation of German Crimes in Poland, *German Crimes in Poland* (NY: Howard Fertig, 1982).

Conot, Robert, *Justice at Nuremberg* (NY: Carroll & Graf, 1983).

Datner, Szymon, *Crimes Against POWs* (Poland: Zachodnia Agencja Prasowa, 1964).

Dawidowicz, Lucy, *The War Against the Jews* (NY: Bantam Books, 1986).

Durand, Arthur, *Stalag Luft III* (LA: Louisiana State University Press, 1988).

Eisner, Jack, *The Survivor* (NY: William Morrow, 1980).

Feingold, Henry, *The Politics of Rescue* (NJ: Rutgers University Press, 1970).

Foot, MRD, *SOE in France* (MD: University Publications of America, 1984).

Foreman, Paul, "Buchenwald and Modern Prisoner of War Detention Policy," *Social Forces* (May 1959), pp. 289–298.

Foy, David, *For You the War Is Over* (NY: Stein and Day, 1984).

Friedman, Philip, ed., *Martyrs and Fighters* (NY: Praeger, 1954).

Gilbert, Martin, *Atlas of the Holocaust* (Eng: Pergamon Press, 1988).

———, *The Holocaust* (NY: Henry Holt And Co., 1985).

———, *Auschwitz and the Allies* (NY: Holt Rinehart Winston, 1981).

Heimler, Eugene, *Night of the Mist* (Bodley Head, 1959).

International Military Tribunal, *Trial of the Major War Criminals* (Nuremberg, 1947).

Kalman, Sam, "An Ex-POW Remembers," *The Jewish Veteran* (July-August 1986).

Kaufman, I., *American Jews in World War II* (NY: Dial Press, 1947).

Kennan, George, *Memoirs: 1925–1950* (MA: Little Brown, 1967).

Kogon, Eugen, *The Theory and Practice of Hell* (NY: Berkley Books, 1980).

Kowalski, Isaac, ed., *Anthology on Armed Jewish Resistance, 1939–1945*, Vol. 1 (NY: Jewish Combatants Publishers House, 1984).

Le Chene, Evelyn, *Mauthausen* (London: Methuen and Co., Ltd., 1971).

Lipstadt, Deborah, *Beyond Belief* (NY: Free Press, 1986).

Mark, Ber, *Uprising in the Warsaw Ghetto* (NY: Schocken Books, 1975).

Meed, Vladka, *On Both Sides of the Wall* (NY: Holocaust Library, 1979).

Miller, Judith, *One by One by One* (NY: Simon and Schuster, 1990).

Nazi Conspiracy and Aggression, Vol. IV (DC: Government Printing Office, 1946).

Nir, Yehuda, *The Lost Childhood* (NY: Harcourt Brace Jovanovich, 1989).

Richarz, William, et al., eds., *The 390th Bomb Group Anthology,* Vol. 1 (AZ: 390th Memorial Museum Foundation, Inc.).

Roy, Morris, *Behind Barbed Wire* (NY: Richard R. Smith, 1946).

Simon, Bob, *Forty Days* (NY: G.P. Putnam's Sons, 1992).

Sommers, Stan, *The European Story* (WI: American Ex-Prisoners of War, Inc., July 1980).

Spanjaard, Barry, *Don't Fence Me In!* (CA: B&B Publishing, 1981).

"The Special Treatment of Jewish POWs," *Wiener Library Bulletin* (April 1964).

Strong, Tracy, "Prisoners of War," *Survey Midmonthly* (August 1944).

Trials of War Criminals (DC: Government Printing Office, 1950).

Tusa, Ann and John, *The Nuremberg Trial* (NY: Atheneum, 1986).

United States, 79th Congress, first session, May 15, 1945, Senate Document No. 47: Report of the Committee requested by Gen. Dwight D. Eisenhower through the Chief of Staff, Gen. George C. Marshall to the Congress of the United States Relative to Atrocities and Other Conditions in Concentration Camps in Germany.

Vietor, John, *Time Out* (NY: Richard R. Smith, Inc., 1951).

Weinstock, Eugene, *Beyond the Last Path* (NY: Boni And Gaer, 1947).

Weiss, Ray, "Soldiers Of Berga," *Fort Myers News-Press* (May 1, 1983).

Whiting, Charles, *Massacre at Malmédy* (NY: Stein And Day, 1971).

Winograd, Leonard, "Double Jeopardy: What an American Army Officer, A Jew, Remembers of Prison Life in Germany," *American Jewish Archives* (April 1976), pp. 3–17.

Wyman, David, *The Abandonment of the Jews* (NY: Pantheon Books, 1984).

About the Author

Mitchell G. Bard is the executive director of the American-Israeli Cooperative Enterprise (AICE) and a foreign policy analyst who lectures frequently on U.S.–Middle East policy.

For three years he was the editor of the *Near East Report,* the American Israel Public Affairs Committee's (AIPAC) weekly newsletter on U.S. Middle East policy.

Prior to working at AIPAC, Dr. Bard was a postdoctoral fellow at the University of California at Irvine, where he collaborated on a book examining the politics behind the rescue of Ethiopian Jews. He also served as a senior analyst in the polling division of the 1988 Bush campaign.

Dr. Bard's work has appeared in academic journals, magazines, and major newspapers. He is the author of *The Water's Edge and Beyond: Defining the Limits to Domestic Influence on U.S. Middle East Policy, Partners for Change: How U.S.-Israel Cooperation Can Benefit America,* and *U.S.-Israel Relations: Looking to the Year 2000* and coauthor of *Myths and Facts: A Concise Record of the Arab-Israeli Conflict.*

Bard holds a Ph.D. in political science from UCLA and a master's degree in public policy from Berkeley. He received his B.A. in economics from the University of California at Santa Barbara.

Index